A CALORIE
IS A CALORIE
IS A CALORIE,
RIGHT?
WRONG!

New research in biochemistry shows that many of our old ideas about the caloric value of foods to the human body were wrong. All calories are not the same to the human body. When it comes to being overly fat or overweight, it's primarily the fat calories that count, *not* the carbohydrate and protein calories.

And many forms of physical activity used by overweight persons in their quest for weight reduction, *in combination with the typical mix of nutrients in their diets,* can have little or no impact on their stores of body fat.

The T-Factor Diet is based on recent scientific discoveries that show how you can activate your body's innate, natural fat-burning potential and melt away excess body fat without actually cutting back on your total caloric intake. It is based on concepts that are going to revolutionize our thinking about the metabolism of energy in the human body as well as about weight management.

Bantam Books by Martin Katahn
Ask your bookseller for the books you have missed

THE ROTATION DIET
THE T-FACTOR DIET

THE
T-FACTOR
DIET

Martin Katahn, Ph.D.

DIRECTOR OF THE VANDERBILT
WEIGHT MANAGEMENT PROGRAM
AT VANDERBILT UNIVERSITY

BANTAM BOOKS
NEW YORK • TORONTO • LONDON • SYDNEY • AUCKLAND

THE T-FACTOR DIET
*A Bantam Nonfiction Book / published by arrangement with
W. W. Norton & Company, Inc.*

*PRINTING HISTORY
W. W. Norton edition published April 1989
Bantam rack edition / April 1990*

BANTAM NONFICTION *and the portrayal of a boxed "b" are trademarks of Bantam Books, a
division of Bantam Doubleday Dell Publishing Group, Inc.*

ISBN 0-553-28508-4

Published simultaneously in the United States and Canada

*Bantam Books are published by Bantam Books, a division of Bantam Doubleday
Dell Publishing Group, Inc. Its trademark, consisting of the words "Bantam Books"
and the portrayal of a rooster, is Registered in U.S. Patent and Trademark Office
and in other countries. Marca Registrada. Bantam Books, 666 Fifth Avenue, New York,
New York 10103.*

PRINTED IN THE UNITED STATES OF AMERICA

OPM   16 15

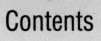

Contents

Acknowledgments

◆

This book and the research in the Vanderbilt Weight Management Program that confirms the validity and usefulness of its concepts are made possible by many people. I would like to express my appreciation to:

Jamie Pope-Cordle, M.S., R.D., for designing the basic menus and analyzing nutrient values, developing many of the recipes, helping to lead the T-Factor research groups, supplying much of the material for the chapter on childhood and adolescent nutrition, and for her comments and suggestions on the manuscript.

James O. Hill, Ph.D., for developing Vanderbilt University's calorimetry chamber, designing our metabolic research program, and for reading critically and commenting on the manuscript.

David G. Schlundt, Ph.D., for directing the Vanderbilt Weight Management Research Program and for helping to design and evaluate the clinical research on which the T-Factor Diet is based.

Tracy Sbrocco for developing the nutrient data bank for the Fat and Fiber Counter.

Harriette Simpkins for coordinating groups, supplying information and encouragement to the thousands of persons who have called the Vanderbilt program for help from all over the country during these past several years, and being ready to jump in and do anything we need done any time we need it.

Veronica Petta, M.A., *Family Circle* home economist and nutritionist, for developing a batch of delicious, nutritious recipes for the T-Factor Diet, six of which are included here: Corn Chowder, Pasta and Shrimp with Ricotta Cheese Sauce, Pork Tenderloin with Orange Marmalade, Picadillo and Cornbread Wedges, Saucy Pastitsio, and Bean-and-Corn Chili over Puffed Tortilla.

Terri Katahn for helping to develop the menus and recipes, supplying the helpful information contained in the introductions to all the recipe sections, and for her critical comments and suggestions during the writing of the manuscript.

Enid Katahn for undying love and patience during the unavoidable stressful periods that arise with every book I write—the final stages always seem to occur at the end of a fall semester at the University, and while I am trying to complete several other projects.

Mary Bomar, who is really Enid's Personal Representative, for tending the home office and doing everything from analyzing nutrient data to booking concerts and walking the dog when necessary.

Joyce Weingartner for her excellent bread recipes, which I include once again in the book.

ESHA Research for the Food Processor II Nutrient and Diet Analysis System which supplies the program we use to analyze our menus and recipes and especially to Elizabeth Geltz for always being Johnny-on-the-spot whenever I have a question.

Starling Lawrence, my editor at W. W. Norton, with whom I've worked so closely on the five books going on six, for making it his business to know as much about the field I work in as possible, which in turn enables him to help me clarify the often complex concepts I work with.

Artie and Richard Pine, my literary agents, for their help in tending to all the matters authors are so poor at, but mostly for friendship and enthusiasm for my work during the many years we have worked together.

All my other friends and helpers at W. W. Norton: Fran Rosencrantz, for handling all the publicity arrangements for all of my books, working me to death and then worrying about me, just like my mother would have done; Debra Makay, my manuscript editor for several books, who always demands accuracy and consistency; Anthony Levintow, Jeannie Luciano, and Iva Ashner, for their editorial assistance; Tara Phethean, for her work on the brochure; Kevin O'Neill, under the guidance of art director Hugh O'Neill, for the design and production of the striking computerized jacket; Margaret Wagner, for the design of the text; and production manager Andrew Marasia, for producing the books on an impossible schedule.

Dona Tapp for being ready on a moment's notice to put everything else in her life on hold in order to do the final proofreading so that Andrew Marasia could meet his impossible schedule.

Doug Stallings, Ralph Kirkland, and the entire staff at the Tandy Computer Center and the Tandy Area Training and Support Group for their attention to my personal needs as well as to the needs of the research group in the Weight Management Program at Vanderbilt University.

Again, thank you all very much.

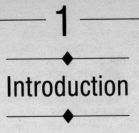

1

Introduction

A calorie is a calorie is a calorie. Right?

WRONG!

The T-Factor Diet is based on recent scientific discoveries in the fields of biochemistry and physiology that reveal major differences in the way our bodies process, utilize, and store the calories in our food. These studies also show how you can activate your body's innate, natural fat-burning potential and melt away excess body fat without actually cutting back on your total caloric intake.

First, research in the biochemistry field shows that many of our old ideas about the caloric value of foods to the human body were wrong. All calories are not the same to the human body. When it comes to being overly fat and overweight, it's primarily the fat calories that count, *not* the carbohydrate and protein calories.

Second, research in the field of physiology shows that many forms of physical activity used by overweight persons in their quest for weight reduction, *in combination with the typical mix of nutrients in their diets,* can have little or no impact on their stores of body fat. While the research shows how to maximize the fat-burning power of exercise, it also explains how certain common combinations of exercise and diet can work against you and actually encourage the transformation of dietary fat to body fat.

The two lines of research that have inspired this book show that there is a particular combination of diet and physical activity that can work against you and actually encourage the transformation of dietary fat to body fat.

1

The two lines of research that have inspired this book show that there is a particular combination of diet and physical activity that can lead you to a permanent reduction in body fat, *without cutting calories and without counting them.*

You will find that combination in the T-Factor Diet.

The T-Factor Diet is based on concepts that are going to revolutionize our thinking about the metabolism of energy in the human body as well as about weight management. Obviously, such claims require an explanation. Here is a brief summary of the scientific background; I will furnish more details in Chapter 2.

In the laboratory, when the caloric value of foods is measured, all calories are by definition equal. In the measurement of the energy of foods, a calorie[1] is the amount of heat it takes to raise the temperature of 1 kilogram of water 1 degree Celsius. Calories are measured in the laboratory by burning carefully measured portions of food in special instruments which in turn measure the amount of energy released. Up until a few years ago, most experts considered that the human body extracted the energy from fat, carbohydrate, and protein with about equal efficiency. By this I mean that when we measured certain amounts of carbohydrate, protein, or fatty foods in the laboratory, and found that each contained 100 calories, we assumed that the human body also extracted 100 calories from those quantities and that the entire 100 calories would be available either for sustaining basal metabolic processes[2] or for powerful physical activity.

To use some actual examples: As measured in the laboratory, we assumed that 100 calories' worth of carbohydrate foods such as apples, carrots, potatoes, and whole-grain bread and 100 calories' worth of fat or fatty foods such as butter, margarine, french fries, and prime

---

[1] When used as a measure of energy in food, the word *calorie* was originally capitalized or referred to as a kilocalorie. It was equal to 1000 "small" calories as used in the field of chemistry, where it is equal to the heat required to raise the temperature of 1 gram of water 1 degree, from 15 to 16 degrees Celsius.

[2] Basal metabolic processes refer to those maintenance functions that are essential to life, such as vital cellular activity, the circulation of blood, and respiration, to name a few. The basal metabolic rate is the energy required to maintain these functions in a fasting, resting organism.

cuts of meat *each supplied the same amount of energy—100 calories—for activity or metabolic functions.*

THIS IS FALSE!

A hundred calories of baked potatoes and 100 calories of french fries are not equal, *except* in the laboratory! They have a very different impact on the human body.

The human body extracts and accumulates much more usable energy from fat than from any other nutrient. In addition, the body seems far, FAR more efficient at converting dietary fat into body fat than it is at converting carbohydrate or protein into body fat. Indeed, the differences in the way your body metabolizes fat compared with protein and carbohydrate are so great that except for a small percentage of persons who suffer from some metabolic abnormality, YOU CAN'T GET FAT EXCEPT BY EATING FAT!

And the precise way in which you get fat is by taking in more fat in your daily diet than you are burning up in the fuel mixture that keeps you alive each day.

I am going to present the facts behind these statements and explain them in full detail in Chapter 2 and, for all people who fall within the range of a normal metabolism, I make this promise:

The T-Factor Diet will turn on your body's innate, hidden potential for melting off excess body fat. If you will stick with the T-Factor formula for the control of fat intake that I'll give you in Chapter 3, you will be able to completely satisfy your appetite and you will still lose weight painlessly and easily.

DO YOU HAVE TO CUT CALORIES TO LOSE WEIGHT?

It's traditional nutritional doctrine and, indeed, it seems only logical: If you want to lose weight you have to cut your caloric intake, and if you want to maintain your weight loss after you've lost weight you have to consume fewer calories forever. This logic is based on the belief that energy in the human being follows a simple rule: A given caloric intake yields a predictable surplus or deficit in fat storage depending on the amount of energy expended in daily life.

Thus, to lose weight you have to unbalance the energy equation so that calories "in" are fewer than calories "out."

The research to which I have already referred has shattered this logic and this belief. The total number of calories you eat may be less important than the source of those calories. As I said earlier, if you have surplus fat on your body, you are probably eating too much fat, not necessarily too many calories. In fact, the reason that most overweight persons are overweight is that they eat *four or five times more fat than is essential, and about twice as much as is necessary to make a tasty, healthy, lifelong weight-maintenance diet.*

Of course, all health professionals are encouraging us to eat less fat—as the former United States Surgeon General, Dr. C. Everett Koop, pointed out, fat is Western society's greatest nutritional hazard. Why is it, however, that all this advice and exhortation is only marginally successful?

Let's make it personal! What about you? If you're one of the vast majority of Americans who are still consuming too much fat—the fat that's making you fat, and possibly contributing to premature heart disease and other ills— why haven't you followed this advice and cut back to desirable levels?

Believe me, there is no need to feel guilty over your preference for fatty foods. If your appetite turns on to the prime cuts of meat, the fried foods, the rich sauces, and the tasty desserts, it's not a moral issue. It's a biological issue. And I will explain all of this in Chapter 10 with the hope of helping you combat a perfectly normal predisposition that kept primitive humans alive when they faced periodic food shortages, but which does not serve you well in a society where rich foods are continually and easily available.

We must all face the fact that fat makes many foods, including many carbohydrate and protein foods, *taste better!* That's why so many of us choose those french fries and prime steaks over the baked or boiled potato and the flank or round steak.

But, there are ways to deal effectively with our innate liking for fat, and for that matter, with our innate liking for sweet-tasting things as well. All of us at the Vanderbilt Weight Management Program have worked very hard on the T-Factor Diet to create a *livable* diet as well as a *workable* diet. I say this because just about any semi-starvation, reduced-calorie diet will *work temporarily* when it comes to losing weight; the real issue is, can you *live* with it?

Yes, you are going to have to change—you can't continue to do precisely as you have been doing in the way of diet and exercise and expect any change in the ease with which you manage your weight. But the T-Factor Diet can succeed for you where other diets have failed because, in addition to its fat-burning potential, it gets you off the ersatz, artificial products that research shows are little, if any, help for weight control. We are going to return to the foods that are much more satisfying to the human appetite, including the genuine, natural fats, oils, and sweeteners.

I promise you a satisfying diet as well as a healthier diet. And, of course, it's going to solve your weight-management problems. As the saying goes, "Try it—you'll like it!"

WHAT ABOUT EXERCISE?

I know I am going to surprise those of you who are familiar with my previous work in the obesity area with the following statement because I am such a strong proponent of physical fitness as a key to weight management, and I continue to be a strong proponent, but:

Yes! You can reduce your body fat without additional exercise by following the nutritional principles of the T-Factor Diet. I am very pleased to be able to say this, because, for the first time, there appears to be real hope for persons who suffer from limitations in their ability to be active.

But I want to emphasize that the healthiest way to permanent weight management, *and the easiest and quickest*, is through a combination of the T-Factor Diet and its associated T-Factor forms of physical activity. Besides, physical activity has a special impact on our self-esteem and psychological well-being that cannot be matched by any other change in a sedentary person's life-style.

WHAT TO EXPECT IN THIS BOOK

In the next chapter (Chapter 2) I will explain what the T-Factor is and summarize the scientific research that led to the development of the T-Factor Diet and how it works. It is the healthiest diet there is for all normal persons and you do not have to cut calories to burn off the unhealthy excess fat.[3]

And then we won't waste time. In Chapter 3 I'll explain each of the principles of the T-Factor Diet fully and simply. If you are the kind of person who wants to just sit back and watch as the fat gradually falls off, there will be no calorie counting and no need to follow fixed menus unless you want my specific recommendations. Your excess fat will simply and naturally melt away, that is, be burned as fuel, until your body establishes a new equilibrium with the minimum of fat storage that was meant for you by mother nature. Because I am interested in helping you to eat a nutritious diet I will, however, give suggestions for several basic breakfasts, lunches, and dinners. I also include three weeks of specific daily menus. I want to show you that exactly the same principles apply to permanent weight management as to weight loss—*no more on-and-off diets!*

In Chapter 4 I will present some personal experiences and hints from persons who have been following the T-Factor Diet and who have permanently incorporated it into their life-style—including myself.

Although I hope you realize from your own past experience that the race may not go to the hare but to the tortoise, I know that some of you—especially thóse who have more than a few pounds to lose—are in a hurry! I was when I lost my own excess 70 pounds some twenty-six years ago. As long as you use a quick-loss plan that incorporates the principles you must incorporate permanently into your diet, a quick-loss plan need not be counterproductive and need not encourage a quick regaining of lost weight (as so many quick-loss plans do). It's really a matter of temperament and personal choice.

---

[3]Because the research is so new and has to date appeared only in scientific journals and has not been incorporated into the nutrition textbooks, I present a much more in-depth and detailed discussion, with references, in Appendix A.

The Quick Melt plan, which I present in Chapter 5, is for those of you who want a safe head start on your weight-management program. If you are considerably overweight, the Quick Melt can take off up to a pound a day. In contrast with the basic T-Factor Diet, the Quick Melt plan is calorie reduced in order to pull extra fat from your fat cells. To make sure you are eating well during your Quick Melt, I present twenty-one days of sample menus. Incorporated in these menus are six special recipes developed by Ms. Veronica Petta, M.A., *Family Circle* home economist and nutritionist, specifically for the T-Factor Diet. I think they are delicious and that they will appeal to you.

If you choose to start with the Quick Melt, stick with it for three weeks. Then, if you have more weight to lose, use either the principles or the sample menus in Chapter 3 to continue to your weight-loss goal. *You do not have to continue to cut calories to burn off excess body fat, and the sooner you begin to incorporate T-Factor principles and practice into your permanent eating plan WITHOUT cutting calories, the more certain you are of lifelong success.*

After you have been on a reduced-calorie diet, there is always the danger of a rapid gain should you increase calories too quickly. Chapter 5 closes with transitional menus that will prevent you from regaining the weight you have lost when you switch to maintenance after using the Quick Melt.

In Chapter 6 I present many recipes to show you that the diet I am recommending is truly something you can live with for the rest of your life. Some of these recipes come from my own household, others from the director of nutrition of the Vanderbilt Weight Management Program, Ms. Jamie Pope-Cordle, M.S., R.D., and others were developed by Ms. Veronica Petta at *Family Circle* magazine. Still others demonstrate how participants in the Vanderbilt Weight Management Program responded to the challenge of modifying their own favorite dishes to fit the principles of the diet. Before being included in this book all recipes were repeatedly tested and, in addition to being delicious, they are designed to serve as an education. I want to show you how to use T-Factor principles to prepare everything from soup to nuts, including your own favorite dishes. I want everyone in your family to be happy about the changes you are making. Two things are certain: If you don't like what I'm encouraging you to do, you will find it hard to stick with, and if everyone in your family feels as though you're forcing THEM to go on a diet because you're trying to lose weight, you're not going to get much cooperation.

Going on to my recommendations for physical activity in Chapter 7, I will explain why some kinds of exercise do so little to help with weight control and how some forms of exercise, in combination with the typical American diet, may actually encourage your body to gain fat. I will, of course, describe an activity program that can make sure your body fat is at its healthiest, lowest minimum.

In Chapter 8 I will explain how psychological factors can play a key role in maintaining your motivation for physical activity. Our research shows that physical activity contributes more to the development of a positive self-concept than does weight loss itself.

With the help of Ms. Pope-Cordle I have prepared a special chapter (Chapter 9) on childhood and adolescent nutrition. Here I will explain how to help overweight children lose weight without going on a diet. Of course, even if your children are not overweight, the way to prevent weight problems in later life is to develop healthy eating and activity habits early in life.

In Chapter 10 I'll discuss some important myths and misunderstandings about obesity. I'll explain the likely origins of carbohydrate cravings and why we tend to have a preference for fatty foods. I'll also explain the real meaning of the term *set point* and how you can control it.

In order to help guarantee your success in losing weight, this book includes a fat-gram counter. If you really want to know how much fat you are eating, on which your body's fat storage depends, all you need to do is count your fat grams. When you reach the limit, you can eat just about anything you want in case you're hungry, but it must *not* contain additional fat! The counter also includes the values for dietary fiber because the consumption of fiber can help assure that you obtain the maximum fat-burning impact of the T-Factor Diet, as well as a number of other health benefits.

HOW IS THE T-FACTOR DIET AN IMPROVEMENT OVER THE ROTATION DIET AND ANY OTHER WEIGHT-LOSS DIET?

The Rotation Diet was designed in 1984–1985 by my colleagues and me in the Vanderbilt Weight Management Program to help people lose weight quickly without encountering the metabolic slowdown that often accompanies quick losses. It's a good, fast weight-loss diet that has helped millions of people lose weight. Our research results show that about 25 percent of the people have lost weight permanently, and at least half of the users are remaining physically more active than before.

That's an excellent record, but the scientific discoveries that led to the development of the T-Factor Diet have now provided a way to improve on it. I will discuss the improvements in detail when I compare it with the Quick Melt in Chapter 5. In brief, the T-Factor Diet is more nutritious, easier to follow, has a much greater variety of foods, and does not require low-calorie dieting for a quick loss. In particular, I'm concerned with the maintenance of weight loss, and while the Rotation Diet has done extremely well, it is a calorie-based and calorie-restricted diet. We now know the essential role that dietary fat plays in obesity, and that the key to permanent weight control has less to do with calories than with the fat in your diet. When people fail to keep their weight off after losing it on any diet, it's because they begin to consume more fat than they can burn off each day. When you fully understand this point and learn to incorporate its practical application into your own diet, you will never have a weight problem again.

HERE IS WHAT'S IN STORE FOR YOU ON THE T-FACTOR DIET

"I can't believe I'm eating like this and losing weight!"

This is the most frequent comment that people on the T-Factor Diet make from Day 1. I wish I didn't have to call the T-Factor Diet a "diet" because of the calorie-cutting associations that people make to that word. YOU ARE NOT GOING ON A DIET TO LOSE WEIGHT.

You are not going to be cutting calories or counting them.

Except for fat, you are going to be eating just about as much of everything as you want.

"I'm never hungry! There's always something good to eat!"

That's another frequent comment made by people on the T-Factor Diet.

Right from the first day you will be losing weight AND eating delicious food according to the principles that will make it easy for you to maintain ideal weight for life. No more on-and-off diets. No more deprivation. No more obsessions with food. No more guilt feelings. And no more wild desires to binge that can follow constant restraint.

I'll say it once again and then let you find out for yourself:

There is always something good to eat on the T-Factor Diet. You can lose weight and you can keep it off, and YOU'LL NEVER GO HUNGRY AGAIN!

2

◆

The Thin-Factor: The Scientific Background of the T-Factor Diet[1]

◆

The T-Factor is your THIN-Factor!

Essentially, the term "T-Factor" refers to the energy-using processes by which your body turns food into fuel and burns fuel during exercise. These natural processes, labeled in the scientific field with unusual terms like "thermic" and "thermogenesis," can be harnessed to help you lose weight. I've grouped all of these processes under the term *T-Factor* (the "T" being the first letter of the words thermic and thermogenesis) and I'm going to explain why and how you can maximize your T-Factor so that you can actually eat more and weigh less! This is not an idle claim. Here's how it works.

There are three aspects to the T-Factor:

1. *The Thermic Effect of Food.* It takes energy to get energy! Your body burns up a certain number of calories simply turning the protein, carbohydrate, and fat in your food into the form your body needs to stay alive and keep moving. *The amount of calories required in the conversion process is different for protein, carbohydrate, and fat.*

---

[1] In this chapter I present the conclusions from the most important research that led to the development of the T-Factor Diet. The actual studies are discussed in detail and referenced in Appendix A.

Adaptive Thermogenesis. Your body also has the to adapt to changing circumstances. It can either *conserve* or *waste* a certain number of calories while it's turning your food into fuel and performing all the other functions necessary to life.

In its conservation mode, the metabolic processes are slow or sluggish. The body switches to conservation mode and slows down to protect a person against fat and protein loss in times of famine, but, when plenty of food is available, this slowdown leads to easy weight gain.

In its wasteful mode your body's metabolic rate speeds up; the wasteful mode is nature's way of preventing weight gain and keeping people thin.

Without realizing it, however, overweight people keep their bodies in the conservation mode with an unwise choice of foods, going on and off diets, and, often, a lack of exercise! Obviously, if you want to lose weight and stay lean, you want to switch modes. That is, if you want to lose weight and never regain it, you want to rev up and waste fuel. Fortunately, as you will soon discover, turning on your wasteful mode by speeding up your metabolism is good for your health as well as your spirits and energy level!

3. *The Thermic Effect of Exercise.* Quick, explosive physical movements are powered by your body's carbohydrate energy stores, while sustained repetitive movements use primarily fat. This is why certain kinds of activity tend to be better for losing weight than others. We'll talk more about the T-Factor Exercise Program in Chapter 7.

You can take advantage of your body's natural fat-burning T-Factor in a number of ways, from how your body turns food into fuel to how it stores fuel and how it burns fuel.

HOW THE BODY TURNS FOOD INTO FUEL

Until quite recently, experts in the field of nutrition assumed that the energy in different food sources, that is, protein, carbohydrate, and fat, was extracted with about equal efficiency. Thus, if we overate on *any* source, all the surplus energy would end up in our fat cells. Calories contained in carbohydrate foods would make you just as fat as calories from fatty foods. Recent research in the area of biochemistry is about to revolutionize our views about how energy is extracted from the different foods and used by our bodies.

This new biochemical research has shown more clearly than ever that IT'S THE FAT IN YOUR DIET THAT MAKES YOU FAT.

This statement probably comes as no surprise to you, at least in part. Anyone who has ever been on a diet knows to stay away from fatty foods, including fried foods and rich desserts. But what about grains, breads, muffins, pasta, beans, rice, corn, and all those starchy foods? How about those high-calorie natural sweets like dried fruits? Do we have to cut back on those foods in order to lose weight?

The answer is NO! Carbohydrate foods, including starchy foods and dried fruits, actually turn on your T-Factor and help you stay thin. Protein also turns on your T-Factor, but animal protein is often found together with a great deal of fat, and a diet high in protein is not recommended.

How do protein and carbohydrates affect your T-Factor? Why is it virtually impossible to get fat, or stay fat, when you follow the low-fat dietary guidelines in the T-Factor Diet?

Here are the facts:

1. First of all, protein is not a major factor in weight regulation. Within the normal range found in the typical American diet, all of the energy contained in the protein is burned in our daily fuel mixture and none is converted for fat storage. Indeed, it takes 25 percent of the energy contained in protein just to transform it into the form our bodies need, so only 75 percent is available for building and repairing cells and other metabolic functions.

2. Fat is another story. It takes hardly any energy at all to convert fat into a source of fuel for our bodies. A whopping 97 percent of the calories in fat can be placed in permanent storage just where you don't want it if you overeat even a tiny bit on fat. REMEMBER THAT!

3. The real news pertains to carbohydrate. Until recently, we thought that while the body may not be quite as efficient at converting excess carbohydrate to body fat as it

is in converting dietary fat to body fat, any extra calories still ended up in your fat storage. WE NOW KNOW THAT THIS IS NOT TRUE. EXCEPT UNDER VERY, VERY UNUSUAL CIRCUMSTANCES, THE BODY CONVERTS ALMOST NO CARBOHYDRATE TO FAT!

THE T-FACTOR CARBOHYDRATE STORY

A bit of history first. We have known for some time that it takes more energy to convert carbohydrate to fat than it takes to convert dietary fat to body fat. The cost of converting dietary fat to body fat is only 3 percent, which means that only 3 out of every 100 calories of dietary fat will be burned as the body converts fat for storage. In comparison, the cost of going through the various steps that convert carbohydrate to fat is about 25 percent. That is, whenever the body converts carbohydrate to fat, it takes about 25 percent of the energy content of the carbohydrate to fuel the conversion process. This leaves about 75 percent available for fat storage.

Based on these costs as determined in the laboratory, we used to think that should you consume more energy than you customarily expended in a given day, part of it in carbohydrate and part in fat, 97 percent of the fat and 75 percent of the carbohydrate ended up in your fat cells.

NOT SO!

Within a very wide range, which I'll discuss below, the body finds a way to burn off just about every single bit of the carbohydrate you give it or to enter it into temporary glycogen[2] storage, and only the fat goes to fat. Under normal circumstances, in any given day, *a maximum of only about 4 percent of the carbohydrate is converted to fat.*

Here are some other facts which I hope will convince you of the weight-management value of cutting fat in your diet and substituting carbohydrate.

The body expends from two to three times more energy metabolizing carbohydrate compared with fat. By

[2]Glycogen is a polysaccharide, a different form of the carbohydrate that your body stores so that it can be retrieved easily and quickly when needed. After retrieval it is transformed to glucose before being burned as fuel.

this I mean it burns two to three times more calories just getting it from your intestines into your bloodstream and transforming it to glycogen for storage in your liver and muscles (and eight times more calories to convert any part of it to fat).

If you customarily eat a high-carbohydrate diet, your metabolic rate over a twenty-four-hour period is likely to be higher than the metabolic rate of a person eating a high-fat diet. Although you are not consciously aware of it, a high ratio of carbohydrate to fat in your diet causes your body to work a bit harder after every meal than a high ratio of fat to carbohydrate. This thermic effect of a high-carbohydrate diet can average as much as 200 or even 300 calories each day. These calories are simply burned off and wasted.

In addition, should you ever go out on the town and celebrate with a big meal, your metabolic rate will go even higher in an effort to burn off the extra calories if you normally eat a high-carbohydrate diet rather than a high-fat diet.

Even if you take in a large amount of carbohydrate, practically none of it will be turned to fat. In fact, in one of the studies I describe and reference in Appendix A, the research subjects ate a single meal containing 2000 carbohydrate calories. Only 81 of those calories were turned to fat, and, because the body burns a mixture of fat and carbohydrate for fuel, the subjects had to burn stored body fat in the hours that followed that meal. In other words, in spite of consuming 2000 carbohydrate calories in a single sitting, they began to lose body fat!

This sounds so unbelievable that I'm sure you want to know whether there are any conditions at all under which the body will begin to convert carbohydrate to fat. The answer is yes, but the conditions are so extreme that I don't think you or anyone else would want to create them intentionally. Here's why.

Because the body seems to resist converting carbohydrate to fat, you must force it to do so. This requires that you out-eat your daily energy needs for carbohydrate by hundreds or even thousands of calories every day for many successive days. The first few hundred carbohydrate calories of your overconsumption will be fit into your liver and muscle storage sites. But these sites fill rather quickly. Then, in an effort to burn off any additional carbohydrate, your body gradually increases its metabolic rate. To maintain the conversion of carbohydrate to fat, you have to keep on increasing your food consumption, eating more and more carbohydrate every day! Overeating in this way is not at all like overeating at a single meal. Most of us would not voluntarily wish to endure the experience! I discuss the research that demonstrates this in Appendix A.

HOW THE BODY STORES FUEL

Carbohydrate is transformed into glucose, a form of sugar that your body can use directly as fuel. But then, since we use only a part of the carbohydrate we eat at any given meal immediately, most of it is transformed to another form of sugar, called glycogen, for storage. Your body has limited room for glycogen storage: About 400 calories are normally stored in the liver plus 1200 to 1600 calories in muscle tissue. That amount can be increased by a few hundred calories through exercise, which encourages your muscles to store some extra energy, or, as I described above, by greatly overeating on carbohydrate, which saturates all storage sites.

The glycogen is stored in a solution of water, about 3 to 4 parts water to 1 part glycogen. For every 500 calories of glycogen stored, enough water is combined with it to equal 1 pound of body weight. Thus, whenever you increase or decrease just 500 calories of your glycogen stores, you gain or lose a pound of body weight, but it's mostly water. Part of the daily weight fluctuation we all experience is due to variation in our carbohydrate intake, as well as our salt intake, which also influences water retention.

Quick-weight-loss diets that cut out carbohydrates in the diet capitalize on glycogen depletion, to give you a spurious weight loss; the water weight is regained immediately upon any increase in calorie consumption.

Fat, in contrast with glycogen, can be stored in almost unlimited quantities. A woman of normal weight may have 85,000 to 100,000 calories in fat storage, and with a high-fat diet and a lack of physical activity, fat storage is easily increased. A person who is 30 pounds overweight has about 105,000 extra calories in fat storage, on top of the average of 85,000 to 100,000 in the person of normal weight!

Fat is stored in a ratio of 4 parts fat to 1 part water. This is almost the exact *opposite* ratio of carbohydrate to water. And, because there are 9 calories contained in each gram of fat, compared with only 4 in each gram of glycogen, this means that each pound of fat contains about 3500 calories. Do you see what this energy concentration in fat storage implies for weight loss? While you will lose a pound of mostly water for every 500-calorie deficit in carbohydrate intake, it takes a deficit of 3500 calories to lose a pound of fat. But don't jump to conclusions! When you cut back on calories, you deplete glycogen stores quickly and lose a lot of water weight, but since you have only about 2000 calories in your glycogen stores, this rate of loss is severely limited. It cannot last.

Fast-weight-loss diets that cut back on carbohydrates count on the water loss that accompanies the depletion of your glycogen stores to make the diets more attractive and encourage you to try them. They also count on the cutback in sodium intake that accompanies a reduction in calories, which also leads to a large water loss. But, at the end of one to two weeks, you've reached a new low point in glycogen storage and in water balance. At that time, weight loss, while now all fat,[3] is about seven times slower than it was when you first began the diet. If you don't understand how the nature of your diet affects water balance and weight loss, this slowdown can be very discouraging.

HOW THE BODY BURNS FUEL

Under normal circumstances your body burns all the protein energy you can eat in a day. As I described above, the new research shows that, short of "force feeding," we also burn all the carbohydrate we eat. Since, within a very wide range, we tend to burn in our fuel mix each day all the protein and carbohydrate that we obtain in our diets, the

[3] When people who are greatly overweight lose weight they also lose a certain amount of lean tissue simply because they don't need as much muscle to carry excess weight around. This is perfectly normal.

difference between our total daily energy needs and the combined amount of energy that was supplied by protein and carbohydrate must be made up by burning fat.

THE FAT CAN COME FROM OUR DIETS OR OUT OF OUR FAT CELLS!

This is a very important point. It is essential that you understand what it means for weight control. Let me show you how it works with a real example from an important research study.

In this study the research subjects ate two breakfasts, on different days, that had exactly the same amount of protein and carbohydrate, but varied in fat content.

On each of the two days, the diet had 120 calories in protein and 292 calories in carbohydrate.

On the low-fat day it had only 54 calories in fat.

On the high-fat day it contained 414 calories in fat.

Following each of the breakfasts, the researchers measured the amounts of protein, carbohydrate, and fat that were burned by these subjects in their fuel mixtures during the next nine hours.

On both days the total energy needs over nine hours were quite similar—the research subjects burned about 760 to 780 calories. On each of the days they burned almost exactly the same number of protein and carbohydrate calories as were contained in the breakfast, that is, about 120 protein calories and about 292 carbohydrate calories. The really interesting results concern fat, because on both days the subjects burned approximately 360 calories of fat in their fuel mixtures.

That is, regardless of the fat content of the breakfast—it didn't matter if it was high or low—the body still burned the same total calories and the same amount of fat.

But, as you can see illustrated in Figure 2-1, ON THE LOW-FAT DAY, THE BODY TOOK ABOUT 300 CALORIES OUT OF FAT STORAGE.

ON THE HIGH-FAT DAY, THE BODY USED THE DIETARY FAT IN ITS FUEL MIXTURE AND HAD ABOUT 50 CALORIES LEFT OVER TO BE PUT IN FAT STORAGE!

The research I have just discussed, together with the other studies I present in Appendix A, has led us to the amazing conclusion that when it comes to the amount of fat you have in storage—the fat that's making you over-weight—the calories that you consume in the form of protein and carbohydrate don't really count for very much. You, as well as everyone else concerned with remedying the problem of obesity, must revise your way of thinking. It's not a question of total calories and you don't have to cut them down and go on low-calorie diets in order to lose weight!

The reason you got fat in the the first place is that you took in more calories in the form of dietary fat than you were burning off in your daily fuel mixture.

AND THE KEY TO LOSING WEIGHT, IN THE SIMPLEST OF TERMS, IS TO EAT LESS FAT IN YOUR DAILY DIET THAN YOUR BODY BURNS EACH DAY!

THE FAT IN YOUR DIET DETERMINES YOUR AMOUNT OF BODY FAT

The research I have discussed above has led leading biochemists to the conclusion that body fat may be more closely related to the fat in your diet than to total calories. As in the study I just described, within a wide range, you will burn up the protein and carbohydrate you eat each day. Then, if the fat in your diet exceeds your remaining needs for energy, it goes into fat storage. As long as you continue to eat more fat than you burn in your fuel mix each day you will keep getting fatter and fatter until you reach a new equilibrium where the expanded energy needs of your fatter, heavier body match your high fat intake. In one animal study where calories and the mixture of nutrients could be controlled carefully, an increase from 20 percent of calories in fat to 40 percent of calories in fat led to A DOUBLING OF BODY-FAT CONTENT!

THEREFORE, THE KEY TO A PERMANENT LOW AMOUNT OF BODY FAT IS NOT CUTTING CALORIES OR "DIETING." IT'S A PERMANENT LOW-FAT DIET!

The T-Factor Diet makes sure that you are burning more fat calories in your fuel mixture than you are consum-

FIGURE 2-1

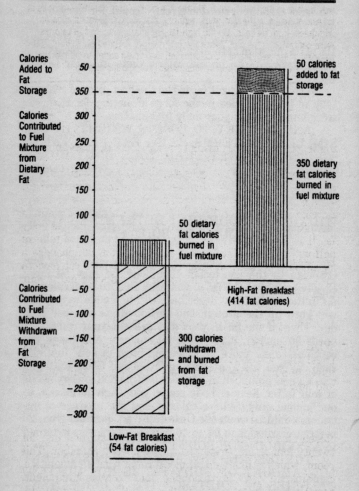

Calories
Added to
Fat
Storage

Calories
Contributed
to Fuel
Mixture
from
Dietary
Fat

50 calories
added to fat
storage

350 dietary
fat calories
burned in
fuel mixture

50 dietary
fat calories
burned in
fuel mixture

High-Fat Breakfast
(414 fat calories)

Calories
Contributed
to Fuel
Mixture
Withdrawn
from
Fat
Storage

300 calories
withdrawn
and burned
from fat
storage

Low-Fat Breakfast
(54 fat calories)

Source of fat burned in fuel mixture following low- and high-fat breakfasts. In the nine hours following both breakfasts an average of 350 calories in fat was burned in the fuel mixture. On the low-fat day only about 50 calories in fat was supplied in the diet, thus requiring that about 300 fat calories be withdrawn from fat cells. On the high-fat day approximately 400 calories were contained in the diet. Since the fuel mixture required only about 350 calories, there were about 50 calories left over to be added to fat storage (figures are rounded for ease of illustration; see text for details).

ing in your diet. This leads to weight loss of *fat* even if you increase your carbohydrate consumption.

The T-Factor Diet also shows you how to maintain a permanent low-fat diet that you can like and enjoy forever. This means that you will have a permanently lower body-fat content when you finish losing the weight you want to lose. Since we all start with a different percentage of body fat, I can't promise that everyone who cuts fat intake in half will cut body-fat content in half! But I can promise a significant, permanent reduction, and the more you have to lose, the greater will be the impact of reducing fat in your diet.

RESEARCH AT VANDERBILT

What, in actual practice, occurs when you use the T-Factor Diet? Can we determine the amount of body fat you are likely to burn off each day? How much weight will you lose and how fast?

Research in the Calorimetry Chamber

Research subjects in one phase of our studies live for twenty-four-hour periods in a calorimetry chamber. This room, which is like a small motel room with all amenities, contains a TV, VCR, telephone, and exercise equipment, together with other facilities, such as a commode, sink, and small refrigerator. It is also airtight. Since we supply the air to the room, we can measure the change in the expired gas as the subjects breathe throughout the day and night. The room is also equipped with radar and we can monitor the amount of physical activity that occurs spontaneously. This provides us with a means of determining with great accuracy the daily metabolic rate, the response to different diets and exercise levels, and the proportions of fat and carbohydrate that are burned each day in the fuel mixture.

Subjects in our research are accustomed to each of two diets, a high- or low-fat diet (T-Factor fat-gram intake), for a full week at a time. We measure the daily energy needs and the nature of the fuel mixture during two days each of these weeks in which they spend twenty-four hours in the chamber. We then repeat the process again with the same subject in order to verify and replicate the findings of the first two weeks.

We have determined that the thermic effect of food—that's the amount of energy it takes to metabolize food over and above the resting metabolic rate—can average as much as 200 calories or more on a high-carbohydrate diet each day compared with as little as 50 calories on a high-fat diet *in the same individual*. That's energy that is not available for sustaining metabolic functions or for storage. It's wasted.

In addition, when the same individual switches to the low-fat T-Factor Diet, the fuel mixture still requires considerably more fat than is contained in the diet. During the week on the T-Factor Diet, an average of over 100 calories more each day is withdrawn from the fat cells, compared with a high-fat diet for the same subject.

Obviously, the greater thermic response to the high-carbohydrate diet and the need for more fat in the fuel mixture than is contained in the diet can lead to weight loss! This helps explain the fine results we have obtained with the T-Factor Diet in our clinical studies.

Clinical Studies at Vanderbilt

In our clinical studies with two different groups of women, we contrasted the weight loss and reactions to the T-Factor Diet in its two forms, the basic, no calorie counting or cutting form, and the Quick Melt.

The Quick Melt is calorie controlled around a core menu of about 1000 calories per day. A snack is permitted (in fact, recommended so that subjects will not feel deprived and can maintain the diet for as long as they choose). As implemented by our research subjects in actual practice, the Quick Melt ended up at about 1250 calories per day. Subjects in the no counting or cutting group ended up eating about 1500 calories a day. For identification purposes in our study, we called this latter group the Lifestyle group.

Both groups followed the T-Factor fat-gram formula and, over time, both groups averaged approximately 30 grams of fat per day, or about 270 calories. The extra 250 calories eaten by the Lifestyle group were almost entirely in the form of carbohydrate snacks. All subjects were encouraged to gradually increase physical activity until they could walk comfortably at a brisk pace for forty-five minutes.

The average amount overweight according to standard weight-for-height tables in our groups was 60 pounds, and the average age of the women was thirty-nine. Just about all were quite sedentary before beginning this program.

As you might expect, the Quick Melt group lost weight rapidly, averaging 11 pounds the first three weeks, and then slowing to an average of between 1.5 and 2 pounds per week thereafter. The Lifestyle group lost an average of 7 pounds the first three weeks, and then slowed to around 1 pound a week thereafter. Several of the women in the Lifestyle group lost over 15 pounds the first five weeks. This was a great surprise to me. I never anticipated that our research subjects would achieve that speed of loss without making a conscious effort to curtail eating and cut calories. Of course, by reducing fat they did end up eating fewer calories than before, *but they also ate far more food in terms of bulk and weight than ever before. They were never hungry.* Needless to say, our research subjects were very pleased. In Chapter 4 I will reproduce some of their personal reactions, as well as my own and those of the Vanderbilt Weight Management Program's director of nutrition as we adopted the T-Factor Diet.

A Field Study

There is always a problem extrapolating from a controlled study, in which seriously overweight research subjects are guided and monitored by a professional staff, to what might happen to that great mass of people "in the real world" who want to lose only a small amount of weight. What can we expect when people adopt the T-Factor fat-gram formula on their own and follow the general recommendations that I give in Chapter 3?

Although not planned as a formal study, after two lectures on nutrition and obesity given by Ms. Pope-Cordle and me, eight young women and one man between the ages of nineteen and twenty-two decided to count fat grams and follow the T-Factor formula for a minimum of two weeks as part of their term project in a health-promotion course at Vanderbilt University. The women were all within the normal weight range, with weights lying between the mid and upper points of the suggested weight table. The man was 8 pounds above the upper limit. Thus, these women (and the man) were all concerned with what has been called the "final 5 to 15" pounds that millions of people, but especially women, struggle with all their lives and never seem to be rid of once and for all.

The women averaged a loss of 1.25 pounds per week during the project. Out of curiosity alone, since this was not a research study, I decided to survey the group without prior warning at the end of the semester. You can imagine how pleased I was to discover that they had ALL stuck with the T-Factor Diet and that they had averaged, *and maintained,* exactly the loss they set out for: 5 pounds. The man lost 11 pounds in one month, and he, too, had maintained that loss at follow-up. EVERY SINGLE PERSON WAS SUCCESSFUL.

It is important in considering these results to note that the persons who achieved them did so without participating in a formal research study. Thus they had no external motivation or supervision supplied by a group leader, and there was no external motivation to continue sticking with the program in anticipation of a follow-up.

Why—indeed HOW—had all of these students continued to stick with the T-Factor Diet? If you have ever tried to eat a healthful diet as a college student living on campus, you will know what I mean when I emphasize that word "how." Well, as one of the young women remarked in the comments section of her follow-up form, "It's easy and it works!"

3

♦

Putting the T-Factor Diet to Work: How to Lose Weight Without Cutting Calories

♦

It's not how much you eat, but WHAT you eat.

If you've ever been on a diet I'm sure you remember the *energy equation* the experts refer to when they suggest that you cut back on your calorie intake to lose weight. This equation states that you maintain your weight when

ENERGY IN = ENERGY OUT.

Then, in order to lose weight, you are told to "unbalance the energy equation." *Energy in* must be less than *energy out*.

Energy in is considered to be the energy content of the food in your diet, as measured in the laboratory. These are the calories that get listed in your calorie counters. In the previous chapter I explained that this is not an entirely correct way to view energy balance when it comes to weight management. The energy that is available for use or that gets stored in the human body from protein and carbohydrate, compared with fat, IS NOT EQUAL! And, similarly, all *energy out* is also not equal when it comes to losing body fat, but I'll get into this issue when I discuss physical activity in Chapter 7.

The key to losing excess body fat is not simply a

question of the total energy in your diet relative to total energy expenditure. Changes in body fat depend primarily on that portion of the energy in or out that is supplied by fat. If you eat less fat each day than the fat you are burning up in the fuel mixture required to sustain your basal metabolic processes and the fat you are using to power physical activity, you end up losing body fat. In other words, when

FAT *IN* is less than FAT *OUT*

you will lose weight and 100 percent of the weight you lose will be FAT.

I must emphasize this fact—the way to lose body fat is to eat less fat than you burn up each day.

Of course you can rush the process and cut back on calories, too, if you want to lose weight even more quickly. This will pull calories out of both your carbohydrate and fat stores, and I'll discuss the best way to do this when I talk about the Quick Melt in Chapter 5. But when you follow the T-Factor Diet as I will outline in this chapter, we are concerned only with the fat in your diet, not cutting calories.

DO YOU KNOW HOW MUCH FAT IS CONTAINED IN THE FOOD YOU EAT EACH DAY?

I'll bet you don't! Our research shows that the great majority of people do not know how much fat they eat each day. Even those of us who are most nutrition and weight conscious think "calories," not "fat." We know that butter, ice cream, mayonnaise, and salad dressings are fatty foods, but we don't realize that 50 to 75 percent of calories in many meat products, dairy products, snack foods, condiments, and desserts are fat calories.

Once you know where the fat is coming from in your diet and become aware of how much you consume each day, it's not hard to make some modifications and design a satisfying diet that will start melting off *all* your surplus body fat. Follow the general principles that I will outline in this chapter. Within a matter of weeks I think you will find that you are able to modify your present diet and develop a new approach to eating that will become the most satisfying diet you've ever eaten. You will never feel hungry because you can add anything you want to the basic diet as long as it isn't a fatty food. And, as a bonus, if you have been eating a typical American diet and suffering from any kind of gastric distress, you will probably feel better than you have ever felt before.

FORGET ABOUT CALORIES!

The first thing you need to do when you follow the T-Factor Diet without cutting calories is to forget about them! When you follow the T-Factor Diet you need make no effort to count calories. Don't even think calories. This way you never feel that you are "dieting." We are only going to make some substitutions!

You will be amazed at the freedom from food obsessions that this will give you. Rather than feel guilty over every deviation from a calorie goal, you will be feeling good over the easy switches from high- to low-fat foods that will soon become habitual.

But there is still some work to do. At first you will need to count fat grams, so you are not entirely free from counting. You must learn where the fat in your diet is coming from, and we are concerned with grams of fat. I'll explain how we do this in a moment when I give you our "magic"[1] formula for losing fat without dieting.

Counting grams of fat, however, lasts only until you learn the fat content of the different foods and recipes that will become part of your customary diet. The major difference between the T-Factor Diet and other diets is that you don't have to restrain yourself to fit within some calorie limit. Our only concern is with fat. You are free to make healthy substitutions for fatty foods *and to keep on eating healthy foods until your appetite is satisfied.* No more guilt feelings!

Strangely enough, an interesting issue arose when the T-Factor Diet was first introduced to our research participants at Vanderbilt. I was greeted by a roomful of skeptical faces. They couldn't believe that they could lose weight simply by substituting nutrients—carbohydrate for fat—and still eat pretty much to their heart's content.

---

[1] My colleagues and I debated the use of the word "magic," which I have put in quotation marks, because we don't want to be misunderstood. There is no magical cure for obesity. Permanent changes in diet and/or activity level are necessary to achieve a permanent change in weight. I made a decision to keep the word, in quotation marks, to communicate an "as if" quality. The T-Factor concept is so simple to implement, compared to calorie counting and cutting, that the results may seem truly unbelievable, if not "magical," to you.

Well, as the saying goes, the proof of the pudding is in the eating!

I will describe my own experience switching to the T-Factor Diet, and those of some other individuals, in Chapter 4. According to the weight charts, I did not need to lose weight. I was right in the middle of the desirable weight range. But I certainly did not want to talk about this fascinating new dietary concept without living it out myself. I lost 7 pounds in seven weeks simply by changing the composition of my diet, and all of it from my nice little extra store of fat around my hips! The others whom I interviewed had lost as much as 50 pounds or more. The T-Factor Diet has led to some remarkable changes in our lives, and together we'll give you some useful tips.

THE "MAGIC" NUMBERS

I've been talking about grams, not calories, and it's grams of fat that we are concerned with in the T-Factor Diet. Perhaps some of you have counted carbohydrate grams as part of a weight-control effort in the past, thinking that it was carbohydrate that was responsible for your weight problems. We now know that it's the fat that counts, almost to the exclusion of other forms of energy.

A gram of fat contains approximately 9 calories, compared with approximately 4 contained in a gram of carbohydrate. You will soon get a feeling for where the fat lies in the foods you customarily eat. The menus in this chapter all contain fat-gram counts and there are a number of discussions below that will alert you to the differences in foods as you begin to make low-fat for high-fat substitutions. You will, of course, study the fat-gram counter in Appendix C.

Our studies show that the average overweight woman is eating between 80 and 100 grams of fat each day. That, translated into calories, is between 720 and 900 calories in fat. The average man is taking in about 20 grams more, or between 900 and 1080 calories in fat.

The T-Factor formula for weight loss is:

20 to 40 grams of fat per day for women
30 to 60 grams of fat per day for men

Men can eat more fat than women and still lose weight because they have higher energy needs. The range is large to allow for flexibility. Even at 40 grams a day, most women will be cutting their fat intake in half, and will lose weight, although not as fast as they would if they chose to stay near the bottom of the range.

Only fat grams are limited. When you have reached your quota of fat grams for the day, you may substitute no-fat foods for foods with fat at any time until your appetite is satisfied. I'll give more details on how to implement this formula as we go along.

It's not wise to go below the ranges that I suggest because fat supplies some essential nutrients that cannot be obtained from other foods and a minimal amount is necessary for the transport of fat-soluble vitamins. Besides, fat makes food taste good! If you don't get enough fat, you are likely to feel deprived. *Deprived people are more likely to binge.* Do not deprive yourself. The T-Factor Diet is be enjoyed. It's not a penance.

With respect to protein, the T-Factor Diet recommends levels and types of protein foods that are common in this country, although I will be showing you healthy and tasty ways to switch a portion of your animal protein intake to vegetable sources. So, assuming an adequate protein intake, you are, as I've indicated, free to compensate for the reduction of fat in your diet with whatever increase in carbohydrate foods feels good and satisfies your appetite.

Because of the greater weight and volume of carbohydrate foods, compared with fatty foods, you probably will automatically cut back a bit in calories, too. This automatic cut is another benefit that accrues from the T-Factor Diet without conscious effort, and it serves to foster a speedier loss of weight.

Since you don't have to cut fat to unreasonable levels, food still tastes good. You obtain yet another big plus because your diet will improve immensely in its nutritional value. Calorie for calorie, carbohydrate foods, especially the complex carbohydrates in fruits, vegetables, and whole grains, have far more vitamins and minerals than fatty foods.

FIRST STEPS FIRST

I realize, of course, that you probably are not accustomed to thinking in terms of fat grams rather than calories. So, when you first start to implement the T-Factor Diet you will need to do several things to make it easy for yourself.

1. As you read along in this chapter, be sure to study carefully the list of foods in Table 3-1 and plan how you will make the suggested low-fat substitutions for any high-fat foods that are contained in your present diet. A study of that table will give you a feeling for food fat content in general, high versus low, and start you thinking about how you will make substitutions.

2. Study my discussions on food preparation and menu design below. These will provide you with your first steps toward gaining more specific information on the fat-gram content of different foods.

I will present you with some specific suggestions for a selection of "standard" breakfasts and lunches (all with fat-gram content of the suggested foods). Most people eat about three different kinds of breakfasts and, similarly, a rather restricted number of different lunches. I will want you to think in terms of several kinds of breakfasts and lunches that you can live with just as comfortably as your present selection. If you don't care for my specific suggestions, you will be able to design your own using the fat and fiber gram counter in Appendix C. You can use my suggestions as models. Not that you will be unable to deviate on occasion and have an old-style country breakfast. Of course you will. Preferably before doing an old-country-style day's work! But the standard low-fat breakfasts and lunches will assure that you fall within the fat-gram limits on most days.

3. I also present suggestions for five standard dinners that you can include in your diet whenever the spirit moves you. Each includes a different, easily prepared main course that is commonly found in the American diet. My recipes will show you how to select and prepare these dishes, which most of us already include in our diets, but from now on with a minimum of fat.

However, for a full introduction to the great variety and gastronomic pleasure offered in the T-Factor Diet, I encourage you to try the entire twenty-one days of menus that I present as models in this chapter (pages 51-68). My colleagues and I have designed these menus to take you through a large range of different foods and styles of cooking. In a way, we intend these menus to furnish a practical education in nutrition. Represented in these menus you will find just about everything available in your grocery store. All common fruits, vegetables, low-fat meats, and so on. We have recipes to help you learn how to prepare these foods in a healthful manner. AND IF YOU THINK HEALTHY, LOW-FAT COOKING IS A BORE AND A BOTHER, I WANT YOU TO TRY EVERY SIN-GLE ONE OF THE VEGETABLE, GRAIN, AND MEATLESS MAIN COURSE RECIPES! Let us show you the way to increase your culinary repertoire and help everyone around you stay slim and healthier.

You will notice that our menus specify portion sizes only for foods that contain more than trace amounts of fat; other foods are unlimited, although you can adjust your intake to promote whatever speed of weight loss you prefer.

4. Until you have a good idea of how to construct a diet that falls within 20- to 40-gram fat limit for women or the 30- to 60-gram range for men, you must count fat grams every day. Before you begin the T-Factor Diet, it is a good idea to skim the more complete list in the fat and fiber gram counter in Appendix C, which gives fat grams per serving of over 1100 common foods. You need to know where the fat grams are and this list will give you a good guide to food selection, especially when you desire to make substitutions for anything in the menus. NOTE THAT SOME FOODS HAVE SO LITTLE FAT THAT THEY CAN BE EATEN IN UNLIMITED QUANTITIES AT ANY TIME, AS PART OF YOUR MEALS OR AS UN-LIMITED SNACKS.

WHY THE EMPHASIS ON FIBER IN THE T-FACTOR DIET? WHICH FATS ARE BEST?

Before giving you specific instructions for the T-Factor Diet I must make a digression and talk about the health benefits of increasing fiber in your diet and the reasons for replacing some of the animal fat with fats from vegetables, nuts, and seeds.

I am sure you are aware of the efforts that are being made by health professionals to get Americans to increase their fiber intake. Certain forms of fiber, such as the non-soluble kinds found in whole-grain wheat and wheat bran, seem to help reduce the likelihood of intestinal cancer. Others, such as the water-soluble kinds contained in whole oats and oat bran, rice bran, many fruits, peas, legumes, and corn, seem to help reduce cholesterol and thus the likelihood of cardiovascular disease. Almost every month another article is published in some medical or nutrition journal that reports health benefits for one or another of the high-fiber foods. Similarly, just about as frequently you will find another article reporting the dangers of high-fat consumption, especially of saturated fats, which are found primarily in products of animal origin or in palm or coconut oil. While there is evidence that fiber may help counteract to some slight extent the effects of too much fat in the diet by binding with it and preventing some of it from being absorbed, most of us would do well to attack the problem directly and reduce fat in general.

Although a reduction in total fat should be your primary consideration, you may obtain additional health benefits by replacing a good part of the animal fats in your diet with mono-unsaturated and poly-unsaturated fats. Fats of animal origin are highly saturated and encourage the body to increase its production of cholesterol. Some experts believe saturated fat is an even greater danger in its ability to foster cholesterol production than is dietary cholesterol itself, in part because we tend to consume so much of it. Saturated fats tend to be solid at room temperature. Except for palm and coconut oil, which are also highly saturated, fats from vegetables, nuts, and seeds are mono- and poly-unsaturated, and liquid at room temperature. Soft margarines tend to be less saturated than hard margarines. I use primarily the mono-unsaturated oils, such as olive oil for my salads and peanut oil for cooking. The flavor of olive oil makes for the best salad dressings, while peanut oil withstands higher temperatures in cooking. Research reports suggest that consumption of both these oils, as well as other mono-unsaturated oils, can lower your cholesterol level.

By reducing saturated fat, switching to the use of mono- and poly-unsaturated fats, and increasing soluble fiber in the diet, you may achieve a significant reduction in cholesterol level. Reductions of 20 percent or more are common, and the process is accentuated when you lose weight.

But the role of fiber in the T-Factor Diet is important for many other reasons. Fiber is most commonly found in exactly the foods you can eat in virtually unlimited quantities without gaining weight. When you reduce the fat in your diet, it is next to impossible to eat enough of these foods—the complex carbohydrates—to interfere with gradual weight loss.

The goal for fiber is 20 to 40 grams a day for a woman, and as high as 50 grams for a man. Many people find they can eat even more than that without any ill effects.

However, be sure not to go hog wild over fiber and immediately make a drastic increase. If you have been eating a typical American low-fiber diet (10–12 grams a day), YOU MUST INCREASE GRADUALLY. If you triple your intake overnight you may suffer some intestinal distress, including gas, possibly diarrhea, or even constipation if you don't drink enough liquid. The digestive system can adapt, at least partially if not completely, to an increase in fiber *over time*. So, any distress you notice is likely to disappear as your body adjusts to a change in diet.

While fiber can prevent the absorption of about 10 percent of the fat you eat each day, certain forms of fiber in very large quantities can also interfere with the absorption of certain vitamins and minerals. This is a very complex subject and there is no need to get into the specifics because they are not relevant to the T-Factor Diet. I want to be sure you understand, however, that there is no danger of harmful absorption interference with the T-Factor Diet. The recommended fiber intake is within the safe range, and, because you end up eating so many healthful foods as you reduce your fat intake, the "nutrient density" of your diet increases dramatically. That is, when fat goes down in the diet and whole grains, fruits, and vegetables increase, the amount of vitamins and minerals in the diet per 1000 calories is significantly increased.

The key to getting enough of the several different

TABLE 3-1

FAT SUBSTITUTION GUIDE

USE	INSTEAD OF
Skim or low-fat milk	Whole milk or cream
Evaporated skim milk (canned)	Cream, whipping cream
Plain low-fat or skim-milk yogurt	Sour cream
Blenderized low-fat cottage cheese	Cream cheese or sour cream
Skim milk or low-fat cheeses	High-fat cheeses
½ can soup and 4 ounces skim milk	1 can cream soup in recipes
Sherbet, frozen low-fat desserts	Ice cream
Low-fat yogurt with fresh fruit	Commercial yogurts with fruit, sugar
2 egg whites or egg substitute	One whole egg
Reduced-calorie mayonnaise,[a] mustard, ketchup	Regular mayonnaise
No-cal or low-cal salad dressings	Regular salad dressings
½ or less of the fat called for in recipes, with the remainder in suitable liquid	Regular amount of fat in recipes
Blend of yogurt and mayonnaise	Salad dressing for tuna, chicken
Lean, well-trimmed meats, under 15% fat (flank, round)	Regular heavily marbled cuts, over 15% fat
Ground turkey	Ground beef
Chicken, turkey without skin	Poultry with skin, duck
Water-packed fish	Fish canned in oil
Fresh fish, broiled, baked, poached, steamed	Fried fish, frozen breaded fish
Measured portions of meat women: up to 7 ounces/day men: up to 9 ounces/day	Large portions of meat
Low-fat sauces and marinades	High-fat sauces and gravies
Bouillon, herbs, wine, juices	Gravy, fatty sauces
Low-fat cooking methods: broil bake, boil, poach, steam	High-fat cooking methods: fry, cook in own fat
Legumes, beans, peas, tofu	Meats
Meatless sauces	Sauces with meats

USE	INSTEAD OF
Steamed or microwaved vegetables seasoned with herbs, spices, lemon juice, low-fat sauces	Vegetables in margarine/butter or cheese sauce, or fried vegetables
Water chestnuts	Nuts in vegetable casseroles
Unsweetened water- or juice-packed fruits	Sweetened or syrup-packed fruits
Fresh or dried fruits	High-fat snacks or desserts
Fresh fruit with pancakes	Butter on pancakes
Water, club soda, tea, coffee	Milk shakes
Unbuttered popcorn (preferably air popped), with seasonings such as nutritional yeast	Buttered popcorn, chips, nuts
Pretzels	Chips, nuts, snack crackers
Raw vegetables, low-fat dips	Chips, high-fat dips
Low-fat yogurt dips, salsa	Sour-cream dips
Whole-grain bread, bagel, muffins	Doughnuts, pastry
Low-fat crackers (matzohs, Rye Krisp, flatbread, saltines)	High-fat, flavored snack crackers
Lower-fat cookies (gingersnaps, fig bars, graham crackers, animal crackers)	Higher-fat cookies
Angel food cake	Higher-fat cakes
Fresh fruit	Higher-fat desserts
Puddings made with skim milk	Puddings made with whole milk
Jelly or jam on toast or bread	Butter or margarine on toast or bread

^aOr use less of the regular variety, and compensate for loss of volume with other liquid, if necessary.

TABLE 3-2

FRUIT, VEGETABLES, AND GRAIN FOODS HAVING LITTLE OR NO FAT[a] *(you do not need to control your consumption of these foods)*

FRUIT

Fresh

Apple	Honeydew melon	Persimmon
Banana	(and other melons)	Pineapple
Blackberries	Kiwi	Plum
Blueberries	Mango	Raspberries
Cantaloupe	Orange	Strawberries
Cherries	Papaya	Tangerine
Grapefruit	Peach	Watermelon
Grapes	Pear	

Dried

Apples	Mango	Pineapple
Apricots	Papaya	Prunes
Dates	Peach	Raisins
Figs	Pear	

VEGETABLES

Asparagus	Dandelion greens	Rhubarb
Bean sprouts	Eggplant	Rutabaga
Beets	Endive	Spinach
Beet greens	Escarole	String beans
Broccoli	Green pepper	Summer squash
Brussels sprouts	Kale	Tomatoes
Cabbage	Lettuce	Turnips
Carrots	Mushrooms	Turnip greens
Cauliflower	Mustard greens	Watercress
Celery	Okra	Wax beans
Chard	Onions	Winter squash
Chicory	Parsley	Zucchini
Collards	Pumpkin	
Cucumbers	Radishes	

[a]Fruits and vegetables that contain only trace amounts (less than 0.5 gram) of fat per serving. The grain and other starchy foods usually have less than 1 gram of fat per serving. Be sure to check the labels on all commercially prepared foods for added fat.

GRAINS, LEGUMES, AND OTHER STARCHY FOODS

Breads

Bagel	Hard dinner rolls	Tortilla
Bread (per slice)	Melba toast	Zwieback
English muffin	Pita bread	

Breakfast Cereals

Except for granola-style cereals, most cold and hot breakfast cereals contain no fat to 1 gram of fat per serving. Check the labels of your favorite brands.

Crackers

Animal crackers	Oyster crackers	Saltines
Bread sticks	Pretzels	Venus (brand) crackers
Graham crackers	Rice cakes	

Grains and Grain Foods

Corn	Noodles	Spaghetti
Macaroni	Rice	Wheat (bulgur, etc.)

Legumes and Other Starchy Foods

Kidney beans	Peas, chick	Red beans
Lentils	Peas, green	White beans
Lima beans	Pinto beans	Yams
Navy beans	Potatoes, sweet	
Peas, blackeye	Potatoes, white	

kinds of healthy fiber is to eat a wide variety of foods. Once again, there is no need to become obsessed with getting enough of each kind. You will find the variety you need in my menus and in my recipes, where I make use of different grains in breads and muffins, and in side dishes, often with legumes. Of course, there's plenty of fruit and vegetables. As long as you eat a wide variety of foods, there is no need to become obsessed about *anything* in your diet. And that goes for fat and fiber, too! Once you see where the fat and fiber lie, eating healthy foods will become a matter of habit and you won't need to count grams of fat and fiber anymore, just as there is no need to count calories.

CUTTING BACK ON FATS

The T-Factor Diet does not require you to cut out any particular group of foods in order to meet the fat-gram goal of 20 to 40, or 30 to 60, grams a day. I will show you how to use butter, oil, and other fats in moderation. But there is also a large amount of hidden fat in many cuts of meat, dairy products, seafood prepared in rich sauces, sweets, and snack foods. Since we want to keep low-fat versions of these foods in the diet, you will want to learn how to make low-fat substitutions for the high-fat foods in the same food group.

On the right-hand side of Table 3–1, which I have already suggested that you study carefully, you will find a list of high-fat foods commonly found in the diets of overly fat persons. On the left-hand side are good low-fat substitutions. This table contains my general suggestions for making a real dent in your fat intake. It's intended to give a gut feeling for where the fat lies in your diet. We will get into fat-gram specifics in a moment.

Looking at Table 3-1, do you see how you can keep on eating all kinds of meat and dairy products and certain snacks and desserts and still make a great dent in your fat intake? By making good choices it is very easy to cut out half the fat in most diets without causing any feeling of deprivation at all!

Table 3-2 contains a list of grains, fruits, and vegetables that contain no more than a trace of fat—that is, less than 0.5 gram in the case of the fruits and vegetables, and less than 1 gram in the grains. There is generally a small amount of fat in a whole-grain food, which is contained in the germ or husk. That's why even dry cereal products made without added fat but which contain whole grains usually list 1 gram per serving (it's usually only about half a gram, but anything half a gram or over must be rounded up to 1 gram on the label). Watch out for certain cereals, however, which contain considerable added fat in spite of their healthy-sounding names (such as granola types)! Read the labels.

ADDITIONAL HINTS FOR CUTTING FATS

Here are some more specific hints for cutting fats. In part, these explain and amplify some of the suggestions in Table 3-1 and I expand on them here because they constitute my personal strategies for controlling fat intake. They work!

1. If you are eating more beef, lamb, or pork than you are fowl or fish, reverse that ratio! And when you do eat beef, lamb, or pork, use the leanest cuts and trim all fat. The fat and fiber gram counter will inform you of the relative fat content of various cuts, but, best of all, make friends with your butcher. I really like my butcher! When I don't see exactly what I want prepackaged on the shelf at the supermarket where I do all of my shopping for meats, I tell him what I want and he cuts it specially for me. Use my recipes to discover that low-fat substitutions and low-fat food preparation can be even more satisfying than your present way.

2. *Don't eat fried foods. Period.* Frying can turn a wonderfully healthy food into a junk food! For example, a potato contains no fat, but turn even a small one into just one cup of french fries and you end up with about 24 grams of fat. That's about 200 calories of fat that could come out of your fat cells instead of going in! It's even worse when you fry chicken or fish with a crumb or batter crust. So, when it comes to these foods, bake, broil, steam, poach, or occasionally stew or grill in place of frying.

3. Cultivate your taste for meatless dinners and lunches. Or try dishes in which the animal products are used as condiments, as in Oriental cooking. This is one of the easiest ways to cut back on fats. Because Oriental and similar styles of cooking are less well known in America and most people think it's a bother to cook this way, try my recipes to get the hang of it.

4. Switch from whole milk to either low-fat or skim milk. Use low-fat cottage cheese and yogurt, and part-skim cheeses whenever possible. You may like the lower-fat processed cheese foods, and if you do, I have no objection to them. I don't care for them, however, and I prefer to use the best-tasting cheeses more moderately rather than use the less satisfying, reduced-fat varieties.

5. Substitute fruit (including dried fruit!) or unbut-

tered popcorn (preferably air popped) for most of your desserts, sweets, and snacks.

6. Do not use gravies and sauces made with more than minimal amounts of butter and cream. See my low-fat recipes for instruction on how to use just enough of the fatty ingredients to keep you satisfied.

7. Use all fat and oil in moderation.

But what about diet spreads and commercial calorie-reduced salad dressings? Once again, if you like them, use them. It's a matter of personal choice. We include a couple of recipes that use calorie-reduced products, which got excellent ratings from our tasters. But, to tell the truth, I don't use most of these products myself. Besides, why pay for water? That's what's often added and homogenized to reduce the fat content while maintaining the weight or volume of the product. When it comes to spreads, or fats like butter and margarine, I think you get more flavor from the real thing even if you use less. As for salad dressings, many people do find a commerical variety that they like, at 35 calories or less per tablespoon. That's fine. However, I suggest you try my own recipes for reduced- or no-fat salad dressings. They will illustrate what the best ingredients, including oil used in moderation, can do to satisfy your palate.

HOW TO DEVELOP YOUR DAILY MENU PLAN

Most people alternate among several standard breakfasts and lunches. I think it's a good idea to include no more than half the fat you plan to eat in a given day in these two meals combined, if you plan to have your main meal at night, as most of us do. Remember, however, that most health experts recommend against eating a large meal before going to sleep. It can interfere with sleep as well as make managing your weight more difficult, and it may be dangerous for people with cardiovascular disease. The size and fat levels of the dinners I recommend are well within good health limits.

Here's an important suggestion: The menus below, as well as my discussion of other foods, contain fat-gram information. Begin to compile your mental storehouse of fat-gram counts. These are the common foods that you will be eating every day. Within a few weeks you will have all the important, everyday fat-gram information in memory. Choosing low-fat foods will become easy and second nature. You will have to look up fat-gram counts only when you deviate from your customary diet.

Basic Breakfasts

Breakfast in particular can be very low in fat. Here are four of my own standards, plus a yogurt combination suggested by one of my nutritionist friends. Remember, the only thing you must limit is fat—you can eat the fat-free foods in whatever quantity satisfies you. I include the general, basic fat-gram counts to help you plan your own combinations, but *be sure to check the labels of the brands you use.* There can be considerable difference in the fat content from brand to brand in cereals that have similar names. Normally we recommend you drink coffee and tea without cream, but if you like half-and-half in your coffee (as I do) it contains 0.5 gram of fat per teaspoon. There's room for this on the T-Factor Diet, if you don't overdo it! Be sure to count it in your fat-gram total.

1

Your choice of fruit or juice
Choice of cereal, cold or hot
(about 1 gram of fat per ounce of cold, or ½ cup of hot)
Skim or low-fat milk
(no or 1 to 2 grams of fat per ½ cup)
Coffee or tea

2

Choice of fruit or juice
Toast and jelly
(whole grain preferred, 1 gram of fat per slice)
Coffee or tea
Add a poached or boiled egg occasionally
(about 5 grams of fat)

3

Choice of fruit
Cheese toast
(figure 9 grams of fat per ounce of hard cheese,
1 gram of fat per slice of bread)
Coffee or tea

4

Choice of fruit
Choice of muffin
(about 3 grams of fat; see my
several muffin recipes)
Coffee or tea

5

Low- or no-fat yogurt, mixed with
choice of fruit and cold cereal
(2 to 4 grams of fat; check labels of yogurt and cereal)

When I am really saving fat grams, I may have a couple of slices of hearty whole-grain bread or homemade muffins, plain or toasted, for breakfast. I include several recipes for breads, as well as for different grain muffins, that are relatively low in fat content and filled with a variety of good fibers. They are great to nibble on at any time. Watch out for commercially baked muffins, however. If they feel heavy and sticky to the touch, they can contain 10 or more grams of fat (compared with only 3 grams in my recipes).

Basic Lunches

Lunches pose a bit of a problem if you have to eat out every day and cannot carry your own. While I frequently order salads when I eat out, or soup and salad or a sandwich, I prefer to make my own lunches. The tuna, chicken, or shellfish salads in restaurants will often contain between

12 and 24 grams of fat unless they have been specifically designed as low-fat recipes. If you pour additional dressing on the lettuce and other vegetables that accompany the salad, it's 9 to 10 grams of fat per tablespoon of the regular varieties.

Hearty soups—I mean with potatoes, lentils, rice, and plenty of vegetables—are great for lunches. See my recipes; they contain no fat.

Here are some basic fat-gram figures to help you plan your own luncheon combinations. Once again, be sure to check the labels of the products you like to use.

1. Tuna fish, packed in water, contains only 1 gram of fat per 3-ounce serving (packed in oil it contains about 20 grams).

2. Low-fat varieties of cottage cheese contain from 2 to 3 grams of fat per ½ cup (I know you get tired of seeing cottage cheese and tuna on weight-management menus, so see my suggestions for seasonings on pages 125-126.

3. Soups, bouillon based with added vegetables and potatoes, are practically fat free.

4. Vegetable or vegetable beef and chicken soups will contain about 3 grams of fat per cup (the popular cream of broccoli and cheddar/potato soups served in restaurants and from salad bars may contain up to 25 grams of fat).

5. Sardines, oil all drained off, will contain about 6 grams of fat per ½ tin (about 2 ounces).

6. Fruits and vegetables that are virtually fat free (see my lists in Table 3-2), which you can add in unlimited quantities.

7. Bread for sandwiches contains about 1 gram of fat per slice.

8. Mayonnaise is 4 grams per *teaspoon*.

9. Use ketchup and mustard for flavoring.

10. Use lemon juice and vinaigrette dressings, or my own low-fat salad dressings at 4 grams per tablespoon.

11. My sandwich spreads (see pages 138-139) contain little or no fat.
12. White meat of chicken or turkey contains about 1 gram of fat per ounce; dark meat contains about 2.5 grams of fat per ounce.
13. Sliced beef, extra lean (see page 177), contains about 2.5 grams of fat per ounce; regular cut, about 6 grams per ounce.
14. Venus (brand) wafers have 1 or 2 grams of fat per serving of 8 crackers, as do saltines.

With these data in mind, here are some suggestions for lunches that you can repeat over and over again as your standards. Note that even the menus with higher fat contents have only about 25 percent of the day's fat allowance.

1

Choice of soup
(0 to 3 grams of fat)
Crackers or toast
(1 to 2 grams of fat per serving)
Unlimited no-fat vegetables and fruits
(see Table 3-2)
No- or low-fat salad dressing
(0 to 3 grams of fat per 2 tablespoons)

2

Choice of salad, fruits, and vegetables
(unlimited quantity of the no-fat kind)
Choice of tuna, low-fat cottage cheese, sliced chicken
(1 to 3 grams of fat)
No- or low-fat salad dressing
(0 to 3 grams of fat per 2 tablespoons)

3

Choice of sandwich
(1 gram of fat per slice of bread;
1 to 3 grams of fat per ounce of chicken or lean beef—
see pages 164, 177;
unlimited greens, tomato, etc.;
ketchup and mustard have no fat;
4 grams of fat per teaspoon of mayonnaise)
Soup
(unlimited quantity of the no-fat kind)
Beverage

4

Unlimited fruit mixed in blender with
no- or low-fat yogurt
(no fat for fruit;
0 to 4 grams of fat per cup of yogurt)
Beverage

Compare the fat counts of these luncheon suggestions with the 53 grams of fat that are found in the fast-food restaurant versions of a *small* cheeseburger (31), *small* french fries (12), and 1 cup of a comparatively low-fat soft-serve milk shake (10). Regular ice cream milk shakes will have 12 to 16 grams of fat!

What about soft drinks, regular and diet? They don't contain fat, so are they permissible?

As a general rule, I don't approve of either one. The sweetness of both regular soft drinks and diet drinks keeps your sweet tooth alive and in many people it leads to an overconsumption of sweet FATTY foods. The intense sweetness also deadens your ability to appreciate natural sweetness in fruits and vegetables (there are 10 teaspoons of sugar in one 12-ounce cola drink). The diet varieties stimulate your system to expect honest-to-goodness calories, only nothing is there! This may stimulate appetite and lead to greater hunger than normal. (One important study showed that people who use diet drinks tend to end up gaining more weight over time than those who don't. It really pains me to see the consumption of diet drinks increasing so rapidly in this country.) Both diet and regular soft drinks may lead to a large insulin reaction that can block fat from leaving your fat cells temporarily, making it harder to lose fat weight.[2]

Now that I have said all this, I don't think an *occasional* soft drink or diet drink will harm you. However, if you are a slave to them, then they may be playing a key role in your overeating of sweetened *fatty* foods. You will do much better if you switch to fruit juice, seltzer, or plain fresh water instead of soft drinks!

Dinner

I think you can see that breakfast and lunch combined can easily be designed to have from 10 to 20 grams of fat. If you are a woman, this leaves half or more of your fat count of 20 to 40 grams available for the evening meal (men should add a little more fat to each meal because they are aiming for a total of 30 to 60 grams).

It is easy to design main courses of meat, fish, or fowl. Just see what you can do with lean cuts (fat grams for cooked portions):

Lean beef (see page 177) is about 2.5 grams of fat per ounce.

Breast of chicken (skinned) is about 1 gram of fat per ounce.

Dark meat of chicken (skinned) is 2.5 grams of fat per ounce.

Tenderloin of pork (the only lean on the pig) is 1 gram of fat per ounce.

Ham, lean and trimmed, is 3 grams of fat per ounce.

---

[2] Insulin helps move glucose out of the bloodstream into your body cells. Even though diet drinks contain no sugar they are capable of stimulating an insulin response in some people simply because of their sweet taste, just like regular soft drinks. A high circulating level of insulin signals your system that plenty of energy is present and tends to inhibit the mobilization of fat from your fat cells. This is one reason people with hyperinsulinemia (high insulin levels) tend to have difficulty losing weight.

Fish (most varieties) is about *1 gram of fat per 4 ounces*.

Fatty varieties of fish (trout, swordfish) are about 1 gram of fat per ounce.

High-fat cuts of meat can have two to three times the fat content of the lean cuts, and anything fried may have seven or eight times the fat content! Thus, if you build main courses around low-fat cuts you can eat a great deal of meat if you wish and still have a dinner under 20 grams of fat! That's impossible to do with fatty cuts. Add all the vegetables, potatoes, rice, other grains, or pasta you want, plus fruit or unbuttered popcorn, preferably air popped, for dessert. Fat in the form of butter or margarine is 12 grams per tablespoon, so, when preparing vegetables, allow 1 tablespoon of added fat for every serving for four—that's 3 grams per serving if none stuck to the pot. But I'll show you ways to cook many vegetables without any extra fat.

At cooked weights, 6-ounce portions of chicken and the leanest pork will amount to only 6 grams of fat, and fish is almost always much, much less. Six ounces of lean meat will contain about 12 grams of fat. If you add little or no fat to your vegetables you still have room for standard oil-in-the-pot popcorn, at about 2 grams of fat per cup, if you prefer it to air-popped popcorn. I do, so I save fat elsewhere. A choice of fish, poultry, or a meatless dinner instead of beef will generally leave room for an ounce of cheddar or some similar cheese (about 9 grams of fat) with fruit.

Here are a few dinner suggestions. Notice in my first suggestion how easy it is to think "fat grams" and design a simple, basic American-style dinner with a total of 20 grams of fat or less. Notice in the other selections how quickly and easily you can prepare different popular international dishes with minimum fat. These five dishes or styles of food preparation are basic for most people. You will find many different recipes for meat, fish, and fowl in the recipe chapter of this book (Chapter 6). While the other main courses listed below suggest specific dishes and refer you to specific pages for the recipes, you will find several variations on each theme in the neighboring pages of the recipe chapter.

1

Main course is choice of any of the lean meats (see pages
177, 186, 188), fish, or fowl, up to 6-ounce serving
(2 to 12 grams of fat)
Unlimited vegetables, potatoes, rice,
other grains, or legumes
(if fat added, 4 grams per teaspoon; no- or low-fat salad
dressings, 0 to 3 grams per 2 tablespoons)

2

Main course is pasta
Choice of sauces (pages 159-161)
(4 to 12 grams of fat)
Large salad
(dressings, pages 148-151, fat grams 0 to 3)

3

Indian Spiced Beans, with rice,
topped with choice of chopped fresh vegetables, salsa,
and cheese
(1 gram of fat, page 155, plus 4 grams of fat for each
tablespoon of grated cheese)

4

Pot Roast
(page 181; 12 grams of fat)

5

Chili-Bean Meat Loaf
(page 179; 9 grams of fat)
Large salad
(0 to 3 grams of fat for no- or low-fat dressing)

HOW TO USE THE T-FACTOR MENUS

The T-Factor Diet menus below are meant to introduce you to the wide variety of foods and styles of food preparation that will make your diet interesting and satisfying. Remember, however, that you can substitute any of the basic breakfasts and lunches listed above for the selections in the following menus. You can substitute one vegetable for another, one fruit for another, one meat for another, etc. You don't need to follow the specific recipes that I recommend each day; instead, you may prepare any similar food in the manner I suggest in my other recipes in Chapter 6. You can alternate days or eat breakfast for dinner and dinner for breakfast if your day is normally topsy-turvy! Snacks can be eaten at any time of the day.

This flexibility may seem confusing to you at first. Such flexibility is possible because the only nutrient that concerns us, *assuming that you will eat a wide variety of foods from the different food groups,* is FAT! When you control fat intake, holding it in the 20- or 40-gram range if you are a woman and the 30- to 60-gram range if you're a man, you achieve an unbelievable freedom in your choice of other foods. But if such flexibility confuses you at first, start out by following the daily menus as closely as possible until you get a feeling for what this freedom implies.

USE THE FAT-GRAM COUNTER IN APPENDIX C WHEN YOU MAKE SUBSTITUTIONS.

KEEP TRACK OF FAT GRAMS EACH DAY IN THE MANNER I SUGGEST ON PAGES 279-311 IN APPENDIX C.

ADD FAT-FREE FOODS AT MAIN MEALS OR FOR SNACKS UNTIL YOUR APPETITE IS SATISFIED. DON'T GO HUNGRY!

DAILY T-FACTOR MENUS

Many of these daily menus come out at the low end of the spectrum of 20 to 40 fat grams per day for women, leaving plenty of room for extra low-fat snacks or an occasional dessert. Men may increase the portion sizes of the foods that contain fats by up to half to meet their goal of 30 to 60 grams of fat per day. Where applicable, you will notice the

fat-gram count in parentheses next to the foods listed
(abbreviated for the menus as "g."). For ease in counting,
the grams have been rounded up or down to the nearest
whole gram in some instances.

Rice, pastas, and all vegetables are prepared without
any added fat unless specified. Even if package cooking
directions call for fat for rice, just omit it; you won't miss
it! When cereal is listed, I recommend a cereal mix. Try
combining ½ ounce of a high-fiber, all-bran-type cereal
with ½ ounce of a more highly fortified cereal, such as
Product 19 or Total.

WEEK 1

DAY 1
Breakfast

Banana or fresh fruit of choice; dry cereal (1 g. per
ounce); 1 cup of skim or 1% milk (0–2 g.); coffee or tea.

TOTAL FAT: 1–3 G.

Lunch

½ cup of low-fat cottage cheese (3 g.); assorted raw
vegetables; whole-wheat crackers (5 = 1 g.); fresh
fruit; no-cal beverage

TOTAL FAT: 4 G.

Dinner

1 serving Baked Chicken with Tarragon and Fennel
(pages 164-165; 4 g.) or 3.5 ounces of baked chicken;
brown or wild rice (1 g. per ½-cup serving); green
beans; whole-grain bread (1 g. per slice); tossed salad;
no- or low-cal salad dressing (2 tablespoons = 0–3 g.);
fruit of choice; no-cal beverage

TOTAL FAT: 6–9 G.

Snack

1 cup of plain, nonfat yogurt; fresh strawberries; graham crackers (2 = 1 g.)

TOTAL FAT: 1 G.
TOTAL FAT FOR DAY 1: 12–17 G.

DAY 2
Breakfast

Grapefruit or fruit of choice; 1 egg, poached (5 g.); whole-grain bread (1 g. per slice); 1 cup of skim or 1% milk (0–2 g.); coffee or tea

TOTAL FAT: 6–8 G.

Lunch

2 ounces of sliced cooked chicken for sandwich (2 g.); 2 slices of whole-grain bread (2 g.); lettuce and sliced tomatoes; mustard; pear; no-cal beverage

TOTAL FAT: 4 G.

Dinner

1 serving of Sea Bass with Red Bell Peppers (page 174; 3 g.); broccoli; tossed salad; no- or low-cal salad dressing (2 tablespoons = 0–3 g.); whole-grain bread (1 g. per slice); fruit of choice; 1 serving of Cocoa Pudding Cake (page 198; 4 g.); no-cal beverage

TOTAL FAT: 8–11 G.

Snack

Dry cereal (1 g. per ounce); 1 cup of skim or 1% milk (0–2 g.); sliced fruit

TOTAL FAT: 1–3 G.
TOTAL FAT FOR DAY 2: 19–26 G.

DAY 3

Breakfast

Honeydew melon or seasonal fruit; English muffin (1 whole = 2 g.); jelly; 1 cup of skim or 1% milk or nonfat, plain yogurt (0–2 g.); coffee or tea

TOTAL FAT: 2–4 G.

Lunch

2 ounces of water-packed tuna (1 g.); 1 teaspoon of mayonnaise (4 g.); 1 whole bagel (1 g.); alfalfa sprouts and assorted raw vegetables; orange; no-cal beverage

TOTAL FAT: 6 G.

Dinner

3 ounces of Baked Flank Steak (page 178; 12 g.); baked potato; asparagus; tossed salad; no- or low-cal salad dressing (2 tablespoons = 0–3 g.); whole-grain bread (1 g. per slice); fruit of choice; no-cal beverage

TOTAL FAT: 13–16 G.

Snack

Air-popped popcorn (4 cups popped = 2 g.)

TOTAL FAT: 2 G.
TOTAL FAT FOR DAY 3: 23–28 G.

DAY 4
Breakfast

Dry cereal (1 g. per ounce); raisins; 1 cup of skim or 1% milk (0–2 g.); coffee or tea

TOTAL FAT: 1–3 G.

Lunch

Broth-based, vegetable-type soup (2 g. per cup); chef salad; assorted raw vegetables, 1 ounce of turkey, ½ ounce of hard cheese, croutons (7–8 g.); no- or low-cal salad dressing (2 tablespoons = 0–3 g.); apple; no-cal beverage

TOTAL FAT: 9–13 G.

Dinner

1 cup of spaghetti (2 g.) with 1 cup of Meat Sauce (page 160; 12 g.); steamed zucchini; whole-grain bread (1 g. per slice); fresh fruit; no-cal beverage

TOTAL: 15 G.

Snack

1 cup of plain, nonfat yogurt; banana; graham crackers (2 = 1 g.)

TOTAL FAT: 1 G.
TOTAL FAT FOR DAY 4: 26–32 G.

DAY 5

Breakfast

Assorted fresh fruit; oatmeal or other hot cereal (1 g. per ½ cup); 1 cup of skim or 1% milk (0–2 g.); whole-grain toast (1 g. per slice); jelly; coffee or tea

TOTAL FAT: 2–4 G.

Lunch

Toasted pita pocket: 1 ounce of shredded hard cheese (8–10 g.), 1 6-inch whole-grain pita (1 g.), sliced tomato, assorted raw vegetables; orange or grapefruit; no-cal beverage

TOTAL FAT: 9–11 G.

Dinner

1 serving of Simple Fish in Foil (pages 175–176; 1.5 g.) or 4 ounces of sole or flounder, sliced onions, carrots, potatoes, and green beans (4 g.); whole-grain bread (1 g. per slice); 1 serving of Lemon Meringue Pie (pages 199–200; 6 g.) or Chocolate Meringue Pie (page 197; 6 g.); no-cal beverage

TOTAL FAT: 7.5–10 G.

Snack

Dry cereal (1 g. per ounce); 1 cup of skim or 1% milk (0–2 g.); sliced fresh fruit

TOTAL FAT: 1–3 G.
TOTAL FAT FOR DAY 5: 19.5–27 G.

DAY 6
Breakfast

Seasonal fruit; 1 whole bagel (1 g.); jelly; 1 cup of skim or 1% milk (0–2 g.); coffee or tea

TOTAL FAT: 1–3 G.

Lunch

2 ounces of sliced turkey for sandwich (2 g.); 2 slices of whole-grain bread (2 g.); lettuce and tomato slices; mustard; apple; no-cal beverage

TOTAL FAT: 4 G.

Dinner

Basic Better Beans (page 152; 5 g. per ½ cup); brown rice (1 g. per ½ cup); spinach or other greens; Massachusetts Corn Muffin (page 131; 3 g. each); tossed salad; no- or low-cal salad dressing (2 tablespoons = 0–3 g.); fresh fruit; no-cal beverage

TOTAL FAT: 9–12 G.

Snack

Air-popped popcorn (4 cups popped = 2 g.); fresh fruit

TOTAL FAT: 2 G.
TOTAL FAT FOR DAY 6: 16–21 G.

DAY 7

Breakfast

Grapefruit or fruit of choice; dry cereal (1 g. per ounce); 1 cup of skim or 1% milk (0–2 g.); coffee or tea

TOTAL FAT: 1–3 G.

Lunch

Minestrone (page 144; 1 g. per serving); Massachusetts Corn Muffin (page 131; 3 g.); peach or pear; no-cal beverage

TOTAL FAT: 4 G.

Dinner

3 ounces of lean, well-trimmed pork loin (9 g.); Apple-Sweet Sweet Potatoes (page 190; 1 g. per serving); tossed salad; no- or low-cal salad dressing (2 tablespoons = 0–3 g.); whole-grain bread (1 g. per slice); fruit of choice; no-cal beverage

TOTAL FAT: 11–14 G.

Snack

1 cup of plain, nonfat yogurt; sliced banana; graham crackers (2 = 1 g.)

TOTAL FAT: 1 G.
TOTAL FAT FOR DAY 7: 17–22 G.

WEEK 2

DAY 8
Breakfast

Blueberries or other seasonal fruit; plain, nonfat yogurt; high-fiber cereal (1 g. per ounce; stir in with yogurt and berries); whole-grain bread (1 g. per slice); coffee or tea

TOTAL FAT: 2 G.

Lunch

2 ounces of sliced turkey (2 g.); whole-grain bread (1 g. per slice); lettuce and tomato slices; mustard; orange; no-cal beverage

TOTAL FAT: 3 G.

Dinner

4.5 ounces of Royal Indian Salmon (pages 171–172; 8 g.); 1 cup of green beans; brown or wild rice (1 g. per 1/2 cup); tossed salad; no- or low-cal salad dressing (2 tablespoons = 0–3 g.); whole-grain bread (1 g. per slice); fruit of choice; no-cal beverage

TOTAL FAT: 10-13 G.

Snack

1 cup of skim or 1% milk (0–2 g.); graham crackers (2 = 1 g.); apple

TOTAL FAT: 1–3 G.
TOTAL FAT FOR DAY 8: 16–21 G.

DAY 9

Breakfast

Sliced banana; dry cereal (1 g. per ounce); 1 cup of skim or 1% milk (0–2 g.); coffee or tea

TOTAL FAT: 1–3 G.

Lunch

2 ounces of water-packed tuna (1 g.); 1 teaspoon of mayonnaise (4 g.); whole-grain pita pocket (½ = 1 g.); assorted raw vegetables; grapefruit or orange; no-cal beverage

TOTAL FAT: 6 G.

Dinner

1 serving of Oysters Rockefeller (page 176; 5 g.); cooked pasta (2 g. per cup); ½–1 cup of meatless tomato spaghetti sauce with mushrooms, bell peppers, etc. (0.5 g. for ½ cup of sauce); whole-wheat roll (1 2-inch roll = 2 g.); tossed salad; no- or low-cal salad dressing (2 tablespoons = 0–3 g.); no-cal beverage

TOTAL FAT: 9.5–12.5 G.

Snack

Air-popped popcorn (4 cups popped = 2 g.); fresh fruit

TOTAL FAT: 2 G.
TOTAL FAT FOR DAY 9: 18.5–23.5 G.

DAY 10

Breakfast

Fresh fruit of choice; English muffin (1 whole = 2 g.); jelly; 1 cup of skim or 1% milk (0–2 g.); coffee or tea

TOTAL FAT: 2–4 G.

Lunch

Chicken noodle soup: 1 ounce of diced, cooked chicken, ⅓ cup of noodles, ½ cup of diced vegetables, chicken broth (2 g.); Applesauce-Bran Muffin (page 130; 3 g.); apple; no-cal beverage

TOTAL FAT: 5 G.

Dinner

1 serving of Light and Easy Lemon Chicken (page 167; 4 g.) or 3.5 ounces of chicken breast; steamed zucchini, yellow squash, and green peppers; brown rice (½ cup = 1g.); tossed salad; no- or low-cal salad dressing (2 tablespoons = 0–3 g.) whole-grain bread (1 g. per slice); fruit of choice; 1 serving of Poppy-Seed Cake (page 200; 7 g.); no-cal beverage

TOTAL FAT: 13–16 G.

Snack

1 cup of plain, nonfat yogurt; sliced peaches; dry cereal (1 g. per ounce)

TOTAL FAT: 1 G.
TOTAL FAT FOR DAY 10: 21–26 G.

DAY 11
Breakfast

Fresh fruit of choice; dry cereal (1 g. per ounce); 1 cup of skim or 1% milk (0–2 g.); coffee or tea

TOTAL FAT: 1–3 G.

Lunch

Spinach salad: fresh spinach, sliced fresh mushrooms, ½ hard-boiled egg (3 g.), ½ ounce of part-skim white cheese (4 g.), chopped onions, no- or low-cal salad dressing (2 tablespoons = 0–3 g.); Applesauce-Bran Muffin (page 130; 3 g.); orange; no-cal beverage

TOTAL FAT: 10–13 G.

Dinner

4.5 ounces of Baked Turkey Loaf (page 165; 12 g.); fresh, steamed broccoli; baked acorn squash; tossed salad; no- or low-cal salad dressing (2 tablespoons = 0–3 g.); whole-grain bread (1 g. per slice); apple; no-cal beverage

TOTAL FAT: 13–16 G.

Snack

Air-popped popcorn (4 cups popped = 2 g.); fresh fruit

TOTAL FAT: 2 G.
TOTAL FAT FOR DAY 11: 26–34 G.

DAY 12
Breakfast

Honeydew melon or other seasonal fruit; 1 egg cooked without fat (5 g.); whole-grain toast (1 g. per slice); 1 cup of skim or 1% milk (0–2 g.); coffee or tea

TOTAL FAT: 6–8 G.

Lunch

3 ounces of leftover Baked Turkey Loaf for sandwich (8 g.); 1 whole-grain bun (2 g.); lettuce and tomato slices; grapes; no-cal beverage

TOTAL FAT: 10 G.

Dinner

1 serving of Spinach Lasagna (pages 157–158; 8 g.) or Eggplant Parmesan (page 154; 8 g.—add side dish of 1/2 cup of pasta, and 1 fat gram, with Eggplant Parmesan); whole-grain roll (1 2-inch roll = 2 g.); tossed salad; no- or low-cal salad dressing (2 tablespoons = 0–3 g.); fresh fruit; no-cal beverage

TOTAL FAT: 10–14 G.

Snack

Dry cereal (1 g. per ounce); 1 cup of skim or 1% milk (0–2 g.); banana

TOTAL FAT: 1–3 G.
TOTAL FAT FOR DAY 12: 27–35 G.

DAY 13
Breakfast

Oatmeal or other hot cereal (1 g. per ½-cup serving); raisins; dash of cinnamon; 1 cup of skim or 1% milk (0–2 g.); coffee or tea

TOTAL FAT: 1–3 G.

Lunch

2 ounces of canned salmon (4 g.); 1 teaspoon mayonnaise (4 g.); 1 whole bagel (1 g.); alfalfa sprouts and assorted raw vegetables; pear; no-cal beverage

TOTAL FAT: 9 G.

Dinner

3 ounces of Round-Roast Oriental (page 182; 9 g.); baked potato; Brussels Sprouts with Caraway Seeds (p. 192; 1 cup = 1 g.) or other green vegetable; whole-grain bread (1 g. per slice); tossed salad; no- or low-cal salad dressing (2 tablespoons = 0–3 g.); fresh fruit; no-cal beverage

TOTAL FAT: 11–14 G.

Snack

1 cup of plain, nonfat yogurt; fresh strawberries; graham crackers (2 = 1 g.)

TOTAL FAT: 1 G.
TOTAL FAT FOR DAY 13: 22–27 G.

DAY 14
Breakfast

Grapefruit; 1 whole bagel (1 g.); jelly; 1 cup of skim or 1% milk (0–2 g.); coffee or tea

TOTAL FAT: 1–3 G.

Lunch

½ cup of low-fat cottage cheese (3 g.); assorted fresh fruit; whole-wheat crackers (5 = 1 g.); assorted raw vegetables; no-cal beverage

TOTAL FAT: 4 G.

Dinner

Broccoli Soup (pages 141–142; 1 cup = 3 g.); 1 serving of Grilled Tuna Mediterranean (p. 170; 9 g.); steamed carrots; brown or wild rice (1 g. per 1/2 cup); whole-grain bread (1 g. per slice); fresh fruit; no-cal beverage

TOTAL FAT: 14 G.

Snack

Dry cereal (1 g. per ounce); 1 cup of skim or 1% milk (0–2 g.); fresh fruit

TOTAL FAT: 1–3 G.
TOTAL FAT FOR DAY 14: 20–24 G.

WEEK 3

DAY 15
Breakfast

Banana; dry cereal (1 g. per ounce); 1 cup of skim or 1% milk (0–2 g.); coffee or tea

TOTAL FAT: 1–3 G.

Lunch

Tuna-stuffed tomato: 2–3 ounces of water-packed tuna (1 g.), 1 teaspoon mayonnaise (4 g.), chopped celery, whole tomato; whole-wheat crackers (5 = 1 g.); orange; no-cal beverage

TOTAL FAT: 6 G.

Dinner

1 serving of Quick Turkey Chop Suey (pages 168–169; 8 g.); brown or wild rice (1 g. per 1/2 cup); whole-wheat roll (1 2-inch roll = 2 g.); tossed salad; no- or low-cal salad dressing (2 tablespoons = 0–3 g.); 1 serving of Elegant Pears (pages 198–199, 2 g.); no-cal beverage

TOTAL FAT: 13–16 G.

Snack

1 cup of plain, nonfat yogurt; fresh fruit of choice; graham crackers (2 = 1 g.)

TOTAL FAT: 1 G.
TOTAL FAT FOR DAY 15: 21–26 G.

DAY 16
Breakfast

Grapefruit; English muffin (1 whole = 2 g.); jelly; 1 cup of skim or 1% milk (0–2 g.); coffee or tea

TOTAL FAT: 2–4 G.

Lunch

2 ounces of cooked chicken (2 g.); whole-grain bread (1 g. per slice); lettuce and sliced tomatoes; mustard; pretzels (1 ounce = 1 g.); apple; no-cal beverage

TOTAL FAT: 4 G.

Dinner

3 ounces of Swedish Meatballs (pages 185–186, 14 g.); brown, wild, or saffron rice (1/2 cup = 1 g.); green beans; tossed salad; no- or low-cal salad dressing (2 tablespoons = 0–3 g.); whole-grain bread (1 g. per slice); fresh fruit; no-cal beverage

TOTAL FAT: 16–19 G.

Snack

Air-popped popcorn (4 cups popped = 2 g.); fresh fruit

TOTAL FAT: 2 G.
TOTAL FAT FOR DAY 16: 24–29 G.

DAY 17

Breakfast

Oatmeal or other hot cereal (½ cup = 1 g.); raisins; whole grain bread (1 g. per slice); jelly; 1 cup of skim or 1% milk (0–2 g.); coffee or tea

TOTAL FAT: 2–4 G.

Lunch

Broth-based, vegetable-type soup (1 cup = 0–2 g.); chef salad: assorted raw vegetables, 1 ounce of turkey, ½ ounce of hard cheese, ¼ cup of croutons (7 g.); no- or low-cal salad dressing (2 tablespoons = 0–3 g.); whole-wheat crackers (5 = 1 g.); pear; no-cal beverage

TOTAL FAT: 8–13 G.

Dinner

1 serving of Scallop-and-Clam Pasta (pages 163–164; 9 g.); whole-grain roll (1 2-inch roll = 2 g.); tossed salad; no- or low-cal salad dressing (2 tablespoons = 0–3 g.); fresh fruit; no-cal beverage

TOTAL FAT: 11–14 G.

Snack

Dry cereal (1 g. per ounce); sliced fresh fruit; 1 cup of skim or 1% milk (0–2 g.)

TOTAL FAT: 1–3 G.
TOTAL FAT FOR DAY 17: 22–34 G.

DAY 18
Breakfast

Fresh fruit of choice; dry cereal (1 g. per ounce); 1 cup of skim or 1% milk (0–2 g.); coffee or tea

TOTAL FAT: 1–3 G.

Lunch

½ cup of seasoned low-fat cottage cheese (3 g.); 1 whole bagel (1 g.); alfalfa sprouts and raw vegetables; assorted fresh fruit; no-cal beverage

TOTAL FAT: 4 G.

Dinner

1 serving of Pork Chops Parmesan (pages 186–187; 12 g.); cooked cauliflower; unsweetened applesauce; spinach noodles (1/2 cup = 1 g.); tossed salad; no- or low-cal salad dressing (2 tablespoons = 0–3 g.); whole-grain bread (1 g. per slice); fresh fruit; no-cal beverage

TOTAL FAT: 14–17 G.

Snack

1 cup of plain, nonfat yogurt; fresh fruit of choice; graham crackers (2 = 1 g.)

TOTAL FAT: 1 G.
TOTAL FAT FOR DAY 18: 20–25 G.

DAY 19

Breakfast

Fresh fruit of choice; 1 whole bagel (1 g.); jelly; 1 cup of skim or 1% milk (0–2 g.); coffee or tea

TOTAL FAT: 1–3 G.

Lunch

2 ounces of sliced turkey for sandwich (2 g.); whole-grain bread (1 g. per slice); lettuce and tomato slices; mustard; pretzels (1 ounce = 1 g.); strawberries or seasonal fruit; no-cal beverage

TOTAL FAT: 4 G.

Dinner

Burrito: canned refried beans (½ cup = 2 g.), whole-wheat 8-inch tortilla (2 g.), chopped onions and peppers, chopped lettuce and assorted raw vegetables, ½ ounce or 2 tablespoons of shredded cheddar cheese (5 g.), picante or taco sauce; apple; no-cal beverage

TOTAL FAT: 9 G.

Snack

Air-popped popcorn (4 cups popped = 2 g.); fresh fruit

TOTAL FAT: 2 G.
TOTAL FAT FOR DAY 19: 16–18 G.

DAY 20

Breakfast

Grapefruit; 1 egg, cooked without fat (5 g.); whole-grain toast (1 g. per slice); 1 cup of skim or 1% milk (0–2 g.); coffee or tea

TOTAL FAT: 6–8 G.

Lunch

Broth-based, vegetable-type soup (1 cup = 0–2 g.); Gingersnap Muffin (pages 130–131; 3 g.); assorted raw vegetables; grapes; no-cal beverage

TOTAL FAT: 3–5 G.

Dinner

3.5 ounces of Barbecued Chicken (pages 165–166; 5 g.); 1 serving of Scalloped Potatoes (p. 194; 4 g.); steamed seasoned zucchini; tossed salad; no- or low-cal salad dressing (2 tablespoons = 0–3 g.); whole-grain bread (1 g. per slice); fresh fruit; no-cal beverage

TOTAL FAT: 10–13 G.

Snack

Dry cereal (1 g. per ounce); banana; 1 cup of skim or 1% milk (0–2 g.)

TOTAL FAT: 1–3 G.
TOTAL FAT FOR DAY 20: 20–29 G.

DAY 21

Breakfast

Sliced fresh fruit; dry cereal (1 g. per ounce); 1 cup of skim or 1% milk (0–2 g.); coffee or tea

TOTAL FAT: 1–3 G.

Lunch

Toasted pita pocket: 1 ounce of shredded hard cheese (8–10 g.), 1 6-inch whole-grain pita (1 g.), sliced tomato, assorted raw vegetables; orange; no-cal beverage

TOTAL FAT: 9–11 G.

Dinner

1 serving of Shrimp Florentine (pages 174–175; 7 g.) or 3–4 ounces of broiled fish; greens of choice; brown or wild rice (1/2 cup $1eq g.); whole-grain bread (1 g. per slice); apple; no-cal beverage

TOTAL FAT: 9 G.

Snack

1 cup of plain, nonfat yogurt; sliced peaches; graham crackers (2 = 1 g.)

TOTAL FAT: 1 G.
TOTAL FAT FOR DAY 21: 20–24 G.

4

What to Expect When You Use the T-Factor Diet

As I reported in Chapter 2, the overweight women who used the basic fat-gram formula of the T-Factor Diet, without making any effort to count or cut calories, had an average weight loss of slightly over 7 pounds the first three weeks of the diet and right around a pound a week thereafter. Two of the women lost a pound a day the first week, but obviously it would be nearly impossible to lose that much fat weight that quickly. These women had been retaining a great deal of water and they lost it when they began the diet.

However, all of the women in the group started off with a bang because, as is generally the case, the speed of weight loss correlates with existing weight. Even without making an effort to cut calories, women who are as overweight as they were, and retaining water, can lose as much as a pound a day in the first few days of the T-Factor Diet. From then on, it's the difference between your fat intake and the fat you burn in your fuel mixture.

In this chapter I want to report some of the experiences that people have had with the diet, especially those of a young married couple who were among the first that tested the diet over a year ago. Both husband and wife have each lost over 50 pounds and kept them off. I will talk about this couple later in the chapter because they illustrate what a family can do when it works together.

WHAT ABOUT "FINAL 5 TO 15"?

But what about those persons who have only 5 to 15 pounds to lose—what can they expect? Those final 5 to 15 are often the hardest pounds to lose. They are a source of aggravation and distress for millions of people throughout their lives.

As I reported in Chapter 2, the T-Factor Diet proved to be 100 percent successful with a group of young women who had been struggling with this small amount of excess fat and who went on the diet after hearing about it in a health promotion course. In losing an average of 5 pounds, they now have an average weight that places them right in the middle of the suggested weight charts.

In addition to these women, the entire professional staff of the Vanderbilt Weight Management Program has also adopted the T-Factor Diet. I want in particular to report the experiences that Ms. Jamie Pope-Cordle, the director of nutrition in the Vanderbilt Weight Management Program, and I have had with the diet. We both fit the "final 5 to 15" category, and we kept records of our experience. We will talk about ourselves first, and then we will report the experiences of heavier participants in the Vanderbilt Program.

MY EXPERIENCE IMPLEMENTING THE T-FACTOR DIET

I couldn't possibly recommend a diet that I hadn't tried myself, especially when the diet is supposed to embody health-enhancing principles that I recommend you follow for the rest of your life.

So I did exactly what I suggest you do, with the intention of making a lifetime life-style change. Here is my personal report.

I surveyed my ongoing eating habits to determine how much fat I was eating. I counted fat grams. At first, I often had to look them up.

To my surprise, I was eating, on the average, about 100 grams of fat a day! Now, I am normally a very active person—jogging or playing tennis just about every day. Before adopting the T-Factor Diet I usually averaged about 3000 calories to maintain my weight at around 160 pounds, which, at 5 feet 10½ inches, is smack in the middle of the range of suggested weight in the charts. (If you have read my previous books you will know that I lost 70 pounds twenty-five years ago and have never regained that weight.) One hundred grams of fat is right around 30 percent of my total intake and that percentage of calories in fat would be considered well within the healthy range by most experts. As an absolute amount, however, it is far more than necessary for good health.

When I decided to begin living by the principles of the T-Factor Diet, I wanted the answers to several questions:

1. If I cut back to 60 grams of fat per day and ate freely of anything I wanted in the carbohydrate category, would I lose weight?

2. Considering that I was making no effort to cut calories, how fast would I lose?

3. If I adopted the T-Factor Diet permanently, where would my weight stabilize? I didn't think that I could afford to lose more than 5 or 10 pounds. The one time I got below a weight of 150 after spending two weeks on an experimental very-low-calorie diet, I didn't feel well and my friends and colleagues all remarked on my poor appearance.

4. Where was the fat coming from in my ongoing diet, and if I cut back, would I be able to make healthy substitutions and end up with a more healthful diet?

5. How would I feel?

6. Would I enjoy it?

7. Would I be able to continue eating in my favorite restaurants?

The Changes I Made

When I surveyed my eating habits looking for the excess fat calories, two things stood out: cheese and mayonnaise.

Since I don't care for milk as a beverage, and, except for butter and cream, other dairy products in general are good to excellent sources of calcium, I had chosen cheese as my primary calcium-containing food. But I was eating as much as 4 to 6 ounces a day, using varieties like cheddar or Monterey Jack when I made cheese toast or cheese sandwiches.

Before you read any further, do you know the fat-gram count in 4 to 6 ounces of cheddar cheese? We're talking 36 to 54 grams of fat, or 324 to 486 calories from fat in the cheese component of my daily diet. I was not fully conscious how that one food item, all by itself, contributed the major part of my fat intake each day.

As for the mayonnaise, on the two or three days each week when I made sandwiches using mayonnaise—well, let's just say I've had a love affair with mayonnaise all of my life! When I was a fat adolescent, I would sneak down to the kitchen at night and have mayonnaise sandwiches, with or without Bermuda onions, on thick slices of pumpernickel bread. To this day, I really like mayonnaise, and I was spreading each sandwich with at least a tablespoonful and eating two at a sitting. I might finish up with a slice or two of bread and mayonnaise after eating the two sandwiches. That's another 24 to 36 grams of fat—or 216 to 324 calories.

In other words, about half the fat in my diet was coming from these two sources, cheese and mayonnaise!

When you survey your own eating habits I think you, too, will find that a major part of the fat in your diet is coming from just two, or possibly three, sources. It's not hard to change once you've located the main culprits because there are so many healthy substitutions possible.

This is what I did.

About six out of seven days a week I began substituting either cereal and low-fat milk for the cheese toast or a full cup of variously seasoned low-fat cottage cheese[1] with a bagel or whole-grain toast. Thus, even with two bowls of cereal, with fruit, such as a banana, a cup of berries, or a sliced peach, and with 8 ounces of low-fat milk, I was at 6 to 8 grams of fat, not 36 to 54. A full cup of low-fat cottage cheese, which I most frequently began to eat with a variety of different spicy salsas in place of the hard cheeses, also comes to about 6 grams of fat. Whenever I did eat cheddar or other hard cheeses that are high in fat I made sure it was never over 2 ounces a day. In order to guaran-

---

[1] Be sure to try my suggestions on pages 124–126 for flavoring this old standby. Never before did I find cottage cheese to be a particularly inviting food, but these seasonings have made it one of my favorites.

tee that I was getting enough calcium I increased my consumption of leafy greens and other vegetables such as broccoli, and made sure I ate sardines, canned salmon, or canned jack mackerel once a week. These canned fishes are good sources of calcium because they contain the bones in edible form.

Then I discovered something about mayonnaise. When I cut back from a tablespoon to a teaspoon I found that within a couple of days my sensitivity to its taste increased to the point where even a small amount became perfectly satisfying. So, my mayonnaise consumption was cut by two-thirds. I think I was able to cut my consumption of mayonnaise and still enjoy the limited amounts because I continued to use my favorite, full-flavored brands, specifically Hellmann's (or Best Foods', as it's called out west) and Kraft.

You can see that saving over 40 grams of fat in cheese and mayonnaise wasn't all that difficult for me, and I'll bet that you will find similar "savings" are possible in your own case. Here is a short summary of some other things that permitted me to cut my fat grams substantially and end up with an even healthier diet than before:

When I didn't have cereal or cottage cheese for breakfast, I had hearty whole-grain bread, bagels, or homemade muffins (pages 129-135) and, on occasion, the very best jellies. I found it hard to believe I could be eating toast and jelly and losing weight.

Instead of sandwiches for lunch, spread with that blanket of mayonnaise, I began to eat much more soup (pages 139-145) and cottage cheese, if I hadn't had it for breakfast. When I did make sandwiches, I used one-third my previous amount of mayonnaise. At times I skipped the mayonnaise completely and began to use more different-flavored mustards. When having lunch around the university, I found three restaurants that served a variety of salads, soups, and sandwiches, where I could construct lunches totaling 10 grams of fat or less. By our suggestion, one of the restaurants began serving at least one non-creamed homemade soup each day, to go with sliced turkey or lean-meat sandwiches, all made without mayonnaise, but with a variety of mustards. All we had to do was make the suggestion to the owner.

I increased my number of meatless meals for dinner (pages 151–158), and made many more interesting fish and poultry recipes (pages 164–177). But I still had beef about once a week, since I do enjoy a well-seasoned steak (page 178) or pot roast (page 181).

How Fast Did I Lose?

SLOWLY!!

As I have said before, people who are significantly overweight will lose much more quickly than those who are not when they go on the basic T-Factor Diet. If you are one of those persons in the "final 5 to 15" category, you too, like myself, may face the prospect of a slow (but certain) weight loss.

If I had been in a hurry to lose weight I would have used the Quick Melt. I already knew from experimenting with other low-calorie diets that I can lose up to 9 pounds in two weeks if I cut my calories down to the Quick Melt levels. Every other time, however, after finishing the experimental diet, I would resume my old eating habits and my weight would return to its former level.

This time I wanted to experience the real test of nutrient substitution, and see where my weight would end up when I simply changed the proportion of fat in my diet. *This was not going to be a weight-loss diet. It was an experiment to determine whether I could make a lifetime change in my eating habits—the kind of change that's necessary for those who want to lose weight and keep it off permanently. Would this change lead to an automatic downward adjustment in my weight?*

I lost:

Week 1	½ pound
Week 2	½ pound
Week 3	½ pound
Week 4	1½ pounds
Week 5	2¼ pounds
Week 6	1 pound
Week 7	1 pound

By the eighth week I stabilized at this new level.

I learned several things about losing weight in this fashion rather than by "going on a diet" and some of the following details may be of help to you as you lose your "final 5 to 15" on the T-Factor Diet.

My weight would frequently fluctuate as much as 2 pounds a day. It was 2 pounds up after each of the two times we went out for dinner in a Chinese restaurant (we ask for our food to be prepared without MSG, but there is plenty of sodium from table salt in commercially prepared Chinese food even when you order without MSG). My weight was up a pound when I had a pickle—which is why I warn people, "It's a pound a pickle." It was up 2 pounds after an Italian dinner, with wine. Remember this about alcohol: It has a slight diuretic effect in the short term, but many people rebound and rehydrate beyond their baseline water balance. They end up retaining water and weighing more than they did before, twelve to twenty-four hours after drinking any alcohol.

All of these temporary increases that I mention were superimposed on a slowly descending baseline, but if I had gotten on a scale every day expecting to see myself lighter on each succeeding day, I would have been terribly disappointed. I got on the scale only to see the impact on my water balance, knowing that I was losing fat weight even if it was not detected by the scale.

SO—UNLESS YOU HAVE A SCIENTIFIC INTEREST IN WATCHING YOUR WEIGHT FLUCTUATIONS, I SUGGEST YOU GET ON THE SCALE NO MORE THAN ONCE A WEEK. IF THAT!

Perhaps the very best way to implement the T-Factor Diet is to forget about the scale completely. Throw it away so that you will never be its slave again. Trust your body and mother nature. If you follow a healthful diet and activity program, the weight will take care of itself.

But why did I have the sudden loss in the fourth and fifth weeks? First, I had started rather slowly. Second, in some people, there is a tendency for fat cells to take in a bit of water to replace the fat they lose at the beginning of any weight-loss program. This water is sometimes held for several weeks. Then, suddenly, out it goes. Third, in those two weeks of quicker losses, I may have hit the scale at a low point in my water balance. I did hit a plateau in Week 7, and from then on my weight has bounced around this new low point.

How Did I Feel?

Great! I certainly wouldn't be writing about it if I didn't find myself feeling more energetic than before—and I was building on a rather high baseline since I had felt fine on my previous diet. People remarked spontaneously on how good I looked and how energetic I seemed. This turns out to be a common experience for persons who switch to the T-Factor Diet.

Did I Eat as Much as Before?

I was not able to give this a good test at first because I sustained a knee injury playing tennis and was not able to jog or play tennis for fourteen weeks. My calorie intake dropped to about 2400 a day from 3000, BUT THAT LED TO AN INTERESTING, DIFFERENT KIND OF TEST WHICH PROVED THAT WEIGHT LOSS WAS POSSIBLE, IN FACT QUITE EASY, WITHOUT MY USUAL LEVEL OF ACTIVITY.

Because weight loss occurred automatically with the cutback in fat intake, in spite of my inability to continue my customary physical activities, I feel that the T-Factor Diet offers hope to those persons who have physical limitations on the amount of exercise they can pursue. We have not given this a formal test because we feel that exercise is so important to good health, but we have worked with a few individuals who are not able to exercise consistently for one reason or another, with good results, as you will see from my discussion below.

As my injury healed, I gradually resumed jogging, going from short stints of one to three miles, two to three times a week, back up to full steam, mixing five or six miles of jogging on alternate days with tennis. Just as the experts predict, my caloric intake increased approximately 100 calories per mile of activity. (In tennis, according to actual measurements made on many occasions, I move almost exactly five miles in every 1½ hours of singles.) I now eat a few more grams of fat each day, but the major part of that extra intake is in carbohydrate foods.

The T-Factor Diet Is Livable

I found that within a few weeks my low-fat for high-fat substitutions became second nature. Today, I no longer think about it. I've gotten used to small amounts of fat and even the thought of increasing makes me feel a little nauseated. I would find it hard to resume my old way of eating. You, too, will discover how much easier it is to digest low-fat meals and how much better you will feel as you follow the T-Factor Diet.

Eating Out

I have already mentioned how I deal with lunches when I eat out around the university. Most of the restaurants where we like to eat dinner have several low-fat selections on their menus. Look around your own city for restaurants that offer fine low-fat cooking. There is so much interest developing in eating a more healthful diet that more and more restaurants are responding and making it possible to eat out without pigging out.

But in those few cases where suitable things do not appear on the menu, ASK! One of my favorite restaurants NEVER prepares anything on its menu without one-eighth a pound of butter or a rich cream sauce. The owner to this day feels that when people go out to eat they want to kill themselves with "goodness." Yet the excellent chef at this restaurant will make anything I ask for without the fat or the cream, and if I want a taste of the sauce, he puts it in an attractive little cup on the side. Any decent restaurant will be happy to do the same for you. It's important for you to get over any embarrassment you may have about asking for special food preparation: In a recent national survey, 75 percent of restaurants said they would modify their manner of food preparation on request.

If you have any doubt about the restaurant's willingness to prepare food the way you want it, call and ask them in advance. You should have no trouble since just about all fish, fowl, veal, and beef can be prepared without added fat. Even if the food is grilled, a touch of oil is all it takes to prevent sticking and keep the food tender. When it comes to pasta, plain tomato sauce or a clam sauce will generally be lowest in fat. *Except for fast-food establishments, I personally have never found a restaurant that would not make one or more dishes in the low-fat manner that I prefer if I could not find something on the menu.*

THE T-FACTOR EXPERIENCE: A NUTRITIONIST'S VIEWPOINT

Ms. Jamie Pope-Cordle is the director of nutrition for the Vanderbilt Weight Management Program. She, like me, fits into that "final 5 to 15" category. She gave me this summary at a Thanksgiving Day dinner in 1988 (quite appropriately, I thought) of her experience using the T-Factor approach:

> I can remember my freshman year in college and my first nutrition course: "Whether you eat it as chocolate cake or celery, a calorie is a calorie—carbohydrate, fat, and protein created equal." There was no reason to debate the issue. In the mid-seventies scientific evidence did not exist that pinpointed fat as the crucial factor in weight management. The research and clinical findings concerning differences in the metabolism, storage, and mobilization of fat and carbohydrate have only been brought to the scientific community's attention in the last few years. The vast majority of nutrition texts still do not reflect these findings.
>
> I have been a chronic calorie counter ever since that 1975 freshman nutrition course. Battling my own weight against a family history of obesity and a mild obsession with food, I became a walking calculator—I rarely went to sleep without a daily inventory of calories consumed and expended. I was even known to count the calories of persons in front of me in line at convenience stores, silently comparing their caloric purchases

with mine. Sounds crazy, but I bet this hits home with a few others as well!

So, needless to say, switching from counting calories to counting fat grams was quite a switch. I had to add another automatic function to my mental calculator. I started counting fat grams a little over three months ago, although I have been aware of the "proportion" of calories from fat for several years. I had always strived to keep my own intake of fat, along with that of participants in my weight-management programs at Vanderbilt, to less than 30 percent of total calories. However, the importance of a specific number of fat grams became evident to me as I did research for a grant proposal concerning low-fat reducing diets. In addition, we began to notice that participants in our own studies who made the greatest reduction in their fat intake lost the most weight. Of course, calorie reduction facilitated the loss, but fat intake seemed to be the most significant factor. Those who ate the same "type" of diet as they had previously, that is, choosing the same high-fat foods but in smaller quantities to achieve caloric reduction, did not do as well as those who switched their eating style to lower-fat, higher-fiber fare.

When I first started counting fat grams I found I still couldn't resist a nightly calorie inventory. At the beginning, on some days, despite eating three meals and two snacks, I found I was eating only 1300 calories. I lost 5 pounds in two and a half weeks even though I intentionally tried to up my intake to at least 1800 calories per day. The weight loss just "happened" after I began stocking my kitchen with a brand-new variety of low-fat foods. I was rather surprised, though, that I lost this much weight because I was even testing recipes for the book during this period, which meant lots of taste testing!

In the past I used to average around 1800 calories a day and I maintained my weight with running and walking fifteen to twenty miles a week. Now my weight has stabilized at 4 pounds lower than when I started and I have increased my intake to around 2000 calories a day. But I cringe to reveal, as of late, I have not been exercising at that same level. Normally, this would have shown up as a few extra pounds on my thighs and stomach. I am confident that I would have seen my weight stabilize at an even lower point if I had been consistent in my activity AND that I would be eating around 2200 calories and weighing less. It is obvious to me that not only can I eat more food in terms of volume and weight, but in calories, too, as long as they are carbohydrate calories and not fat calories.

And, just for your information, I don't know how many calories I ate today—I don't add them up any more. I had 34 grams of fat—but I am not really counting fat grams any more either. You just learn how to eat differently.

A FINAL WORD ON THE "FINAL 5 TO 15"

The T-Factor Diet is THE certain way to eliminate the final 5 to 15 pounds you may have been struggling with for years. Just as in my own case, and as with the young women whose results I reported in Chapter 2, fat loss may proceed at about 1 to 1½ pounds a week rather than at the faster rate that significantly overweight people achieve. But just as our follow-up with these women showed, WE ARE TALKING ABOUT 100 PERCENT SUCCESS WITH *YOUR* FINAL 5 TO 15 POUNDS WHEN YOU STICK WITH THE T-FACTOR FAT-GRAM FORMULA.

Do remember this: Your fat loss is correlated with your present body composition and diet. If, *like me*, you are already near your healthiest minimum body-fat composition and are eating a reasonably low-fat diet, fat loss will necessarily be slower than for persons with more body fat. It may start out, as with me, at only half a pound a week. Of course, I did not cut much below 60 grams of fat a day in my diet (aren't men lucky!). If you are a woman and wish to lose as quickly as possible, cut your fat intake to the bottom limit of the recommended range, that is, to 20 grams a day (men may cut to 30 grams a day).

Your ultimate guarantee of success in eliminating the final 5 to 15 pounds lie in making sure you include *fat-burning exercise* in your weight-management regimen. As I explain in Chapter 7, many people are unaware that certain forms of exercise can make it very difficult to lose body fat and that these forms of exercise may even facilitate weight gain. If you are already an active person and losing those last few troublesome pounds has been truly difficult, the T-Factor Diet *and* the maximum fat-burning potential of the T-Factor Activity Program are both essential.

WHAT OTHERS SAY ABOUT THE T-FACTOR DIET

In our own narratives, Ms. Pope-Cordle and I tried to describe our experiences on the T-Factor Diet in a way that we hope will be helpful to you. Now I will report the experiences of other persons who have used the diet with the same end in mind.

Ms. K. is a minister in one of our local churches. Her husband works on the national Board of Education for that church denomination. Ms. K. was about 75 pounds over recommended levels and Mr. K. was about 55 pounds overweight when they began the program under Jamie's guidance. I did not meet them until they had each lost in the vicinity of 50 pounds. Mr. K. had been at his goal weight for several months, while his wife was still in the process of losing her last 20 pounds.

When I asked what was different about this time, compared with other times when they had tried to lose weight, they both said, "We were ready together. At other times it was just one of us, but this time we were ready to support each other and both do what it takes."

I have always felt that it is very hard for one family member to make an effort to change her or his eating habits when no one else has an interest in doing so. And this is especially true of the wife and mother. I have seen it happen countless times. The woman announces her desire to begin a weight-management program and the whole family responds, "You mean we have to go on a diet because YOU'RE trying to lose weight?" For some reason, this doesn't often happen to the man in the family! When Pop says he's going to lose some weight, the whole family tends to fall in line.

The nice thing about the T-Factor Diet is that it's a healthy diet for everyone. The basic diet, including all of the menus and recipes, is suitable for the entire family. If you don't want to lose weight, just add more no-fat and low-fat foods. You can all do it together and be healthier even if you have no wish to be slimmer.[2]

I'm always interested in how people solve the three major problems associated with changing eating and activity habits:

1. What substitutes for the high-fat foods they used to eat have they found?

2. How do they manage to eat out and enjoy themselves?

3. What motivates them to continue, since there will always be some situations in which the temptation to return to old habits is very strong?

When Ms. K. began the diet, she was eating a daily average of 144 grams of fat, or 54 percent of her 2400 daily calories. Over 45 percent of 3000 daily calories, or 150 grams, in Mr. K's diet were from fat sources. They ate many meals out at fast-food restaurants, and especially enjoyed Mexican and Italian dishes. Now, according to their latest eating records, they are both consuming in the vicinity of 20 to 25 percent of their total daily intake as fat calories. Ms. K. is holding under 40 grams per day, and is still losing, while Mr. K. is at approximately 50 grams per

---

[2] For people who do not wish to lose weight I suggest starting out by adding fat only to the top of the T-Factor ranges recommended for women and men, together with any amount of no-fat foods to satisfy the appetite. For most people this will result in an intake of about 20 percent of total daily calories in fat. Recent research shows that while this may not lead to any appreciable weight loss in people who are already within the range of desirable weight, it can lead to body composition changes. That is, people at desirable weight lose fat and replace it with lean tissue when they change the composition of their diets by replacing dietary fat with carbohydrate.

day and holding steady. How did they accomplish this? Here are the answers they gave, in condensed form:

> We switched restaurants. There are some places we just don't go anymore. We still continue to eat plenty of Mexican and Italian dishes. We order pizzas without fat meats, and use little or no cheese on the Mexican dishes. We tell our servers how we want the food prepared to make sure they go easy on the fat. We like spicy foods and the spice now is just as satisfying as the fat used to be.
>
> We checked the labels on the crackers we had been using and switched to low-fat varieties. We eliminated cakes and cookies, and substituted popcorn, graham crackers, and fruit. We eat a lot more salads and more Chinese food, but we don't choose dishes that are loaded with oil.
>
> There are times when we don't accept invitations to events where we know there will be nothing but eating going on, and nothing but foods we don't care to eat available. Sometimes we do go to church events where the foods we prefer are not available, but we "save up" and we do have some of the hot dogs and barbecue. Just recently we were at one of these, and I [Mr. K. speaking] skipped the hot dogs and had one of the most delicious chocolate-chip cookies I have ever eaten. I know the woman who makes them, I know how good they always are, and I planned to eat one. But only one. In the past I would have had three, and I calculate they each contain at least 250 calories and 14 or 15 grams of fat from butter and chocolate.

I asked about their levels of physical activity. Since I am such an advocate of activity, I was disappointed in their answers. But these answers are informative.

Mr. K., who had been very active while losing weight, had dropped to "one workout a week, but I do walk a lot every day in my job." I suggested he get a pedometer and see just how far he really goes. Most people who think they move around a great deal don't move nearly as much as they think they do. I know: I move around as much as I can when I'm working, but it only adds up to about one mile per day. Ms. K. had never gotten active at all. "I'm just too busy to take the time, and I'd rather do it with my diet."

Well, on the one hand, they are managing their weight very well by following the T-Factor Diet without becoming more active, which proves once again that the diet can be of help to sedentary people. But, on the other hand, I never feel very confident about the ability of anyone with tendencies to obesity to maintain desirable weight without a daily activity program. As I explain in Chapter 7, physical activity helps regulate appetite. Anyone who does not develop an active life-style will probably always feel a need for restraint, and that restraint can become oppressive.

When I asked the couple whether sticking with their program ever presented any problems, Ms. K. said, "Yes, sometimes. It doesn't happen very often, but we are both very busy. Our work requires that we eat out two-thirds of the time, and we are often pressed for time when we decide to cook at home. However, when we are tempted in a restaurant as the dessert tray comes around, we always split one dessert rather than each take one. And we have learned many new, quick, low-fat recipes for home cooking."

When I asked what motivates them to adhere to the program in spite of temptations, both of them responded enthusiastically about the change in the way they feel. "I am down three dress sizes. I changed my hairdo. I switched from eyeglasses to contact lenses. When I meet people who haven't seen me in a year, they absolutely do not recognize me. I just like myself a whole lot better this way, and I'm not going to change." Mr. K. echoed the exact same sentiments, adding, "It's so much easier to move around now that I'm almost 60 pounds lighter. I automatically take the stairs in our building, covering the three flights many times a day, and I walk wherever and whenever I can on business. I never try to conserve on the number of trips I need to make, as I used to."

Although I am disappointed in their failure to increase and maintain an activity program, I still think the couple will do well, especially for the following reason. They have started a T-Factor group in their church, and have been joined by members from another church. Perhaps the need to be good role models will reinforce their commitment. I think you, too, will find solid extra reinforcement for maintaining the T-Factor program if you, too, recruit friends and co-workers to join you. There is great strength in social support. With all your friends helping you, you won't have any whose behaviors will sabatage your motivation to succeed.

COMMENTS FROM THE RESEARCH PARTICIPANTS IN THE VANDERBILT WEIGHT MANAGEMENT PROGRAM

During the past year we have been testing both versions of the T-Factor Diet at Vanderbilt. Half of our research participants are in the no-calorie-cutting, no-calorie-counting group, and half of our participants use the Quick Melt. Periodically we ask our program participants to write comments and suggestions for their group leaders.

Here are the major comments that have been made by persons who have followed the basic T-Factor Diet without trying to cut or count calories. These comments are distilled from the hundreds of weekly reports in our files.

The most frequent comment we receive from persons who implement the T-Factor Diet without counting calories, or making any effort to control them, is, first and foremost, "I can't believe I'm eating like this and losing weight!" It's phrased in many different ways:

"It doesn't seem like a diet—I'm not counting calories!" A.S.

"I can't believe I can eat some of these high-calorie foods that are low in fat just as I desire, and lose weight." J.I.

For many persons who have resigned themselves to the idea that they must deprive themselves and periodically fight hunger in order to lose weight, it's an almost incredible experience. "There is always something to eat *that tastes good* when I'm hungry." C.R.

Here are some other comments in this vein:

"I have a large family, all working different shifts. I

cook for all of them, and now I can nibble on no-fat foods like crackers and pretzels and not feel like I'm starving myself." F.L.

"I can eat bread! I'm not hungry." D.L.

"I'm not hungry, yet I'm losing weight. Best—I'm changing my life-style." J.I.

For persons who have been a part of the calorie-counting diet culture all of their lives, the T-Factor Diet is a re-education in nutrition and the importance of reducing fat in the diet. Comments such as "I didn't know where the fats are. I'm getting educated in nutrition and exercise and there are nice tips on food" (V.W.) summarize this new awareness quite well.

Of course we want the T-Factor Diet to be effective in helping people who have had difficulty losing weight in other programs, and it's nice to receive comments like this one, from someone who was on a 1200-calorie diet in another program and could not lose weight: "It works. I was in [popular commerical program] for two months before this and lost nothing. I'm thrilled!" J.B.[3] Also "I'm getting a consistent, gradual weight loss—my first success in years. It works!" R.V.

But naturally the most important issue is—*can you live with it?* Here are some quotes that address this important concern:

"This is a diet to live by, not three months on and then back to old eating habits." M.E.

"It's great being able to eat at any time—all you want—so long as you watch the fat. It's wonderful for munchers like me." A.K.

"The flexibility is a strong point. No rigid rules about substitutions and I'm learning the fat content of foods." D.L.

"I was surprised to see how many good things there are that do not contain fat." K.D.

"It's a life-style I can live with for the rest of my life. I never need to feel hungry or deprived. It's a logical, rational, good-health program." R.F.

---

[3] This woman was choosing foods that were high in fat on the commercial 1200-calorie program. An analysis of her eating records in that program showed over 50 percent of calories from fat. She is now eating much more total food and far less fat, and is losing weight.

Many persons comment on the ease of implementing the diet:

"It is less time consuming than counting calories, and I don't feel like I'm dieting when I can eat sandwiches instead of cottage cheese all the time." D.L.

"It's so easy. You absolutely don't feel deprived. It's not confusing." J.B.

We want people to feel good. It's time to be done with obsessions and guilt over your eating habits. Comments like these indicate that we are successful in this regard, and in the case of this last comment, that the diet does have the impact we desire on the digestive systems of people who have clogged themselves up with a high-fat diet:

"I feel better. I can see some increase in energy level. My friends say I look better, especially less tired. Psychologically, I feel better about myself since I'm taking care of myself as well as my family." M.S.

5

The Quick Melt

Having been 70 pounds overweight myself I can certainly understand how you feel if you are eager to lose weight quickly. When I lost those 70 pounds twenty-five years ago I used an alternating approach—three weeks of quick weight loss followed by a vacation period. I would repeat the quick-weight-loss diet whenever I felt motivated to do so, losing about 15 pounds each time. I kept the weight off by becoming a tennis player and jogger, which helped me burn off whatever calories I chose to eat each day. Many years later my approach to losing weight evolved into the Rotation Diet. The T-Factor Quick Melt is an advance over the Rotation Diet, but, like the Rotation Diet, it can be used to give people who want a quick weight loss the safe, fast results they desire.

Because I don't think it's wise from a psychological standpoint, or particularly good for your morale, to restrict food intake for long periods of time, I continue to recommend the appealing, time-limited, quick-weight-loss feature of the Rotation Diet in the T-Factor Quick Melt. Just as in the Rotation Diet, very overweight people may lose up to a pound a day, and, depending on the number of optional snacks chosen (one is recommended), the average dieter will lose 9 to 12 pounds in three weeks.

HOWEVER, THE T-FACTOR QUICK MELT IS A SIGNIFICANT IMPROVEMENT OVER THE ROTATION DIET IN ONE KEY ASPECT—IT'S DESIGNED TO LEAD YOU ALONG THE ROUTE TO LASTING RESULTS RIGHT FROM DAY 1.

Here's why.

Although the Rotation Diet is a low-fat diet as well as a low-calorie diet *in its quick-loss phase*, it has, unfortunately, failed many people in maintenance. With its emphasis on calories, the Rotation Diet and its maintenance program fail to stress the extreme importance of continuing to control fat intake at the level required for permanent weight control. That's because when I created the Rotation Diet, I was unaware of the direct relationship between the fat content of your body and the fat content of your diet. I want to stress this point once again: *The fat content of your body may be less related to your diet's total calories than it is to your daily fat intake.*

When you use the T-Factor Quick Melt, you will be following the basic fat-control principles of the T-Factor Diet. So, although you will be losing weight just about as quickly as with the Rotation Diet, you will still be learning, and, I hope, permanently adopting, the T-Factor fat-gram solution to your weight problem.

I think you will find the Quick Melt much easier and more comfortable to implement than other quick-loss plans because it not only permits you but *encourages* you to eat more of a larger variety of foods. *Unlike most other quick-loss plans, the T-Factor Quick Melt is a nutritious diet that meets the Recommended Dietary Allowances (RDAs) established by the National Research Council.*

The daily menus in this chapter each contain the fat levels I recommend in the T-Factor Diet—that is, 20 to 40 grams of fat per day for a woman and 30 to 60 grams for a man (see pages 29–30 for adapting the menus for men). But, obviously, in order to lose weight even more quickly than you would on the basic T-Factor Diet, you have to cut calories. By cutting calories—not just substituting carbohydrates for fat—you create a deficit that pulls even more fat from your fat cells.

The daily menus in this chapter all contain approximately 1000 calories for a woman, and 1500 calories for a man. With an added snack (shown as optional on the menus) they will total between 1100 and 1300 calories per day for a woman and between 1600 and 1800 for a man.

Although there are twenty-one days of menus, you can repeat them over and over again as long as you wish. My personal preference is to take a vacation after three weeks of cutting calories, but the menus are nutritious enough (even at 1000 calories for women and 1500 for men) to be repeated for long periods of time. You can, occasionally, substitute one day's menu for another, one meal for another, or you can substitute different foods using the rules listed below. This variety will keep the diet interesting and lessen any feelings of deprivation you might have. However, don't eat the same meal or menu over and over, to the virtual exclusion of other foods! The key to a healthful diet is to eat a wide variety of foods and not to slight any particular food group.

HOW FAST WILL YOU LOSE?

Weight loss on the Quick Melt is initially faster than on the basic T-Factor Diet because you are cutting calories and establishing a larger daily energy deficit. The deficit will at first be made up in part from your glycogen (carbohydrate) stores and in part from your fat stores. While the average participant in the Vanderbilt Weight Management Program who tested the Quick Melt and *added the daily snack* lost over 9 pounds in three weeks, people who are considerably overweight can begin with a weight loss of over a pound a day for a few days and end up losing as much as 21 pounds in twenty-one days.

If you are less than 50 pounds overweight, however, do not expect that rate of loss for more than a few days, or a week at most, for the following reasons.

As I explained in Chapter 2, when you cut calories, you burn part of your glycogen storage, as well as fat, in your fuel mixture. This causes an initial water loss. This occurs because there are only about 500 calories of glycogen stored in a pound of the glycogen/water mixture in your liver and muscles (as compared to 3500 calories in a pound of fat). Thus, for every 500 calories of glycogen loss, you lose a pound. In addition, the reduction in calories also means a reduction in sodium, which will increase your water losses.

On reduced calories you can lose several pounds in the first week before you reach a new equilibrium in glycogen storage and water balance. Your new level of glycogen storage will be somewhat lower than your normal standard. At this point your body will begin to draw upon its fat storage to a greater extent, using up more fat relative to glycogen, *and weight loss will slow considerably.* Since fat is stored at around 3500 calories per pound of fat tissue, compared with only 500 calories per pound of glycogen storage, weight loss may slow to about one-seventh the rate of your initial loss by the end of two or three weeks.

Weight loss in people who are not significantly overweight is also slower because they are not as likely to be retaining as much water and the calorie deficit created by the diet is less than it is for a severely overweight person. It only stands to reason that, other things being equal, a heavier person requires more calories to maintain his or her weight. A 250-pound person who cuts from an intake of 3000 calories to 1000 calories creates a deficit that's twice as large as that in a 150-pound person who cuts from 2000 to 1000. The heavier person will lose about twice as fast as the lighter person.

This slowdown in the rate of weight loss tends to be very discouraging to many overweight persons. It will occur no matter what reduced-calorie diet you use. *So please understand how and why it occurs, and be assured that the losses beginning in the second or third week will be entirely fat losses.*

Here is how you can calculate your expected average losses per week once you have established your new glycogen and water balance. Starting Week 3, think in terms of those 3500 calories per pound of fat. That is, you must have an energy deficit of 3500 calories a week to lose a pound of fat per week. If your energy intake is approximately 1000 calories less than your output each day, you will accumulate a deficit of about 7000 calories per week and lose an average of about 2 pounds of fat weight per week. But, that's only "on the average"!

If you count calories while using the Quick Melt, remember that you will actually lose more true fat weight *by cutting fat calories* than by cutting carbohydrate calories. That's because fat is more available for use by the human body than carbohydrate. As I also explained in Chapter 2, 1000 calories of fat has always provided you with more usable energy than 1000 calories of carbohydrate, so your *actual* energy deficit will be greater than it might seem on paper if you cut fat calories rather than carbohydrates.

WEIGHT LOSS WILL NOT PROCEED LIKE CLOCKWORK.

Even if your caloric deficit averages 1000 calories a day, you will not lose exactly 2 pounds per week. Sometimes you will gain! You will think your body is playing tricks on you, but it isn't. Cyclic hormonal changes can lead to several pounds of water retention. Stress can lead to weight gain. Under the severe stress accompanying the outbreak of war, people have been known to gain several pounds overnight, due to water retention. Every pickle means a pound of water retention, and if you happen to use a salty dressing such as a blue-cheese dressing on your salad, together with eating a pickle, it can mean 2 or 3 pounds. A Chinese dinner means 2 pounds for most people, including me, and 3 or 4 pounds for others who have stronger tendencies to retain water.

IN SPITE OF THE SCALE'S VARIATIONS, THE FAT LOSS CONTINUES.

Is there *any* limit to the time you can use the Quick Melt?

There are a number of different ways to use the Quick Melt and you can suit your changing moods and inclinations.

Because the Quick Melt is designed to meet the RDAs and is healthfully low in fat and well balanced, you can, if you like, stick with it until you lose all the weight you wish to lose.

You can take a semi-vacation from dieting if you feel deprived, and you can continue to lose fat weight, by following the T-Factor fat-gram formula. But, ADD CARBOHYDRATE CALORIES SLOWLY!

You can enter into a period of true maintenance BY ADDING CALORIES, INCLUDING BOTH CABOHYDRATE *AND A LITTLE FAT*, TO YOUR DIET VERY SLOWLY!

You must add calories slowly after a restricted-calorie diet in order to prevent water retention and a rapid weight gain. Be sure to read the final section of this chapter on making a transition to maintenance before increasing your intake after the Quick Melt if you want to prevent water retention.

HOW TO USE THE QUICK MELT MENUS

In contrast with the menus for the basic T-Factor Diet (Chapter 3) in which only the fatty foods are portion controlled, the menus here are entirely portion controlled. They are designed to contain between 1100 and 1300 calories per day for women and between 1600 and 1800 calories per day for men, including the snack. Your snack can be eaten at any time (dried and fresh fruit, low-fat crackers, pretzels, and raw vegetables may also be used as substitutes for the suggested snacks for variety).

The Substitution Rule

Follow the menus as closely as you can, but in case you don't like a particular selection, substitute *from within the same food group*. That is, you can substitute one vegetable for another, one fruit for another, one meat for another, etc. Try to stick with similar foods—a green for a green, a citrus fruit for a citrus—when you can. That's because we want you to preserve as much as possible the spectrum of nutrients. You may also settle on three or four favorite breakfasts and lunches, and rotate among them, but keep in mind that a wide variety of different foods helps ensure sound nutrition.

Do You Need Vitamin and Mineral Supplementation?

When you reduce calories there is always the danger that you will be a bit deficient in one or another vitamin or mineral if you plan to stick with that reduction for a long period of time, that is, more than three weeks. The wide variety of foods in the menus below helps assure that you will meet the Recommended Dietary Allowances and obtain sound nutrition. Thus, if you substitute and limit variety beyond my recommendations, I suggest you take a multiple vitamin and mineral tablet that contains from 100 to 150 percent of the RDAs for the key nutrients. DO NOT TAKE MEGADOSES OF VITAMINS EXCEPT FOR

SOME SPECIFIC MEDICAL PURPOSE, AND THEN
ONLY UNDER THE GUIDANCE OF A KNOWL-
EDGEABLE PHYSICIAN.

T-FACTOR QUICK MELT MENUS

WEEK 1

DAY 1
Breakfast

½ banana; 1 ounce of dry cereal (1 g.); 1 cup of skim or
1% milk (0–2 g.); coffee or tea

TOTAL FAT: 1–3 G.

Lunch

2 ounces of water-packed tuna (1 g.); 1 teaspoon of
mayonnaise (4 g.); 1 whole bagel (1 g.); alfalfa sprouts
and assorted raw vegetables; 1 apple; no-cal beverage

TOTAL FAT: 6 G.

Dinner

3 ounces of lean beef (see pages 177; 12 g.); 1 medium
baked potato; 1 cup of zucchini; 2 cups of tossed salad;
no- or low-cal salad dressing (2 tablespoons = 0–3 g.);
no-cal beverage

TOTAL FAT: 12–15 G.

Snack

1 cup of plain, nonfat yogurt; 1 cup of strawberries; 2
graham crackers (1 g.)

TOTAL FAT: 1 G.
TOTAL FAT FOR DAY 1: 20–25 G.

DAY 2
Breakfast

½ grapefruit; 1 whole English muffin (2 g.); 2 tea-spoons of jelly; 1 cup of skim or 1% milk (0–2 g.); coffee or tea

TOTAL FAT: 2–4 G.

Lunch

2 ounces of turkey (2 g.); ½ 6-inch pita pocket (1 g.); sliced tomato; assorted raw vegetables; mustard; no- or low-cal salad dressing (2 tablespoons = 0–3 g.); 1 pear; no-cal beverage

TOTAL FAT: 3–6 G.

Dinner

4.5 ounces of baked or broiled fish (4 g.); ½ cup of brown or wild rice (1 g.); 1 cup of steamed broccoli; 1 cup of carrots; ½ cup of assorted fresh fruit; no-cal beverage

TOTAL FAT: 5 G.

Snack

4 cups of air-popped popcorn (2 g.)

TOTAL FAT: 2 G.
TOTAL FAT FOR DAY 2: 12–17 G.

DAY 3
Breakfast

½ cup of blueberries or other seasonal fruit; 1 ounce of dry cereal (1 g.); 1 cup of skim or 1% milk (0–2 g.); coffee or tea

TOTAL FAT: 1–3 G.

Lunch

Cheese toast: 1 ounce of cheese (8–10 g.), 1 slice of wholegrain bread (1 g.); 1 cup of soup of choice (see recipe section; 0–2 g.); 1 orange; no-cal beverage

Dinner

3.5 ounces of chicken (3.5 g.); ½ cup of boiled new or red potatoes; 1 cup of green beans; 2 cups of tossed salad; no- or low-cal salad dressing (2 tablespoons = 0–3 g.); 1 apple; no-cal beverage

TOTAL FAT: 3.5–6.5 G.

Snack

1 cup of plain, nonfat yogurt; ½ banana; 2 graham crackers (1 g.)

TOTAL FAT: 1 G.
TOTAL FAT FOR DAY 3: 14.5–22.5 G.

DAY 4
Breakfast

½ cup of hot cereal of choice (1 g.); 2 tablespoons of raisins; 1 cup of skim or 1% milk (0–2 g.); 1 slice of whole-grain bread (1 g.); coffee or tea

TOTAL FAT: 2–4 G.

Lunch

2 ounces of leftover chicken for sandwich (2 g.); 1 whole-wheat sandwich roll (2 g.); tomato slices; lettuce leaves; 1 teaspoon of mayonnaise (4 g.); ½ cup of pineapple chunks; no-cal beverage

TOTAL FAT: 8 G.

Dinner

1 serving of Pork Tenderloin with Orange Marmalade (page 187; 3 g.); 1 cup of cauliflower; ½ cup of unsweetened applesauce; 2 cups of tossed salad; no- or low-cal salad dressing (2 tablespoons = 0–3 g.); 1 Massachusetts Corn Muffin (page 131; 3 g.); no-cal beverage

TOTAL FAT: 6–9 G.

Snack

1 ounce of dry cereal (1 g.); ½ cup of sliced peaches; 1 cup of skim or 1% milk (0–2 g.)

TOTAL FAT: 1–3 G.
TOTAL FAT FOR DAY 4: 17–24 G.

DAY 5
Breakfast

1 cup of honeydew melon or other seasonal fruit; 1 egg, poached (5 g.); 1 slice of whole-grain toast (1 g.); 1 cup of skim or 1% milk (0–2 g.); coffee or tea

TOTAL FAT: 6–8 G.

Lunch

1 cup of broth-based, vegetable-type soup (2 g.); chef salad: 2 cups of assorted raw vegetables, 1 ounce of turkey (1 g.), ½ ounce of cheese (4–5 g.), ¼ cup of croutons (1 g.), no- or low-cal salad dressing (2 tablespoons = 0–3 g.); ½ cup of fresh fruit; no-cal beverage

TOTAL FAT: 8–12 G.

Dinner

1 serving of Picadillo and Cornbread Wedges (pages 156–157; 9 g.); 2 cups of tossed salad; no- or low-cal salad dressing (2 tablespoons = 0–3 g.); 1 apple; no-cal beverage

TOTAL FAT: 9–12 G.

Snack

4 cups of air-popped popcorn (2 g.)

TOTAL FAT: 2 G.
TOTAL FAT FOR DAY 5: 25–34 G.

DAY 6
Breakfast

½ cup of sliced fruit; 1 ounce of dry cereal (1 g.); 1 cup of skim or 1% milk (0–2 g.); coffee or tea

TOTAL FAT: 1–3 G.

Lunch

2 ounces of canned salmon (4 g.); 5 whole-wheat crackers (1 g.); assorted raw vegetables; no- or low-cal salad dressing (2 tablespoons = 0–3 g.); 1 orange; no-cal beverage

TOTAL FAT: 5–8 G.

Dinner

3.5 ounces of chicken breast (3.5 g.); 1 cup of brussels sprouts or other green vegetable; 1 serving of Scalloped Potatoes (page 194; 3.5 g.); 2 cups of tossed salad; no- or low-cal salad dressing (2 tablespoons = 0–3 g.); 1 slice of whole-grain bread (1 g.); no-cal beverage

TOTAL FAT: 8–11 G.

Snack

1 cup of plain, nonfat yogurt; 2 tablespoons of raisins; 2 graham crackers (1 g.)

TOTAL FAT: 1 G.
TOTAL FAT FOR DAY 6: 15–23 G.

DAY 7
Breakfast

½ grapefruit; 1 whole English muffin (2 g.); 2 teaspoons of jelly; 1 cup of skim or 1% milk (0–2 g.); coffee or tea

TOTAL FAT: 2–4 G.

Lunch

½ cup of low-fat cottage cheese (3 g.); 1 cup of assorted fresh fruit; 1 bran muffin (see pages 130, 132; 3 g.); assorted raw vegetables; no-cal beverage

TOTAL FAT: 6 G.

Dinner

1 cup of Quick Turkey Chop Suey (pages 168–169; 8 g.); ½ cup of brown rice (1 g.); 2 cups of tossed salad; no- or low-cal salad dressing (2 tablespoons = 0–3 g.); 1 slice of whole-grain bread (1 g.); no-cal beverage

TOTAL FAT: 10–13 G.

Snack

1 ounce of dry cereal (1 g.); ½ banana; 1 cup of skim or 1% milk (0–2 g.)

TOTAL FAT: 1–3 G.
TOTAL FAT FOR DAY 7: 19–26 G.

WEEK 2

DAY 8
Breakfast

½ grapefruit; 1 whole bagel (1 g.); 2 teaspoons of jelly; 1 cup of skim or 1% milk (0–2 g.); coffee or tea

TOTAL FAT: 1–3 G.

Lunch

2 ounces of sliced turkey (2 g.); 2 slices of whole-grain bread (2 g.); sliced tomato; lettuce leaves; assorted raw vegetables; 1 apple; no-cal beverage

TOTAL FAT: 4 G.

Dinner

1 cup of Pasta and Shrimp with Ricotta Cheese Sauce (pages 162–163; 7 g.); 1 cup of green beans; 2 cups of tossed salad; no- or low-cal salad dressing (2 table-spoons=0–3g.); ½ cup of blueberries; no-cal beverage

TOTAL FAT: 7–10 G.

Snack

4 cups of air-popped popcorn (2 g.)

TOTAL FAT: 2 G.
TOTAL FAT FOR DAY 8: 14–19 G.

DAY 9
Breakfast

½ cup of fresh fruit; 1 ounce of dry cereal (1 g.); 1 cup of skim or 1% milk (0–2 g.); coffee or tea

TOTAL FAT: 1–3 G.

Lunch

2 ounces of water-packed tuna (1 g.); ¼ cup of chopped celery and onion; sliced tomato; lettuce leaves; 1 tea-spoon of mayonnaise (4 g.); 2 slices of whole-grain bread (2 g.); 1 orange; no-cal beverage

TOTAL FAT: 7 G.

Dinner

1 serving of Spinach Lasagna (pages 157–158; 8 g.); 2 cups of tossed salad; no- or low-cal salad dressing (2 tablespoons = 0–3 g.); ½ cup of seedless grapes; no-cal beverage

TOTAL FAT: 8–11 G.

Snack

1 cup of plain, nonfat yogurt; ½ banana; 2 graham crackers (1 g.)

TOTAL FAT: 1 G.
TOTAL FAT FOR DAY 9: 17–22 G.

DAY 10
Breakfast

½ cup of hot cereal of choice (1 g.); 2 tablespoons of raisins; 1 cup of skim or 1% milk (0–2 g.); 1 slice of whole-grain toast (1 g.); coffee or tea

TOTAL FAT: 2–4 G.

Lunch

Cheese toast: 1 ounce of cheese (8–10 g.), 1 slice of whole-grain bread (1 g.); 1 cup of Split-Pea Soup (page 145; 1 g.); 1 apple; no-cal beverage

TOTAL FAT: 10–12 G.

Dinner

3.5 ounces of baked or broiled chicken (3.5 g.); 1 serving of Apple-Sweet Sweet Potatoes (page 190; 1 g.); 1 cup of broccoli; 2 cups of tossed salad; no- or low-cal salad dressing (2 tablespoons = 0–3 g.); no-cal beverage

TOTAL FAT: 4.5–7.5 G.

Snack

1 ounce of dry cereal (1 g.); 1 cup of skim or 1% milk
(0–2 g.); ½ cup of peach slices or other seasonal fruit

TOTAL FAT: 1–3 G.
TOTAL FAT FOR DAY 10: 17.5–26.5 G.

DAY 11
Breakfast

½ grapefruit; 1 egg, cooked without fat (5 g.); 1 slice of
whole-grain toast (1 g.); 1 cup of skim or 1% milk (0–2
g.); coffee or tea

TOTAL FAT: 6–8 G.

Lunch

2 ounces of leftover chicken (2 g.); ½ 6-inch pita pocket
(1 g.); assorted raw vegetables; ½ cup of seasonal
fruit; no-cal beverage

TOTAL FAT: 3 G.

Dinner

1 serving of Saucy Pastitsio (pages 182–183; 10 g.); 2
cups of tossed salad; no- or low-cal salad dressing (2
tablespoons = 0–3 g.); 1 pear; no-cal beverage

TOTAL FAT: 10–13 G.

Snack

4 cups of air-popped popcorn (2 g.)

TOTAL FAT: 2 G.
TOTAL FAT FOR DAY 11: 21–26 G.

DAY 12
Breakfast

½ banana; 1 ounce of dry cereal (1 g.); 1 cup of skim or 1% milk (0–2 g.); coffee or tea

TOTAL FAT: 1–3 G.

Lunch

Spinach salad: 2 cups of spinach, ¼ cup of sliced fresh mushrooms, ½ hard-boiled egg (3 g.), ½ ounce of part-skim white cheese (4 g.), ¼ cup of chopped onions, ¼ cup of croutons (1 g.), no- or low-cal salad dressing (2 tablespoons = 0–3 g.); 1 slice of whole-grain bread (1 g.); 1 peach; no-cal beverage

TOTAL FAT: 9–12 G.

Dinner

1 serving of Basic Better Beans (pages 152; 5 g.); ½ cup of brown rice (1 g.); ½ cup of Squash-Zucchini-Mushroom Mix (pages 195–196; 1.5 g.); 1 Massachusetts Corn Muffin (page 131; 3 g.); 2 cups of tossed salad; no- or low-cal salad dressing (2 tablespoons = 0–3 g.); ½ cup of sliced fresh fruit; no-cal beverage

TOTAL FAT: 8.5–11.5 G.

Snack

1 cup of plain, nonfat yogurt; 2 tablespoons of raisins; 2 graham crackers (1 g.)

TOTAL FAT: 1 G.
TOTAL FAT FOR DAY 12: 19.5–27.5 G.

DAY 13
Breakfast

½ cup of berries; 1 ounce of dry cereal (1 g.); 1 cup of skim or 1% milk (0–2 g.); coffee or tea

TOTAL FAT: 1–3 G.

Lunch

1 cup of soup of choice (see recipe section; 2 g.); 1 whole bagel (1 g.); ¼ cup of part-skim ricotta cheese as spread for bagel (4–5 g.); assorted raw vegetables; 1 orange; no-cal beverage

TOTAL FAT: 7–8 G.

Dinner

3 ounces of Royal Indian Salmon (pages 171–172; 5 g.); 1 medium baked potato (or 1 serving of Scandinavian-Style Potato Casserole, page 195; 4.5 g.); 1 cup of green beans; 2 cups of tossed salad; no- or low-cal salad dressing (2 tablespoons = 0–3 g.); 1 slice of whole-grain bread (1 g.); 1 nectarine; no-cal beverage

TOTAL FAT: 6–13.5 G.

Snack

4 cups of air-popped popcorn (2 g.)

TOTAL FAT: 2 G.
TOTAL FAT FOR DAY 13: 16–26.5 G.

DAY 14
Breakfast

½ grapefruit; 1 whole bagel (1 g.); 2 teaspoons of jelly; 1 cup of skim or 1% milk (0–2 g.); coffee or tea

TOTAL FAT: 1–3 G.

Lunch

½ cup of low-fat cottage cheese (3 g.); ½ cup of assorted fresh fruit; assorted raw vegetables; 1 muffin of choice (see recipe section; 3 g.); no-cal beverage

TOTAL FAT: 6 G.

Dinner

3.5 ounces of baked or broiled chicken (3.5 g.); 1 cup of broccoli; ½ cup of brown or wild rice (1 g.); 2 cups of tossed salad; no- or low-cal salad dressing (2 tablespoons = 0–3 g.); ½ cup of melon; no-cal beverage

TOTAL FAT: 4.5–7.5 G.

Snack

1 ounce of dry cereal (1 g.); ½ cup of raspberries; 1 cup of skim or 1% milk (0–2 g.)

TOTAL FAT: 1–3 G.
TOTAL FAT FOR DAY 14: 12.5–19.5 G.

WEEK 3

DAY 15
Breakfast

½ cup of seasonal fruit; 1 whole English muffin (2 g.); 2 teaspoons of jelly; 1 cup of skim or 1% milk (0–2 g.); coffee or tea

TOTAL FAT: 2–4 G.

Lunch

Stuffed tomato: 1 whole tomato, 2 ounces of water-packed tuna (1 g.), assorted raw vegetables, no- or low-cal salad dressing (2 tablespoons = 0–3 g.); 5 whole-wheat crackers (1 g.); ½ cup of seedless grapes; no-cal beverage

TOTAL FAT: 2–5 G.

Dinner

3 ounces of lean beefsteak (see page 177; 7.5 g.); 1 medium baked potato; 1 cup of cooked spinach; 1 slice of whole-grain bread (1 g.); 1 apple; no-cal beverage

TOTAL FAT: 8.5 G.

Snack

4 cups of air-popped popcorn (2 g.)

TOTAL FAT: 2 G.
TOTAL FAT FOR DAY 15: 14.5–19.5 G.

DAY 16
Breakfast

½ cup of peach slices or other seasonal fruit; 1 ounce of dry cereal (1 g.); 1 cup of skim or 1% milk (0–2 g.); coffee or tea

TOTAL FAT: 1–3 G.

Lunch

Toasted pita pocket: 1 ounce of cheese (8–10 g.); ½ 6-inch whole-grain pita (1 g.), sliced tomato, alfalfa sprouts, and other vegetables of choice; 1 orange; no-cal beverage

TOTAL FAT: 9–11 G.

Dinner

4.5 ounces of baked or broiled fish (4 g.); ½ cup of spinach noodles (1 g.); 1 cup of Beets a l'Orange (page 191); 2 cups of tossed salad; no- or low-cal salad dressing (2 tablespoons = 0–3 g.); ½ cup of pineapple chunks; no-cal beverage

TOTAL FAT: 5–8 G.

Snack

1 cup of plain, nonfat yogurt; ½ banana; 2 graham crackers (1 g.)

TOTAL FAT: 1 G.
TOTAL FAT FOR DAY 16: 16–23 G.

DAY 17
Breakfast

½ cup of melon of choice; 1 egg, cooked without fat (5 g.); 1 slice of whole-grain toast (1 g.); 1 cup of skim or 1% milk (0–2 g.); coffee or tea

TOTAL FAT: 6–8 G.

Lunch

Chef salad: 2 cups of assorted raw vegetables, 1 ounce of turkey (1 g.), ½ ounce of shredded hard cheese (4–5 g.), ¼ cup of croutons (1 g.), no- or low-cal salad dressing (2 tablespoons = 0–3 g.); 1 bran muffin (see pages 130, 132; 3 g.); no-cal beverage

TOTAL FAT: 9–12 G.

Dinner

1 serving of Bean-and-Corn Chili over Puffed Tortilla (page 153; 8–10 g.); 1 cup of cooked greens or 2 cups of greens salad; no- or low-cal salad dressing (2 tablespoons = 0–3 g.); no-cal beverage

TOTAL FAT: 8–13 G.

Snack

1 ounce of dry cereal (1 g.); ½ cup of sliced fruit; 1 cup of skim or 1% milk (0–2 g.)

TOTAL FAT: 1–3 G.
TOTAL FAT FOR DAY 17: 24–36 G.

DAY 18

Breakfast

½ cup of hot cereal of choice (1 g.); 2 tablespoons of raisins; 1 cup of skim or 1% milk (0–2 g.); 1 slice of whole-grain toast (1 g.); coffee or tea

TOTAL FAT: 2–4 G.

Lunch

1 cup of Corn Chowder (pages 142–143; 2 g.); 1 whole bagel (1 g.); ¼ cup of part-skim ricotta cheese as spread for bagel (4–5 g.); assorted raw vegetables; 1 apple; no-cal beverage

TOTAL FAT: 7–8 G.

Dinner

3.5 ounces of baked or broiled chicken (3.5 g.); 1 medium baked potato; 1 cup of brussels sprouts or other green vegetables; 2 cups of tossed salad; no- or low-cal salad dressing (2 tablespoons = 0–3 g.); ½ cup of assorted fresh fruit; no-cal beverage

TOTAL FAT: 3.5–6.5 G.

Snack

4 cups of air-popped popcorn (2 g.)

TOTAL FAT: 2 G.
TOTAL FAT FOR DAY 18: 14.5–20.5 G.

DAY 19
Breakfast

½ cup of sliced fruit; 1 ounce of dry cereal (1 g.); 1 cup of skim or 1% milk (0–2 g.); coffee or tea

TOTAL FAT: 1–3 G.

Lunch

2 ounces of leftover chicken breast (2 g.); 2 slices of whole-grain bread (2 g.); lettuce; tomato slices; 1 teaspoon of mayonnaise (4 g.); ½ cup of watermelon or other seasonal fruit; no-cal beverage

TOTAL FAT: 8 G.

Dinner

1 serving of Pork Tenderloin with Orange Marmalade (page 187; 3 g.); ½ cup of green peas; 1 cup of cauliflower; 2 cups of tossed salad; no- or low-cal salad dressing (2 tablespoons = 0–3 g.); 1 slice of whole-grain bread (1 g.); 1 apple; no-cal beverage

TOTAL FAT: 4–7 G.

Snack

1 cup of plain, nonfat yogurt; 1 cup of strawberries; 2 graham crackers (1 g.)

TOTAL FAT: 1 G.
TOTAL FAT FOR DAY 19: 14–19 G.

DAY 20
Breakfast

½ grapefruit; 1 whole English muffin (2 g.); 2 teaspoons of jelly; 1 cup of skim or 1% milk (0–2 g.); coffee or tea

TOTAL FAT: 2–4 G.

Lunch

½ cup of low-fat cottage cheese (3 g.); ½ cup of sliced fruit; 1 muffin of choice (see recipe section; 3 g.); assorted raw vegetables; no-cal beverage

TOTAL FAT: 6 G.

Dinner

4.5 ounces of baked or broiled fish (4 g.); ½ cup of brown or wild rice (1 g.); 1 cup of green beans; 2 cups of tossed salad; no- or low-cal salad dressing (2 tablespoons = 0–3 g.); 1 whole-grain roll (2 g.); 1 pear; no-cal beverage

TOTAL FAT: 7–10 G.

Snack

1 ounce of dry cereal (1 g.); ½ banana; 1 cup of skim or 1% milk (0–2 g.)

TOTAL FAT: 1–3 G.
TOTAL FAT FOR DAY 20: 16–23 G.

DAY 21

Breakfast

½ cup of blueberries; 1 ounce of dry cereal (1 g.); 1 cup of skim or 1% milk (0–2 g.); coffee or tea

TOTAL FAT: 1–3 G.

Lunch

2 ounces of sliced turkey (2 g.); 2 slices of whole-grain bread (2 g.); sliced tomato; alfalfa sprouts; assorted raw vegetables; 1 orange; no-cal beverage

TOTAL FAT: 4 G.

Dinner

3.5 ounces of baked or broiled chicken (3.5 g.); ½ cup of lima beans; 1 cup of summer squash; 2 cups of tossed salad; no- or low-cal salad dressing (2 tablespoons = 0–3 g.); 1 slice of whole-grain bread (1 g.); ½ cup of fresh fruit; no-cal beverage

TOTAL FAT: 4.5–7.5 G.

Snack

4 cups of air-popped popcorn (2 g.)

TOTAL FAT: 2 G.
TOTAL FAT FOR DAY 21: 11.5–16.5 G.

Adapting the Quick Melt Menus for Men

The male version of the Quick Melt calls for 1600–1800 calories per day and a fat-gram range of 30–60 grams. This level is easily obtained by increasing the portion sizes of the main dishes in the above menus, as well as the starchy side dishes, by 50 percent. In addition, men can have two extra slices of bread each day. By increasing the sizes of portions, everyone in the family can stick with the same menu and the person who prepares the food will not need to prepare any special ones.

THE TRANSITION TO MAINTENANCE

WHY SHOULD YOU ADD CALORIES AND CARBOHYDRATES SLOWLY AFTER A RESTRICTED DIET?

Following an increase in total calories, or even in carbohydrate foods exclusively, there is a quick rehydration effect. On reduced calories, your body has been at a low point in glycogen storage and water balance. If you add calories quickly, it's as though your body has been lying in wait for this very opportunity. Your depleted glycogen stores go up about a pound in weight for every increase of 500 calories of glycogen stored. There is also an increase in body fluid due to the additional sodium that occurs naturally in many foods. The carbohydrate itself stimulates a temporary increase in water retention throughout the system. Taken together, your body may even overshoot its normal water balance and take a few days to return to a lower equilibrium.

If you add calories and carbohydrates slowly, you can continue to lose body fat while you slowly rehydrate. For example, if you gradually go up to a maintenance level over a one-week period, you can continue to lose enough additional body fat to equal the increase in body fluid. Only in this way can you come out even on the scale.[1]

Daily exercise will also help prevent water retention. Water will be lost through perspiration. In addition, your breath is 100 percent saturated with moisture, so any increase in breathing rate due to exercise means more water lost.

Remember to drink plenty of water; it helps stimulate kidney action. Of course, avoid foods high in sodium and increase fruits and vegetables, which are high in potassium. A high potassium to sodium ratio in your diet helps prevent water retention.

When you finish the transition, begin to use the fat-gram-controlled menus in the basic T-Factor Diet that are found in Chapter 3. If you have not already reached a low point in your body-fat content you will continue to lose additional weight without attempting to cut or count calories. Keep your fat-gram count in the recommended daily range of 20 to 40 grams for women and 30 to 60 grams for men. Add nonfatty foods in larger portions to your meals and use them as snacks until you reach a new equilibrium in your weight. Only experience can tell just what this weight will be, but remember that you will keep lost weight off forever as long as you stick with a low-fat diet and satisfy your appetite with complex-carbohydrate foods.

---

[1] A complete explanation of how the body stabilizes at a new weight and fat content is given in Appendix A.

TRANSITION MENUS

The first three days of the following menus contain between 1400 and 1500 calories. The last four days contain between 1600 and 1800 calories. The fat-gram count each day is low enough for you to add a teaspoon of extra fat or oil as a spread or for cooking, and not exceed the recommended level.

Men may increase portion sizes of main courses and side dishes by 50 percent and add two extra slices of whole-grain bread or its equivalent each day.

DAY 1
Breakfast

1 serving of fresh fruit of choice; 1 cup of hot cereal (2 g.); 2 tablespoons of raisins; 1 cup of skim or 1% milk (0–2 g.); coffee or tea

TOTAL FAT: 2–4 G.

Lunch

Spinach salad: 2 cups of fresh spinach, ½ cup of sliced fresh mushrooms, 1 hard-boiled egg (5 g.); 1 tablespoons of grated cheese (4 g.); 2 slices of Bermuda onion, no- or low-cal salad dressing (2 tablespoons = 0–3 g.); choice of muffin (see recipe section; 3g.); 1 orange; no-cal beverage

TOTAL FAT: 12–15 G.

Dinner

4 ounces of baked or broiled chicken (4 g.); 1 cup of steamed broccoli; ½ cup of brown or wild rice (1 g.); 1 serving of Elegant Pears (pages 198–199; 2 g.); no-cal beverage

TOTAL FAT: 7 G.

Snack

4 cups of air-popped popcorn (2 g.)

TOTAL FAT: 2 G.
TOTAL FAT FOR DAY 1: 23–28 G.

DAY 2
Breakfast

1 ounce of dry cereal (1 g.); 1 banana; 1 cup of skim or
1% milk (0–2 g.); coffee or tea

TOTAL FAT: 1–3 G.

Lunch

¾ cup of low-fat cottage cheese (4.5 g.); choice of
muffin (see recipe section; 3 g.) or serving of crackers
(1–2 g.); assorted raw vegetables; ½ sliced melon; no-
cal beverage

TOTAL FAT: 8.5–9.5 G.

Dinner

1 serving of Shrimp Florentine (pages 174–175; 7 g.)
or 4 ounces of baked or broiled fish; 1 cup of cooked
green beans; 1 medium baked potato; 1 slice of whole-
grain bread (1 g.); 1 apple; no-cal beverage

TOTAL FAT: 8 G.

Snack

1 cup of plain, nonfat yogurt; ½ cup of fresh fruit of
choice; 2 graham crackers (1 g.)

TOTAL FAT: 1 G.
TOTAL FAT FOR DAY 2: 18.5–21.5 G.

DAY 3
Breakfast

2 Oatmeal Pancakes (page 137; 4 g.); 1 cup of skim or 1% milk (0–2 g.); 1 serving of fresh fruit of choice; coffee or tea

TOTAL FAT: 4–6 G.

Lunch

1 cup of soup of choice (see recipe section; 2 g.); sliced turkey sandwich: 2 slices of whole-grain bread (2 g.), 1 ounce of turkey breast (1 g.), sliced tomato, lettuce, sprouts, 1 teaspoon of mayonnaise (4 g.); 1 orange; no-cal beverage

TOTAL FAT: 9 G.

Dinner

1 serving of Spinach Lasagna (pages 157–158; 8 g.) or Eggplant Parmesan (page 154; 8 g.) (add side dish of ½ cup of pasta and 1 g. with Eggplant Parmesan); 1 whole-grain roll (2 g.); 2 cups of tossed salad; no- or low-cal salad dressing (2 tablespoons = 0–3 g.); 1 serving of fresh fruit of choice; no-cal beverage

TOTAL FAT: 10–14 G.

Snack

1 ounce of dry cereal (1 g.); 1 cup of skim or 1% milk (0–2 g.); 1 banana

TOTAL FAT: 1–3 G.
TOTAL FAT FOR DAY 3: 24–32 G.

DAY 4
Breakfast

½ honeydew melon or other seasonal fruit; 1 egg, cooked without fat (5 g.); 2 slices of whole-grain bread (2 g.); 1 cup of skim or 1% milk (0–2 g.)

TOTAL FAT: 7–9 G.

Lunch

Tuna-stuffed tomato: 2–3 ounces of water-packed tuna (1 g.), 1 teaspoon of mayonnaise (4 g.), chopped celery, whole tomato; 5 whole-wheat crackers (1 g.); 1 orange; no-cal beverage

TOTAL FAT: 6 G.

Dinner

1 serving of Swedish Meatballs (pages 185–186; 14 g.); ½ cup of brown or wild rice (1 g.); 1 cup of steamed broccoli; 2 cups of tossed salad; no- or low-cal salad dressing (2 tablespoons = 0–3 g.); fresh fruit of choice; no-cal beverage

TOTAL FAT: 15–18 G.

Snack

4 cups of air-popped popcorn (2 g.)

TOTAL FAT: 2 G.
TOTAL FAT FOR DAY 4: 30–35 G.

DAY 5
Breakfast

½ grapefruit (or choice of fruit); 1 whole toasted bagel (1 g.); 2 teaspoons of preserves; 1 cup of skim or 1% milk (0–2 g.); coffee or tea

TOTAL FAT: 1–3 G.

Lunch

1 cup of Minestrone (page 144; 1 g.); tuna salad sandwich: 2 slices of whole-wheat bread (2 g.), 2–3 ounces of water-packed tuna (1 g.), chopped celery, ½ ounce of chopped green olives (about 4 medium, 2 g.), 1 teaspoon of mayonnaise (4 g.), sliced tomato, lettuce; 1 apple; no-cal beverage

TOTAL FAT: 10 G.

Dinner

1 cup of Indian Spiced Beans (page 155; 1 g.); 1 cup of brown rice covered with 1 cup of choice of chopped raw vegetables (e.g., romaine, scallions, green peppers, tomatoes) and 2 tablespoons of grated cheese (9 g.), served with Mexican-Style Hot Sauce (page 124); 1 serving of Lemon Meringue Pie (pages 199–200; 5.5 g.); no-cal beverage

TOTAL FAT: 15.5 G.

Snack

Choice of 1 serving of fresh or dried fruit

TOTAL FAT: 0
TOTAL FAT FOR DAY 5: 26.5–28.5 G.

DAY 6
Breakfast

1 ounce of dry cereal (1 g.); sliced peaches (or choice of fruit for cereal); 1 cup of skim or 1% milk (0–2 g.); 1 slice of whole-wheat bread (1 g.); 1 teaspoon of preserves; coffee or tea

TOTAL FAT: 2–4 G.

Lunch

2 ounces of turkey or chicken (2 g.); ½ 6-inch toasted pita pocket (1 g.); sliced tomato; assorted raw vegetables; mustard; no- or low-cal salad dressing (2 tablespoons = 0–3 g.); 1 pear (or choice of fruit); no-cal beverage

TOTAL FAT: 3–6 G.

Dinner

1 serving of Royal Indian Salmon (pages 171–172; 10 g.); ½ cup of green peas; ½ cup of brown or wild rice (1 g.); 2 cups of tossed salad; no- or low-cal salad dressing (2 tablespoons = 0–3 g.); 1 serving of Poppy-Seed Cake (page 200; 7 g.); no-cal beverage

TOTAL FAT: 18–21 G.

Snack

1 cup of plain, nonfat yogurt; 1 banana; 2 graham crackers (1 g.)

TOTAL FAT: 1 G.
TOTAL FOR DAY 6: 24–32 G.

DAY 7
Breakfast

½ cup of sliced fresh fruit; 1 cup of oatmeal or other hot cereal (2 g.); 2 tablespoons of raisins; 1 cup of skim or 1% milk (0–2 g.); 1 slice of whole-grain toast (1 g.); 1 teaspoon of jelly; coffee or tea

TOTAL FAT: 3–5 G.

Lunch

1 cup of soup of choice (see recipe section; 2 g.); chef salad: 2 cups of assorted raw vegetables, 1 ounce of turkey (1 g.), ½ ounce of cheese (4–5 g.), ¼ cup of croutons (1 g.), no- or low-cal salad dressing (2 table-spoons = 0–3 g.); 1 apple; no-cal beverage

TOTAL FAT: 8–12 G.

Dinner

4.5 ounces of Round-Roast Oriental (page 182; 13–14 g.); or other lean beefsteak; 1 medium baked potato; 1 cup of Brussels Sprouts with Caraway Seeds (page 192; 1 g.) or other green vegetable; 1 hard whole-wheat roll (2 g.); 1 serving of Cocoa Pudding Cake (page 198; 4 g.) or other T-Factor dessert recipe of your choice; no-cal beverage

TOTAL FAT: 20–21 G.

Snack

1 serving of fresh or dried fruit

TOTAL FAT: 0
TOTAL FAT FOR DAY 7: 31–38 G.

6

Recipes

INTRODUCTION

All the recipes in this chapter have been tested and tasted repeatedly by family members, friends, and nutritionists at the Vanderbilt Weight Management Program and at the *Family Circle* test kitchen. They are delicious!

Most can be prepared in 10 to 20 minutes (not including cooking time), though there are a few "special occasion" recipes that are more complicated. All oven temperatures are for preheated ovens, unless otherwise specified.

Recipes that have been included in the menu plans have been marked with an asterisk (*).

Microwave Cooking

Just about any of these dishes can be adapted to microwave cooking. Since my wife and I both have busy schedules, our microwave oven gets quite a workout; we cook practically every kind of food in it.

Microwaves vary somewhat, so check the instruction book that came with yours for specific directions on how to cook recipes similar to the ones in this book.

In general, roasts take around 13 minutes per pound, chops take anywhere from 5 to 20 minutes depending on thickness and how many you are microwaving at once, while chicken pieces run about 3 minutes per piece. You can "bake" a batch of muffins in a microwave in less than half the time it takes in a conventional oven, and the same is usually true of fish fillets. Our microwave oven cooks sliced vegetables in about 11 minutes per pound, and of course, you can have a tender baked potato on your plate in about 6 minutes using a microwave.

Nutritional Analyses

The nutritional contents of all recipes were analyzed using the ESHA Food Processor II computer program. After each recipe, you will find information about calories, cholesterol, dietary fiber, fat, and sodium content. Naturally, with the T-Factor Diet, you are primarily interested in watching your fat (which is in boldface type) as well as your fiber intake, but the other amounts are provided for your information. If you are restricting your cholesterol and sodium intake, I believe you will find this helpful.

Cholesterol and sodium values were rounded up or down to the nearest whole milligram, while fat and fiber values were rounded up or down to the nearest half of a gram.

Herbs and spices have such minimal amounts of nutrients in the quantities used that they have been omitted from the analyses.

In recipes calling for beef, chicken, or vegetable stock, the sodium content is estimated because the computer program had only high-sodium bouillons in its database. I prefer homemade stock, and think it's well worth the minimal effort required to make it (see Basic Vegetable Stock, page 140, and Soup Base, pages 140–141). Otherwise, I recommend looking for low-sodium or no-sodium bouillons in your supermarket.

Meat shrinks about 25 percent in cooking. Therefore, in recipes calling for chicken breasts, for example, the nutritional content was analyzed using a standard 3.5-ounce cooked chicken breast.

I hope you'll use these recipes not only for the sake of enjoying the tempting dishes themselves, but as guides to teach you how to modify your own favorite dishes to meet T-Factor standards.

APPETIZERS AND SNACKS

One of my favorite appetizers when we have company is simply a variety of fresh fruits. However, here are a few recipes for dips, chips, and more that are suitable for snacking and for parties. On occasions when you are going to be a guest at someone's house, you might ask if you can bring anything. Then you can be assured that you'll have at least one low-fat food available.

Garbanzo-Bean Dip

1 large can (20 ounces) of garbanzo beans, drained
3 tablespoons of tahini (sesame-seed paste)
¼ cup of lemon juice

3 cloves of garlic, crushed
1 scallion, minced
Dash salt
Parsley sprigs

1. Combine all ingredients except parsley in a blender or food processor and blend into a thick paste. Pour into serving bowl and chill.
2. Garnish with parsley and serve with whole-wheat crackers or raw fresh vegetables.

MAKES ABOUT 40 TABLESPOONS.
Per 2 tablespoons: 62 calories, 0 cholesterol, 2 g. dietary fiber, **2 g. fat,** 13 mg. sodium

Herb Dip

Serve this with toasted pita bread traingles, whole-wheat crackers, Homemade Tortilla Chips (page 123), or cut up fresh vegetables. Or try it on a baked potato in place of sour cream.

8 ounces of plain, low-fat yogurt	¼ teaspoon of basil
¼ teaspoon of garlic powder	½ teaspoon of chives
⅛ teaspoon of dill weed	½ teaspoon of dried parsley
¼ teaspoon of oregano	½ teaspoon of marjoram
	Dash of salt

Combine all ingredients in a medium-sized mixing bowl. Chill for a couple of hours before serving.

MAKES 1 CUP.

Per ¼ cup: 32 calories, 1 mg. cholesterol, 0 dietary fiber, 0 fat, 123 mg. sodium

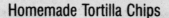

Homemade Tortilla Chips

Keep your eye on these while they are baking, as they brown quickly.

1 or 2 tablespoons of vegetable oil or nonstick vegetable cooking spray	1 package of corn tortillas (10 tortillas)

1. Either spread part of the oil lightly on a foil-covered baking sheet with a pastry brush, or spray with non-stick cooking spray.
2. Stack the tortillas on top of each other and cut into eighths. Spread the tortilla pieces on the baking sheet, and brush or spray lightly with oil.
3. Bake at 350 degrees for about 10 minutes, or until just beginning to turn crispy and brown.

Variations: Sprinkle the chips with garlic powder, Parmesan cheese, paprika, or other seasonings before baking.

MAKES 80 CHIPS.

Per chip: 10 calories, 0 cholesterol, 0 dietary fiber, 0.5 g. fat, 2 mg. sodium

◆

*Mexican-Style Hot Sauce

This is a good salsa-type dip for Homemade Tortilla Chips (page 123), and it adds spice to cottage cheese or any Mexican recipe. It requires no cooking and contains no oil. We like it spicy-hot, but if you prefer a milder sauce, cut back on the Tabasco . . . or the crushed red pepper . . . or the jalapeño!

1 can (28 ounces) of whole tomatoes
1 can (6 ounces) of tomato paste
3 to 4 green onions, finely chopped
½ medium bell pepper, diced
4 jalapeño peppers from a can, finely chopped (use gloves!)

3 tablespoons of juice from jalapeño can
½ ounce (¼ bottle) of Tabasco sauce
1 tablespoon of crushed red pepper
¾ cup of cold water

1. Pour the can of whole tomatoes into a large bowl, along with their juice. Chop the tomatoes into small pieces.
2. Add all the other ingredients, blending well. Store in a glass container in the refrigerator (you must use glass because the acid in the peppers will react with metal or plastic).

MAKES ABOUT 6 CUPS.
Per tablespoon: 4 calories, 0 cholesterol, 0 dietary fiber, **0 fat**, 2 mg. sodium

SEASONINGS

"Salt to taste" can be a dangerous instruction in the hands of some people! Human taste buds adapt to the tastes of salt and sugar, so that the more we use, the less sensitive to the flavor we become.

Although sodium (which comprises 40 percent of table salt, the other 60 percent being chloride) is an essential nutrient, Americans consume about eight to ten times more than our bodies need to stay healthy. Many of us are "salt sensitive" and can develop high blood pressure in response to this overconsumption. Therefore, most health professionals, me included, recommend cutting back on salt. Add less salt in cooking, and eat fewer processed meats, soups, and snack foods. It isn't necessary to cut out table salt completely, however, unless your physician recommends a severely salt-restricted diet. Salt does seem to bring out the flavor in other foods, so many of the recipes in this book do use *small* amounts of it. When a recipe says "salt to taste," go lightly. Let other people add more salt at the table if they wish.

Perhaps the best way to reduce your use of salt is to gradually add less to your food over a period of a couple of weeks, and learn to use herbs and spices. Try some of the seasoning mixtures presented here, and then experiment with your own. Keep a wide variety on hand to inspire your creativity in the kitchen. Mrs. Dash and other commercially prepared sodium-free herb combinations may also appeal to your taste buds. Avoid garlic and onion salts, as they have far more sodium than plain garlic and onion powders.

Herbs and spices are a real boon for people on a low-fat diet who miss the flavor of fat. I always keep a wide variety of seasonings in the cupboard.

By the way, fresh herbs are less potent than equivalent amounts of dried, so triple the amount called for if substituting fresh for dried.

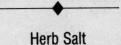

Herb Salt

This is one of my favorite combinations of herbs. Experiment with your own favorites as well. You will soon find that an herb salt is an excellent substitute for plain salt, and instead of about 2000 to 2200 milligrams of sodium per teaspoon, it has only 285 milligrams.

½ teaspoon of basil	¼ teaspoon of celery seed
¼ teaspoon of thyme	¼ teaspoon of salt
¼ teaspoon of dill weed	¼ teaspoon of dried parsley

Combine all ingredients and grind with a mortar and pestle. Store in a small herb jar.

MAKES ABOUT 1¾ TEASPOONS.
Except for the sodium mentioned above, the mixture contains only trace amounts of other nutrients too small to evaluate.

Indian Spice Blend

You can create your own special Indian blend using some of these spices: ginger, coriander, cardamom, cayenne, cinnamon, chilis, mustard seed, turmeric, cumin, black pepper, poppy seeds, fenugreek, fennel, mace, and cloves. Use it any time curry powder is called for. There are many different versions of the blend depending on the type of dish and the preferences of the cook. I like to have the mixture below on hand "in a pinch."

8 teaspoons of cumin
4 teaspoons of ground ginger
2 teaspoons of ground coriander

2 teaspoons of cayenne
4 teaspoons of turmeric
2 teaspoons of black pepper

Combine all ingredients and store in an airtight spice jar.

MAKES ABOUT 7 TABLESPOONS.
This mixture contains trace nutrients too small to evaluate.

SAUCES

Traditional sauces are usually bursting with butter or other fats. Here you will find examples of tasty sauces to accompany your meals that can be made with little or no fat.

◆

*Barbecue Sauce

This sauce will keep for about a week and a half in the refrigerator.

1 12-ounce can of no-salt-added tomato paste
⅓ cup of dry red wine (or substitute water)
1½ cups of water or stock
2 tablespoons of red wine vinegar
2 teaspoons of lemon juice
½ medium onion, chopped fine
½ medium bell pepper, chopped fine
1 tablespoon of Worcestershire sauce
2 tablespoons of brown sugar
1 tablespoon of honey
2 teaspoons of Liquid Smoke
1 teaspoon of garlic powder
1 tablespoon of chili powder
1 tablespoon of dry mustard
Crushed red pepper to taste
Dash of Tabasco
2 tablespoons of fresh parsley, minced
¼ teaspoon of celery seed
½ teaspoon of salt (optional)

1. Combine all ingredients except parsley and celery seed (and salt, if you're using any) in a large kettle or saucepan. Bring to a low boil, then reduce heat and simmer about 20 minutes.
2. Add the parsley, celery seed, and salt (if desired), and simmer for another 5 minutes or so.

MAKES ABOUT 1 QUART.
Per tablespoon: 8 calories, 0 cholesterol, 0 dietary fiber, **0 fat,** 5 mg. sodium

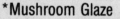

Light Béarnaise

¼ cup of homemade chicken or vegetable stock
¼ cup of flour or 2 tablespoons of cornstarch
2 cups of skim milk
½ cup of nonfat dry milk

1 bay leaf
½ teaspoon of thyme
½ teaspoon of white pepper
1 teaspoon of vegetable seasoning (optional)

1. Heat chicken or vegetable stock over moderate heat in a saucepan.
2. Gradually add flour or cornstarch and blend with a wire whisk or wooden spoon.
3. Simmer and stir until heated through but not browned.
4. Remove from heat and add remaining ingredients.
5. Return to heat and cook, stirring occasionally, until thickened.

MAKES 2½ CUPS.

Per ¼ cup: 42 calories, 1 mg. cholesterol, 0 dietary fiber, 0 fat, 63 mg. sodium (without optional vegetable seasoning; however, a salt-free vegetable seasoning such as Mrs. Dash will add no sodium)

---

*Mushroom Glaze

1 cup of fresh mushrooms (leave whole if small, otherwise slice)
1½ cups of homemade chicken stock

2 tablespoons of cornstarch
1 to 2 tablespoons of cold water

1. Simmer mushrooms in chicken broth for 7 minutes.
2. Add cornstarch to water and mix to a smooth paste. Gradually add the paste to the hot mushroom mixture and cook, stirring occasionally, until thickened.

MAKES 1½ CUPS.

Per 2 tablespoons: 8 calories, 0 cholesterol, 0 dietary fiber, 0 fat, 0 sodium (unless using canned broth, which would be 32 mg. sodium)

◆

"Sour Cream" Topping

Vary this topping endlessly by substituting different herbs and spices for the chives listed below.

¾ cup of low-fat cottage cheese   2 tablespoons of lemon juice
3 tablespoons of skim milk   Chives to taste

Combine all ingredients in a blender or food processor and whir until smooth.

MAKES ABOUT 1 CUP.
Per ¼ cup: 35 calories, 2 mg. cholesterol, 0 dietary fiber, **0.5 g. fat,** 178 mg. sodium

BREADS AND MUFFINS

Except for vitamin B_{12}, bread made from whole wheat contains about the same vitamin and mineral content as beef (beef has more B_{12}). The average slice of whole-grain bread contains about 1 to 2 grams of fat, coming primarily from the grains themselves, not added fats. Plus, the fiber content is much higher than in breads made with refined wheat flour. You will find, however, among the recipes that follow, some that call for a combination of all-purpose and whole-wheat flour, since whole-wheat flour alone tends to have a heavy consistency.

Beware of bran muffins in restaurants and bakeries, which are usually made with tremendous amounts of fat. Try some of the recipes included here for low-fat alternatives. A slice of hot whole-grain bread or a bran muffin makes a great snack, as long as you don't smother it with butter or margarine! You will find your taste buds quickly adapting to unbuttered breads and muffins that are richly flavored with whole grains and dried fruits.

Unless otherwise specified, all bread and muffin recipes call for preheated ovens.

◆

*Applesauce-Bran Muffins

You can vary this recipe by adding ½ cup of raisins or diced apple after Step 4.

1½ cups of 100% bran cereal
1 cup of skim milk
1 egg, slightly beaten
½ cup of unsweetened applesauce
2½ tablespoons of butter or margarine, melted

1 cup of all-purpose flour
2½ teaspoons of baking powder
¼ cup of brown sugar
Nonstick vegetable cooking spray (optional)

1. In a large bowl, combine cereal and milk. Set aside.
2. In another bowl, combine egg, applesauce, and melted butter. Stir into the cereal mixture.
3. Add the dry ingredients, stirring until just blended.
4. Spray a muffin tin with cooking spray or line with baking cups. Fill each cup ¾ full.
5. Bake at 400 degrees for 15 minutes or until nicely browned on top.

MAKES 12 MUFFINS.

Per muffin: 117 calories, 23 mg. cholesterol, 4 g. dietary fiber, 2.5 g. fat, 238 mg. sodium

◆

*Gingersnap Muffins

1¼ cups of whole-wheat flour
1 tablespoon of baking powder
½ teaspoon of salt
2 tablespoons of brown sugar
1 teaspoon of ground ginger
½ teaspoon of cinnamon
¼ teaspoon of ground cloves
½ cup of raisins

½ cup of dates, chopped
1¼ cups of 100% bran cereal
1½ cups of skim milk
¼ cup of molasses
1 large egg
2 tablespoons of peanut oil
Nonstick vegetable cooking spray (optional)

1. Stir together flour, baking powder, salt, brown sugar, spices, raisins, and dates in a large mixing bowl. Set aside.
2. Measure bran cereal into a large measuring cup and combine with milk. Let stand for 2 minutes.
3. In another measuring cup, mix molasses, egg, and peanut oil together until blended. Combine with cereal and milk mixture.
4. Pour the wet ingredients into the large mixing bowl with the dry ingredients and stir only until all is combined and moistened. Spray a muffin tin with cooking spray or line with baking cups. Portion the batter evenly into cups.
5. Bake at 400 degrees for 18 to 20 minutes or until tests done.

MAKES 12 MUFFINS.
Per muffin: 165 calories, 23 mg. cholesterol, 5 g. dietary fiber, 3 g. **fat,** 297 mg. sodium

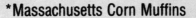

*Massachusetts Corn Muffins

½ cup of honey
2 whole eggs
3 egg whites
1¾ cups of skim milk
¼ cup of vegetable oil
⅓ cup of sugar
2 tablespoons of baking powder

3½ cups of all-purpose flour
1 cup of yellow cornmeal
¼ teaspoon of salt
Nonstick vegetable cooking spray (optional)

1. In a large bowl, whisk together the honey, eggs, egg whites, milk, and oil.
2. Add the dry ingredients and mix with an electric mixer at medium-high speed for 2 minutes.
3. Spray two muffin tins with cooking spray or line with baking cups. Fill each cup ¾ full. Bake at 400 degrees for about 15 minutes, or until tops are golden brown.

MAKES 24 MUFFINS.
Per muffin: 155 calories, 23 mg. cholesterol, 1 g. dietary fiber, 3 g. **fat,** 104 mg. sodium

Mixed Raisin-Bran Muffins

1¼ cups of oat bran
1 cup of whole-wheat pastry flour
¼ cup of brown sugar
½ cup of raisins
2 teaspoons of baking powder
¼ teaspoon of salt

1 cup of low-fat milk
1 egg, beaten
¼ cup of molasses
2 tablespoons of vegetable oil
Nonstick vegetable cooking spray (optional)

1. Combine dry ingredients in large bowl.
2. In separate bowl, mix milk, egg, molasses, and oil.
3. Add liquid ingredients to dry, and mix only until dry are moistened (the mixture should be lumpy).
4. Spray muffin tin with cooking spray or line with baking cups. Fill each cup ¾ full. Bake at 425 degrees for 15 minutes, or until tops are golden brown.

MAKES 12 MUFFINS.
Per muffin: 192 calories, 25 mg. cholesterol, 3 g. dietary fiber, **3 g. fat**, 238 mg. sodium

No-Knead Peasant Bread

1 package (1 tablespoon) of dry yeast
2 cups of lukewarm water
1 tablespoon of salt
1 tablespoon of sugar
3 cups of whole-wheat pastry flour

2 to 3 cups of all-purpose flour
Scant amount of margarine or butter for greasing bowl
Cornmeal
Water

1. Dissolve the yeast in the warm water. Add the salt and sugar and let stand for a minute or two.
2. Add the flours, one cup at a time, beating well after each addition, until dough becomes fairly stiff.
3. Shape dough into a ball and place in a bowl lightly

greased with margarine or butter. Cover with plastic wrap and let rise in a warm place until doubled in bulk, about 1 hour.

4. Turn dough out onto a lightly floured board and shape into two long French-bread-style loaves, or into round loaves.

5. Place loaves on a baking sheet sprinkled heavily with cornmeal. Let rise 5 minutes.

6. Meanwhile, bring about 3 cups of water to a boil in an ovenproof saucepan.

7. Slash tops of loaves with a sharp knife. Brush loaves with cold water. Place them in a cold oven. Put the pan of boiling water in the oven on the rack below the bread. Turn oven to 400 degrees and bake loaves about 45 minutes, until brown and crusty. Cool on a wire rack before slicing.

MAKES 2 LOAVES, 10 SLICES EACH.
Per slice: 120 calories, 0 cholesterol, 2.5 g. dietary fiber, **0.5 g. fat**, 321 mg. sodium

Quick Whole-Wheat Buttermilk Bread

2 cups of whole-wheat flour	1¼ cups of buttermilk
2½ cups of all-purpose flour	¾ cup of water
2 packages of rapid-rising yeast	¼ cup of butter of margarine, melted
½ cup of wheat germ	2 tablespoons of molasses
2 teaspoons of baking powder	Nonstick vegetable cooking spray
2 teaspoons of salt	

1. In a large bowl, mix together 1½ cups of the whole-wheat flour, 1½ cups of the all-purpose flour, the yeast, wheat germ, baking powder, and salt.

2. In a saucepan, heat the buttermilk and water over medium-low heat until warm, not hot. Stir this into the flour mixture.

3. Melt the butter or margarine, and blend into the flour mixture. Blend in the molasses, and stir 100 strokes.

4. Slowly stir in the remaining whole-wheat flour (½ cup) and another ½ cup of all-purpose flour. Add remaining all-purpose flour in ¼-cup increments, mixing well after each addition.
5. Dust your kneading board, hands, and dough with flour. Knead the dough for 8 to 10 minutes. Cover with a damp towel and set aside.
6. Spray 2 loaf pans with nonstick cooking spray, and preheat oven to 425 degrees.
7. Divide the dough into 2 pieces. Pat each piece into a square of about 8 inches, about 1 inch thick. Fold the square in thirds. Seal the seam, and place each loaf, seam down, in a loaf pan.
8. Cover with a damp towel and let rise again until double in size, about 30 minutes.
9. Place the loaves in the center of the oven and bake for 25 minutes, or until the loaves are nicely browned. Let cool on a wire rack.

MAKES 2 LOAVES, 16 SLICES EACH.
Per slice: 86 calories, 4 mg. cholesterol, 1 g. dietary fiber, **2 g. fat,** 182 mg. sodium

Zucchini Muffins

You can create an infinite number of variations on this recipe by substituting grated carrots for the zucchini, for example, or by using chopped fresh or dried fruit instead.

½ cup of whole-wheat flour
½ cup of all-purpose flour
2 teaspoons of baking powder
½ teaspoon of salt
½ cup of sugar
1 egg white

½ cup of skim milk
1 tablespoon of butter or margarine, melted
½ cup of grated zucchini
Nonstick vegetable cooking spray (optional)

1. Stir the dry ingredients together. Beat the egg white just until foamy. Add to the milk, along with the melted butter.
2. Add the liquid ingredients and the zucchini to the dry ingredients, stirring just enough to moisten.

3. Spray muffin tin with cooking spray or line 8 cavities with baking cups. Fill each of the 8 cups ¾ full. Bake at 375 degrees for 15 to 20 minutes.

MAKES 8 MUFFINS.

Per muffin: 124 calories, 0 cholesterol, 1 g. dietary fiber, **1.5 g. fat,** 247 mg. sodium

BREAKFAST FOODS

Many nutritionists feel that breakfast is the most important meal of the day. After all, "breakfast" means to "break your fast": When you wake in the morning you haven't eaten in many hours. If you're trying to lose weight, skipping breakfast can lead to binging later in the day because you may build up a "hidden hunger." As you will discover in Chapter 10, it's the depletion of glycogen that stimulates your appetite. Breakfast can keep that depletion from prompting you to overeat. Here are some recipes that you can use to vary your standard breakfast routine.

These toppings can be used as spreads for toasted bread, bagels, or muffins. They are especially good served on pancakes, for which one recipe follows.

Fruit Topping

1 cup of fresh or unsweetened frozen berries or other fruit	1½ teaspoons cornstarch
¼ cup of unsweetened apple juice	Dash nutmeg, cinnamon, and/or ginger

1. Place the fruit in a saucepan. Stir the apple juice and cornstarch together and pour over the fruit.
2. Heat over medium-low heat, stirring occasionally, until thickened. Add nutmeg or other spices to taste if desired. Serve hot.

MAKES ABOUT 1 CUP.

Per ¼ cup: 31 calories, 0 cholesterol, 1 g. dietary fiber, 0 fat, 3 mg. sodium

Strawberry-Banana Spread

½ pint of strawberries   Dash cinnamon or nutmeg
1 large ripe banana

Mash together the berries and banana. Add the cinnamon and serve immediately, since bananas turn brown when they are left standing.

MAKES ABOUT 1 CUP.
Per ¼ cup: 38 calories, 0 cholesterol, 1.5 g. dietary fiber, **0 fat**, 1 mg. sodium

Tropical Topping

1 cup of sliced fresh or canned apricots, unsweetened, drained
½ cup of canned crushed pineapple, unsweetened, drained

1 teaspoon of unsweetened grated coconut
1½ teaspoons of cornstarch (optional)

1. Place the fruit in a blender or food processor and blend well. Pour the fruit into a saucepan, add the coconut, and heat through over medium-low heat, stirring occasionally.
2. Sprinkle with cornstarch to thicken if desired, or serve as a syrup.

MAKES ABOUT 1½ CUPS.
Per ¼ cup: 28 calories, 0 cholesterol, 1 g. dietary fiber, **0 fat**, 0 sodium

◆

*Oatmeal Pancakes

1¼ cup of oats
  2 cups of skim milk
  1 egg
¼ cup of whole-wheat flour
¼ cup of toasted wheat germ

¼ cup of all-purpose flour
1 tablespoon of baking powder
2 teaspoons of sugar
2 teaspoons of vegetable oil
½ teaspoon of salt

1. Combine the oats and milk and let stand for 10 minutes.
2. Stir in the remaining ingredients.
3. Heat a nonstick pan over medium-low heat. Pour ¼ cup of batter per pancake into the hot pan. Cook, turning once, until golden brown on both sides. Serve with syrup or one of the breakfast spreads immediately preceding.

MAKES 12 PANCAKES.
Per 2 pancakes: 179 calories, 47 mg. cholesterol, 2 g. dietary fiber, 4 g. fat, 232 mg. sodium

LUNCHES

As a change of pace from the basic lunches in the menu plans and as an alternative to high-fat, processed meats and cheeses, here are some sandwich spread ideas (you could also incorporate recipes from the Soups and Salads sections). And don't forget that cottage cheese is much more interesting for lunch when served with fresh fruit, salsa (Mexican-Style Hot Sauce, page 124), or jelly, or seasoned with Old Bay seasoning, Mrs. Dash, celery seed, garlic, or onion powder or a variety of other herbs and spices.

Crabmeat Spread

1 cup of crabmeat
½ cup of celery, diced
1 small onion, diced
Herb Salt to taste (pages 125–126)

½ green pepper, diced
1 cup of sprouts
1 cup of low-fat cottage cheese

Blend all the above ingredients with enough no-fat salad dressing to moisten.

MAKES ABOUT 3 CUPS.

Per ¼ cup: 32 calories, 13 mg. cholesterol, 0.5 g. dietary fiber, 0.5 g. **fat,** 215 mg. sodium

---

Meat Spread

½ pound of cooked meat or fowl
1 small onion, diced
¼ cup of wheat germ (or cooked red beans)
2 tablespoons of soy flour

Herb Salt (pages 125–126) or other herb blend to taste
Fresh-ground black pepper to taste

Blend all ingredients in a food processor. Moisten as needed with ketchup, mustard, or no-fat salad dressing.

MAKES ABOUT 1¼ CUPS.

Per ¼ cup: 99 calories, 38 mg. cholesterol, 0.5 g. dietary fiber, 2 g. **fat,** 85 mg. sodium

◆

Mexican Bean Spread

This can also be used as a Mexican bean dip appetizer. It's great spread on a slice of whole-grain bread and broiled in the oven with slices of tomato and some oregano.

1 can of dark-red kidney beans   ⅛ teaspoon of cayenne pepper
1 small onion   Herb Salt (pages 125–126)
3 tablespoons of ketchup   Fresh-ground black pepper

Blend the above ingredients in a food processor, adding more ketchup if needed for desired consistency.

MAKES ABOUT 1½ CUPS.
Per ¼ cup: 78 calories, 0 cholesterol, 6 g. dietary fiber, 0.5 g. fat, 456 mg. sodium

SOUPS

Some studies have shown that people who often include soup with their meals find it easier to lose weight and maintain their losses. Clear soups are generally lower in fat than cream soups, but you can make low-fat "cream" soups by substituting skim milk for the cream or whole milk, with perhaps some nonfat dry milk, flour, or cornstarch added to make the soup richer and thicker.

I include some recipes for stock, as I like to use my own in recipes calling for bouillon or broth. You can also save any water used for steaming vegetables to use as vegetable stock in other recipes. I use commercial brands in a pinch, but they tend to be much higher in sodium and preservatives. So, in my family, we make a potful of stock and freeze part of it for later use. Try adapting your own favorite soup recipes by cutting fat and experimenting with seasonings.

Basic Vegetable Stock

Here's a basic recipe for a stock made from water and a variety of fresh vegetables. You can add other vegetables, such as parsnips, turnips, leeks, etc., if desired.

3 medium carrots, cut in chunks
2 stalks of celery, cut in chunks
3 medium onions, cut in chunks
3 cloves of garlic, minced

⅓ cup of fresh parsley, minced
1 bay leaf
6 whole peppercorns
½ teaspoon of tarragon and/or other dried herb
6 cups of water

1. Combine all ingredients in a large soup pot, and bring to a boil. Reduce heat to simmer, cover, and let cook for about 1 hour.
2. You may strain the vegetables out and use the clear broth, or put the stock in a blender and puree for a thicker stock, adding a bit more water if necessary.

MAKES ABOUT 8 CUPS.
Per cup: 24 calories, 0 cholesterol, 2 g. dietary fiber, 0 fat, 23 mg. sodium

Soup Base

This basic stock can be used for making all kinds of soups, rice and other grains, and boiled potatoes. It is excellent for soaking and cooking beans.

Save all chicken and turkey giblets (necks, hearts, gizzards, but *not* livers) until you have accumulated the parts of four to six birds. Freeze these parts immediately, first trimming skin and any fat from the necks, and hold in your freezer until you have enough of the makings.

You can also freeze the final product in 2- to 4-cup plastic containers for later use as needed.

You may substitute a beef soup bone or two for the giblets, but I prefer the lighter flavor and lower cholesterol of chicken stock.

Giblets of 4 to 6 birds
8 to 10 cups of water
1 large bay leaf
Salt and pepper to taste
1 teaspoon each: rosemary, sage, thyme, tarragon
1 large onion, coarsely chopped

2 large stalks of celery, cut into 2-inch pieces (include leaves)
2 large carrots, cut into 2-inch pieces

1. Place the giblets in a deep soup kettle, with enough water to cover (about 8 to 10 cups). Bring to a boil and skim as necessary. When finally clear of scum, add the remaining ingredients. You may also throw in any other greens or wilted vegetables you have on hand in your refrigerator (except for asparagus, cabbage, broccoli, or cauliflower, which taste too strong).
2. Bring to a boil once again, then reduce heat and simmer for at least 2 hours.
3. Separate the giblets and vegetables from the water. Blend the vegetables in a blender or food processor until smooth, and return to the stock. Save the cooked giblets for low-calorie snacks.

MAKES ABOUT 10 TO 12 CUPS, DEPENDING ON HOW MANY GIBLETS AND HOW MANY VEGETABLES YOU ADD.
Per cup (10-cup recipe): 31 calories, 20 mg. cholesterol, 1 g. dietary fiber, **0.5 g. fat,** 82 mg. sodium

*Broccoli Soup

This wholesome, nutrient-rich soup warms any evening. Use as a main course topped with 2 tablespoons of grated cheese and croutons. As a side dish, skip the cheese. You can also make Cauliflower Soup by substituting 2 pounds of cauliflower for the broccoli. Add a tablespoon of lemon juice for tanginess.

2 cups of water
1½ pounds of broccoli, stalks separated
¾ cup of chopped celery
½ cup of chopped onion
1 tablespoon of olive oil
2½ cups of water

2 tablespoons of flour
1 tablespoon of instant chicken bouillon
¾ teaspoon of salt
⅛ teaspoon of pepper
⅛ teaspoon of nutmeg
½ cup of evaporated skim milk

1. Heat the 2 cups of water in a large pot till boiling.
2. Add vegetables, cover, and cook till tender (about 10 minutes).
3. Blend vegetables with part of the cooking water in a blender or food processor.
4. Heat olive oil in a small nonstick skillet. Add 2 tablespoons of the 2½ cups of water and sprinkle in the flour. Cook and stir until smooth.
5. Add the remaining water and heat to boiling, stirring constantly. Boil and stir 1 minute.
6. Stir in broccoli mixture, instant bouillon, salt, pepper, and nutmeg. Heat just until boiling.
7. Stir in the evaporated skim milk and heat through without boiling again.

MAKES ABOUT 9 CUPS.
Per 1½ cups: 86 calories, 1 mg. cholesterol, 5 g. dietary fiber, 3 g. fat, 371 mg. sodium

*Corn Chowder

½ cup of chopped green onion
¼ teaspoon of oil
2½ cups of chicken stock
2 cups of 1% milk
3 cups of potato cubes (1¼ pounds)
2 packages (10 ounces each)

of frozen corn kernels
¼ cup of instant nonfat dry milk
¼ teaspoon of dry mustard
⅛ teaspoon of salt
Pinch or ⅛ teaspoon of fresh-ground black pepper

1. Sauté green onion in oil in a large nonstick saucepan. Add chicken stock, milk, and potatoes. Bring to a boil,

lower heat, and simmer until potatoes are tender, about 12 minutes. Add corn and cook 1 minute more.
2. Remove 2 cups of the chowder to a food processor. Puree and return to saucepan.
3. Stir in dry milk, mustard, salt, and pepper. Serve immediately.

MAKES 8 CUPS.
Per cup: 165 calories, 3 mg. cholesterol, 4 g. dietary fiber, 2 g. **fat,** 397 mg. sodium

Gazpacho

Serve this soup chilled in bowls with one of the following assortment of garnishes: chopped hard-boiled egg, finely chopped green onions, chives, or croutons.

1 large tomato
½ small onion
½ cucumber
½ green pepper
1 celery stalk
2 teaspoons of fresh parsley, finely chopped
2 cloves of garlic, minced or crushed
2 cups of tomato juice
3 tablespoons of red wine vinegar
½ cup of white wine
2 tablespoons of basil
1 tablespoon of lemon juice
1 teaspoon of salt
½ teaspoon of white pepper
1 teaspoon of Worcestershire sauce
Dash of Tabasco sauce

Finely chop all vegetables. (A food processor is ideal for this.) Combine with all remaining ingredients and refrigerate 24 hours.

MAKES ABOUT 4½ CUPS.
Per ¾ cup: 42 calories, 0 cholesterol, 2 g. dietary fiber, **0 fat,** 658 mg. sodium (analyses are without garnishes)

*Minestrone

1 medium onion, chopped
1 stalk of celery, chopped
2 medium carrots, chopped
1 cup of fresh or frozen green beans
1 medium zucchini, chopped
1 package (10 ounces) of frozen chopped spinach
1 can (28 ounces) of tomatoes
½ cup of uncooked macaroni (try whole wheat)
1 can (15 ounces) of navy beans with juice
¼ teaspoon of basil
¼ teaspoon of oregano
¼ teaspoon of cayenne pepper
Water as needed

Combine all ingredients in a large pot. Bring to a boil, then reduce heat and let simmer for about 30 minutes, until all vegetables are tender. Add water if necessary to make enough liquid to cover ingredients.

MAKES ABOUT 12 CUPS.

Per 1½ cups: 137 calories, 0 cholesterol, 7.5 g. dietary fiber, **1 g. fat,** 207 mg. sodium

Potato-Vegetable Soup

This is a fast soup—that is, it takes 10 minutes to get everything into the pot. It is a prototype for any quick soup. Just start with stock and add any vegetables, potatoes, rice, lentils, or other grains or legumes, and cook for 1 hour.

2 cups of stock
1 medium potato, cut in eighths
½ cup of onions, sliced
1 cup of carrots, sliced
½ cup of celery, sliced
½ teaspoon of fresh-ground black pepper
1 tablespoon of dried parsley

Place all ingredients in a 4-quart saucepan. Bring to a boil, reduce heat, and cook over low heat for 1 hour.

MAKES 4 CUPS.
Per cup: 91 calories, 0 cholesterol, 3 g. dietary fiber, **0.5 g. fat,** 387 mg. sodium

*Split-Pea Soup

A warming crowd-pleaser. Halve the recipe for a smaller crowd! If you like a smooth-textured soup, you may whir it in a blender or pass it through a sieve.

4 cups of dried split peas	1 teaspoon of salt
18 cups of meat stock or vegetable stock	½ teaspoon of thyme
1 cup of carrots, sliced thin	2 cloves of garlic, minced
1 cup of onions, chopped	⅛ teaspoon of cayenne
2 cups of celery, chopped	2 tablespoons of flour (optional)
½ teaspoon of black pepper	

1. Cook peas in stock for 2½ hours.
2. Add remaining ingredients and cook for 1 additional hour. You may thicken the soup by sprinkling in the flour and blending well.

MAKES ABOUT 16 CUPS.
Per cup: 178 calories, 0 cholesterol, 8 g. dietary fiber, **0.5 g. fat,** 393 mg. sodium

SALADS

Nutritionists recommend that about half the vegetables we eat each day should be raw. Uncooked vegetables are higher in fiber and nutrients than their cooked counterparts. In addition to fresh fruit, raw vegetables in a salad or alone make a great, crunchy, no-fat snack.

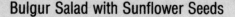

Bulgur Salad with Sunflower Seeds

Bulgur is a cracked wheat used most often in Middle Eastern cuisine. Rather than cooking it, soak it in water as directed below, and you will have a tender, fluffy grain. You can actually use any of your favorite fresh vegetables with any cooked grain to make an interesting meal-in-one luncheon salad such as this one. You can even toss in some leftover cooked greens or other cooked vegetables you might have on hand.

1 cup of bulgur wheat	**DRESSING**
2 cups of water	1 teaspoon of oregano
2 large tomatoes, diced	1 teaspoon of soy sauce
1 medium cucumber, diced	½ teaspoon of salt
1 medium yellow squash, diced	1 teaspoon of black pepper
2 green onions, chopped fine	1 tablespoon of olive oil
1 tablespoon of dried parsley	2 tablespoons of lemon juice
(or 3 tablespoons of fresh)	1 tablespoon of water
¼ cup of dry-roasted unsalted sunflower seeds	

1. Soak the bulgur wheat in a bowl in the water for 3 to 4 hours. The wheat will soak up the water and become puffy and chewable. Drain any excess water if necessary.
2. In the meantime, combine all dressing ingredients.
3. When the wheat is ready, add the chopped vegetables, parsley, and sunflower seeds, mixing well, then add the dressing. Toss and serve.

MAKES ABOUT 8 CUPS.

Per 2 cups: 263 calories, 0 cholesterol, 8 g. dietary fiber, 8.5 g. fat, 363 mg. sodium

Pink Potato Salad

4 large potatoes, skins on,
   diced
1 small can (6 ounces) of diced
   beets, drained
½ bell pepper, diced

½ cup of plain, nonfat yogurt
3 tablespoons of mayonnaise
2 hard-boiled eggs, diced
Salt, pepper, garlic, and onion
   powder to taste

1. Boil the potatoes in a small amount of water until tender. Drain.
2. Combine with remaining ingredients in a large bowl. Chill before serving.

MAKES ABOUT 8 CUPS.
Per cup: 155 calories, 72 mg. cholesterol, 2 g. dietary fiber, **5.5 g. fat,** 161 mg. sodium

Spinach Salad Parmesan

5 cups of fresh spinach leaves,
   washed well and trimmed
½ Bermuda onion, thinly sliced
1 pint of cherry tomatoes
4 ounces of fresh mushrooms,
   sliced

½ cup of radishes, thinly sliced
1 tablespoon of grated
   Parmesan cheese

Toss together all ingredients. Serve with your favorite no- or low-fat dressing.

MAKES ABOUT 6 CUPS.
Per cup: 36 calories, 1 mg. cholesterol, 4 g. dietary fiber, **1 g. fat,** 60 mg. sodium (analyses are for no-fat dressing)

◆

Sweet 'n' Savory Chicken Salad

½ cup of plain, nonfat yogurt
1 tablespoon of lemon juice
¾ teaspoon of dried tarragon, crushed
2 cups of cooked chicken, cut in chunks
1 can (20 ounces) of pineapple chunks, unsweetened, drained

1 can (10½ ounces) of mandarin oranges, unsweetened, drained
1 can (4 ounces) of water chestnuts, sliced, drained
1 small cucumber, diced
1 scallion, finely chopped
Lettuce leaves

1. Mix together the yogurt, lemon juice, and tarragon to make a dressing.
2. In a large bowl, combine the remaining ingredients except the lettuce leaves. Pour the dressing over the chicken salad and toss lightly. Serve on lettuce leaves of your choice.

MAKES 6 CUPS.
Per cup: 195 calories, 40 mg. cholesterol, 2.5 g. dietary fiber, 2 g. fat, 57 mg. sodium.

SALAD DRESSINGS

Many people go to the salad bar in a restaurant, load up on vegetables and fruits, and congratulate themselves on their low-fat food choice. At the same time, though, they often load up on several tablespoonfuls of high-fat salad dressings, adding several hundred calories and many grams of fat to an otherwise healthful meal.

Included here are three no-fat and two low-fat dressings. Creamy dressings usually have a base of plain, nonfat yogurt, while the oil-and-vinegar varieties are "stretched" with the addition of water.

Olive oil is a wonderful base for dressings, especially because it is a mono-unsaturated fat. Studies have shown that such fats (olive, peanut, avocado) in reasonable amounts may have the effect of reducing cholesterol.

Balsamic Dressing

If you don't have balsamic vinegar, you may substitute another kind. But, if this be the case, start with water and vinegar in equal proportions.

¾ cup of water
¼ cup of balsamic vinegar
3 teaspoons of capers
2 teaspoons of Dijon mustard

1½ teaspoons of dried basil
1 tablespoon of fresh parsley, chopped (optional)

Combine the ingredients. Adjust vinegar to taste, since it has a strong flavor. Store in a covered container in the refrigerator.

MAKES ABOUT 1 CUP.
Per tablespoon: 1 calorie, 0 cholesterol, 0 dietary fiber, **0 fat**, 7 mg. sodium

Creamy Dijon Dressing

½ cup of plain, nonfat yogurt
1½ teaspoons of Dijon mustard
2 tablespoons of grated cucumber
½ small scallion, minced

2 teaspoons of fresh parley or cilantro, chopped
Dash of fresh-ground black pepper

Combine all ingredients, mixing well. Serve chilled over your favorite salad greens and vegetables.

MAKES ABOUT ½ CUP.
Per 2 tablespoons: 19 calories, 1 mg. cholesterol, 0 dietary fiber, **0 fat**, 47 mg. sodium

No-Fat Italian Dressing

¼ cup of lemon juice
¼ cup of cider vinegar
¼ cup of unsweetened apple
  juice
½ teaspoon of oregano
½ teaspoon of dry mustard

½ teaspoon of onion powder
1 clove of garlic, cut in half
½ teaspoon of paprika
¼ teaspoon of basil
⅛ teaspoon of thyme
⅛ teaspoon of rosemary

Combine all ingredients. Chill for an hour or two at least to allow herbs to blend. Remove garlic clove pieces before serving.

MAKES 12 TABLESPOONS.
Per 2 tablespoons: 9 calories, 0 cholesterol, 0 dietary fiber, **0 fat,** 1 mg. sodium

Sweet Yogurt Dressing

Fresh chopped fruit becomes a special salad or a light dessert with this dressing.

1 cup of plain, nonfat yogurt
¼ cup of raisins (golden raisins
  are nice)

¼ cup of chopped nuts
  (walnuts, pecans, or other)
1½ tablespoons of honey

Mix all ingredients, and chill overnight. Serve cold.

MAKES ABOUT 1½ CUPS.
Per 2 tablespoons: 45 calories, 0 cholesterol, 0.5 g. dietary fiber, **1.5 g. fat,** 15 mg. sodium

◆

Tarragon-Dijon Dressing

1 tablespoon of olive oil
5 tablespoons of red wine
vinegar
2 tablespoons of lemon juice
6 tablespoons of water
1 teaspoon of Dijon mustard
1¼ teaspoons of tarragon,
crushed

1 garlic clove, crushed
2 tablespoons of shallots or
scallions, finely minced
1 tablespoon of honey
¼ teaspoon of paprika
Fresh-ground black pepper and
salt to taste

Combine all ingredients well. Store in refrigerator.

MAKES ABOUT 1 CUP.
Per 2 tablespoons: 27 calories, 0 cholesterol, 0 dietary fiber, **2 g. fat,** 9
mg. sodium

MEATLESS MAIN COURSES

I usually have at least one meat-free day a week, when my
breakfasts and lunches center around dairy foods, vegetables, and fruits, and my main course at dinner consists of
protein-rich beans and rice or other meatless dishes. Most
Americans eat twice as much protein as they need each
day, with the majority of it coming from meat, which is
higher in fat, cholesterol, chemical additives, and cost than
protein foods from the plant world.

Combinations of legumes, grains, and seeds provide
the same quality of protein as animal protein. Enhance
them with dairy products or small amounts of meat if
desired.

If you're used to eating a good hunk of meat for dinner
each night, try some of these meatless meals for a change,
and discover how satisfying they can be.

Cooking Whole Grains

To cook whole grains such as brown rice, you need about
twice as much liquid (water or stock) as grain—in other
words, about 2 cups of liquid to 1 cup of grain. Simply

bring the liquid to a boil, add the rinsed grain, bring to a boil again, cover, reduce heat, and let simmer for about 40 minutes. Stirring is unnecessary. Especially when cooked in stock, no added fat is needed to make whole grains taste good. You can always add herbs and spices or minced vegetables such as scallions or carrots if you want more flavor.

Toasting Seeds and Nuts

To toast seeds or nuts without added fat, my favorite method is to put them in a dry frying pan over medium heat and brown them, stirring frequently.

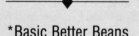

*Basic Better Beans

The use of stock instead of water for soaking and cooking, along with a whole onion stuck with whole cloves, makes beans even more flavorful. Serve with cooked grain for a main course.

2 cups of dried beans, or lentils (your choice)
4 cups of chicken stock
2 large onions

6 whole cloves
2 tablespoons of olive oil
Dash of salt and pepper

1. Soak the beans in the stock, together with the onions that have been stuck with the cloves, overnight in the refrigerator.
2. Remove the onions and cloves (discard cloves), and cook the plumped beans in the stock until just tender.
3. Chop the onions and sauté in the oil until translucent.
4. Place all ingredients (except cloves) in a large casserole dish and bake for 1 hour at 325 degrees.

MAKES 8 SERVINGS.
Per serving: 181 calories, 0 cholesterol, 6 g. dietary fiber, **5 g. fat**, 438 mg. sodium

◆

*Bean-and-Corn Chili over Puffed Tortilla

Check package ingredients for tortillas made with no lard.

4 soft flour tortillas (7 inches in diameter)
1 cup of chopped onion
2 cloves of garlic, finely chopped
½ teaspoon of vegetable oil
1 can (14 ounces) of Italian-style plum tomatoes, drained
¾ teaspoon of ground cumin
⅛ teaspoon of fresh-ground black pepper
⅛ teaspoon of red pepper flakes

1 can (15¼ ounces) of kidney beans (reserve ¼ cup of liquid)
1 can (4 ounces) of chopped mild green chilies, drained, or ½ teaspoon of fresh jalapeño pepper
1 cup of frozen whole-kernel corn, thawed
3 ounces of shredded low-fat Monterey Jack cheese

1. Arrange tortillas on foil-lined baking sheet. Watching carefully, bake tortillas at 450 degrees for 4 to 5 minutes until puffed and lightly golden. Reserve.
2. Sauté onion and garlic in oil in a 12-inch nonstick skillet over medium heat for 3 to 4 minutes.
3. Add tomatoes, cumin, black pepper, red pepper, kidney beans and reserved liquid, and ½ of the green chilies. Simmer for 5 minutes, stirring often. Add corn and cook 1 minute longer.
4. Place a tortilla on each plate. Mound about ¾ cup of chili over each. Sprinkle each with ¼ of the cheese. Serve accompanied by the remaining green chilies.

MAKES 4 SERVINGS.

Per serving: 305 calories, 15 mg. cholesterol, 11 g. dietary fiber, 8 g. **fat,** 979 mg. sodium (if low-fat Monterey Jack cheese is not available and you use regular Monterey Jack, add 18 calories, 2 g. fat, and 5 mg. cholesterol per serving)

◆

*Eggplant Parmesan

Eggplant is known for its ability to absorb huge quantities of oil. This "no-fry" version of a delectable Italian dish eliminates almost all of the oil and therefore, compared with a popular recipe, 75 grams of fat and 675 calories *per serving*. Protein in this recipe comes from the egg, milk, and cheese, along with the wheat germ and bread crumbs.

1 medium eggplant	Nonstick vegetable cooking spray
1 egg, or 2 egg whites	2 cups of Real Italian Tomato
2 tablespoons of skim milk	Sauce (pages 160–161)
¼ cup of wheat germ	¾ cup of part-skim mozzarella
½ cup of bread crumbs	
1 tablepoon of grated Parmesan cheese	

1. Peel the eggplant and cut it into 8 slices, ½ inch thick.
2. Beat together the egg (or egg whites) and milk in a small, shallow bowl.
3. In another bowl, combine the wheat germ, bread crumbs, and Parmesan cheese.
4. Spray a foil-lined baking sheet with cooking spray. Dip the eggplant slices into the egg mixture, coating well. Then dip them into the bread-crumb mixture. Place the slices on the baking sheet, and bake at 350 degrees for 15 minutes. Turn the slices over, and bake for 10 more minutes.
5. Make a layer of eggplant in a casserole dish, top with tomato sauce, then mozzarella cheese. Repeat the layers.
6. Bake covered at 350 degrees for 25 minutes, then uncover and bake 15 minutes more.

MAKES 4 SERVINGS.

Per serving: 256 calories, 81 mg. cholesterol, 9 g. dietary fiber, 8 g. **fat,** 438 mg. sodium

◆

*Indian Spiced Beans

Delicious served with 1 tablespoon of grated cheese per serving, chopped vegetables of choice, and salsa. Add a helping of cooked grain such as rice for a complete meal.

2 cups of dried red or kidney beans	2 dried red peppers
4 cups of stock	1 bay leaf
1 medium onion, sliced	¼ teaspoon of fresh-ground black pepper
1 medium tomato, chopped	¼ teaspoon of ground cloves
1 clove of garlic, chopped	

Wash beans and remove any stones. Place all ingredients in a 4-quart saucepan. Bring to a boil and reduce heat. Cover and cook for 4 hours on low heat.

MAKES 4½ CUPS.
Per ¾ cup: 210 calories, 0 cholesterol, 14 g. dietary fiber, **1 g. fat,** 230 mg. sodium

◆

*Picadillo and Cornbread Wedges

CORNBREAD WEDGES:

Nonstick vegetable cooking spray
⅔ cup of yellow cornmeal
6 tablespoons of unsifted all-purpose flour
1½ teaspoons of baking powder

2 egg whites
⅔ cup of buttermilk
2 tablespoons of vegetable oil

PICADILLO:

1 large sweet green pepper, halved, cored, seeded, and cut into ½-inch pieces (1 cup)
1 large sweet red pepper, halved, cored, seeded, and cut into ½-inch pieces (1 cup)
1 medium onion, chopped (½ cup)
1 clove of garlic, finely chopped

½ teaspoon of reduced-calorie margarine
2 cans (15¼ ounces each) of red kidney beans, undrained
¾ to 1 teaspoon of ground cumin
¼ teaspoon of ground red pepper
½ cup of no-salt tomato sauce
¼ cup of raisins

1. *Prepare cornbread:* Spray an 8 × 1½-inch nonstick round cake pan with cooking spray.
2. Stir together cornmeal, flour, and baking powder in a medium bowl until well mixed.
3. Lightly beat egg whites in a small bowl. Stir in the buttermilk and oil until well combined.
4. Pour the liquid ingredients all at once into the dry ingredients. Stir the mixture briskly with a fork until all the ingredients are just evenly moistened; do not overstir. The batter will be lumpy. Turn into prepared pan.
5. Bake at 400 degrees for 18 to 20 minutes or until wooden pick inserted into center comes out clean. Turn out onto wire rack to cool slightly. Cut cornbread into 4 wedges; put on plates.
6. *Prepare picadillo:* Sauté peppers, onion, and garlic in

margarine in a 12-inch nonstick skillet for 5 to 8 minutes. Stir in kidney beans, cumin, red pepper, tomato sauce, and raisins. Cook to thicken slightly, about 10 to 12 minutes over medium-high heat. Mixture should be saucy.

7. Pour sauce over cornbread, dividing equally. Serve immediately.

MAKES 4 SERVINGS.

Per serving: 451 calories, 2 mg. cholesterol, 17 g. dietary fiber, **9 g. fat,** 994 mg. sodium

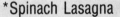

*Spinach Lasagna

1 medium onion, chopped
2 garlic cloves, minced
1 tablespoon of olive oil
2 to 3 tablespoons of water
1 pound of part-skim ricotta cheese
1 pound of tofu, drained and crumbled (optional)
¼ cup of grated Parmesan cheese
1½ pounds of fresh spinach, chopped and packed (about 2 cups), or 1 package of

frozen chopped spinach, thawed and drained
2 egg whites, beaten
¼ teaspoon of fresh-ground black pepper
2 to 3 tablespoons of chopped fresh parsley
½ pound of lasagna noodles, preferably whole wheat
Nonstick vegetable cooking spray
6 ounces of part-skim mozzarella cheese, grated
6 cups of tomato sauce

1. Sauté the onion and garlic in the olive oil, adding water as needed to keep from sticking.
2. Combine the ricotta, tofu (if used), Parmesan, spinach, egg whites, black pepper, parsley, and sautéed onion and garlic, mixing well.
3. Cook the lasagna according to package directions.
4. Spray a 13×9×2-inch casserole with cooking spray. Arrange a layer of cooked noodles on the bottom, top with ⅓ of the ricotta mixture, sprinkle with mozzarella, and spread with tomato sauce. Repeat layers twice more, ending with sauce.

5. Cover pan with aluminum foil, crimping edges tightly. Bake at 350 degrees for 40 minutes, remove foil and bake 10–15 minutes more.

MAKES 12 SERVINGS.
Per serving (minus tofu): 215 calories, 21 mg. cholesterol, 3.5 g. dietary fiber, **8 g. fat,** 918 mg. sodium

Vegetable Stroganoff

This is good served over cooked pasta or grains such as bulgur wheat or rice.

3 cups of mushrooms, sliced
2 medium onions, sliced
1 clove of garlic, crushed
1 teaspoon of vegetable oil
Water as needed
¼ cup of whole-wheat flour
¾ cup of vegetable stock
¼ cup of dry sherry
4 teaspoons of Worcestershire sauce
¼ teaspoon of marjoram

⅛ teaspoon of chili powder
⅛ teaspoon of thyme
Dash nutmeg
Fresh-ground black pepper to taste
3 cups of cooked pinto beans or 2 cans (15 ounces each) of pinto beans, drained
1½ cups of plain, low-fat yogurt
1 teaspoon of lemon juice

1. In a large covered skillet, sauté/steam mushrooms, onions, and garlic in the oil and a little bit of water as needed.
2. In a bowl or measuring cup, mix together the flour, stock, sherry, Worcestershire sauce, and seasonings.
3. When mushrooms are tender, stir in the stock mixture and cook until thickened, stirring occasionally.
4. Stir in the beans and heat through.
5. Remove from heat. Stir in the yogurt and lemon juice and serve.

MAKES 6 SERVINGS.
Per serving: 225 calories, 1 mg. cholesterol, 11.5 g. dietary fiber, **2 g. fat,** 116 mg. sodium

PASTA

High in carbohydrates and low in fat, pasta is one of my favorite T-Factor foods. Cook it *al dente*, not mushy, and enjoy it with some of the wonderful sauces presented here. Sample pastas made from wheat, soy, rice, corn, buckwheat, and other grains.

An average serving of 1 cup of cooked pasta contains about 2 grams of fat.

If you're watching your cholesterol intake, you can use cholesterol-free pasta made from enriched semolina rather than egg noodles, which contains about 50 milligrams of cholesterol per cup.

◆

Red Clam Sauce

2 cups of onions, chopped
12 ounces of mushrooms, sliced
6 cloves of garlic, crushed
2 tablespoons of olive oil
½ teaspoon of salt
¼ teaspoon of black pepper
⅛ teaspoon of cayenne
1 can (10½ ounces) of tomato puree
4 cans (6.5 ounces each) of clams, minced, with liquid

1. In a 4-quart saucepan, sauté onions, mushrooms, and garlic in the oil over medium-low heat for about 5 minutes, or until onions are translucent.
2. Add remaining ingredients and cook, covered, for 45 minutes.

MAKES ABOUT 8 CUPS.

Per cup: 124 calories, 63 mg. cholesterol, 2 g. dietary fiber, **4.5 g. fat,** 185 mg. sodium

*Meat Sauce

2 tablespoons of olive oil
1 cup of sliced onion
8 ounces of mushrooms, sliced
3 cloves of garlic, crushed
1 pound of lean ground beef
1 tablespoon of dried basil
1 can (6 ounces) of tomato
   paste

1 can (28 ounces) of whole
   tomatoes
½ teaspoon of black pepper
½ teaspoon of salt
¼ teaspoon of cayenne or
   crushed red pepper

1. In a 4-quart saucepan, heat the oil and sauté the onion, mushrooms, and garlic over medium-low heat for about 5 minutes or until onions are translucent.
2. Add ground beef and continue to cook for about 5 minutes or until beef is browned. Drain visible fat.
3. Add remaining ingredients and blend well together, breaking up the whole tomatoes with the spoon as you stir.
4. Cover the pan, reduce heat, and cook on low for 1 hour.

MAKES ABOUT 8 CUPS.
Per cup: 198 calories, 37 mg. cholesterol, 2.5 g. dietary fiber, 12 g. fat, 343 mg. sodium

Real Italian Tomato Sauce

Here is our favorite basic marinara sauce. This sauce can be used for any recipe calling for tomato sauce, from pasta to eggplant to fish. You can store this in a tightly sealed container in the refrigerator for up to a week, or freeze it in freezer containers for later use.

Look for the no-salt-added variety of canned tomato products if you're trying to cut down on salt.

1 tablespoon of olive oil
1 medium onion, cut in chunks
8 ounces of fresh mushrooms, sliced or quartered
1 to 3 tablespoons of dried basil (three times more if you use fresh!)
2 large cloves of garlic, crushed or minced

1 large bay leaf
1 can (28 ounces) of tomatoes
1 can (10¾ ounces) of tomato puree
1 can (6 ounces) of tomato paste
Salt and fresh-ground black pepper to taste

1. Heat a large kettle over medium heat. Put in the oil, onion, mushrooms, basil, and garlic. Cover, and reduce the heat to medium low. Stir frequently—you may need to add a tablespoon or two of water to keep it from sticking.
2. When the onions are translucent, add the remaining ingredients, except the salt and pepper. Bring to a boil on high heat, then reduce to simmer and let cook for an hour or so, stirring occasionally and breaking up the whole tomatoes.
3. Add salt and pepper to taste.

MAKES ABOUT 6 CUPS.
Per cup: 110 calories, 0 cholesterol, 4 g. dietary fiber, **3 g. fat,** 326 mg. sodium

Hot Pasta Salad California

This makes a delightful main course for a light supper or special luncheon. It's also good served in smaller portions as a side dish.

2 teaspoons of butter
2 medium-sized yellow summer squash
2 teaspoons of water
1 can (14 ounces) of artichoke hearts, drained and rinsed

6 sprigs of fresh cilantro chopped
Dash of salt
4 cups of cooked vermicelli
4 tablespoons of Parmesan cheese (optional)

1. Melt butter over low heat in a large saucepan. Slice the squash into ⅛- to ¼-inch rounds. Add the squash and water to the butter. Cover and cook for 5 minutes, stirring occasionally.
2. Cut the artichoke hearts into quarters and stir into the squash along with the cilantro and salt. Cover and heat through. Serve hot over hot cooked pasta. Sprinkle with Parmesan if desired.

MAKES 4 SERVINGS AS A MAIN COURSE.
Per serving (including 1 tablespoon of Parmesan and 1 cup of pasta): 257 calories, 9 mg. cholesterol, 6 g. dietary fiber, **4.5 g. fat**, 311 mg. sodium

*Pasta and Shrimp with Ricotta Cheese Sauce

2 large cloves of garlic, finely chopped
¼ teaspoon of crushed red pepper flakes
1 teaspoon of reduced-calorie margarine
½ cup of skim milk
¾ cup of part-skim ricotta
8 ounces of small shrimp, shelled, deveined, and sliced lengthwise
1 package (10 ounces) of frozen

peas, thawed completely
2 tablespoons of chopped parsley
½ teaspoon of salt
⅛ teaspoon of nutmeg
2 to 3 dashes of liquid red pepper seasoning
¼ cup of shredded, low-fat Monterey Jack cheese (1 ounce)
12 ounces of linguine

1. Sauté garlic and red pepper flakes in hot margarine in a 10-inch nonstick skillet for 2 minutes or until garlic is golden.
2. Whisk in milk and ricotta until smooth. Add shrimp, peas, parsley, salt, nutmeg, and liquid red pepper seasoning.
3. Cook over medium-low heat for 3 to 4 minutes or until shrimp turn pink. Stir in cheese.
4. Meanwhile, cook linguine in a large pan of boiling water

following package directions. Drain and rinse quickly in hot water. Transfer to large bowl.

5. Top pasta with hot sauce. Toss well to coat. Serve immediately.

MAKES 6 SERVINGS.

Per serving: 357 calories, 113 mg. cholesterol, 2 g. dietary fiber, **7 g. fat**, 368 mg. sodium

*Scallop-and-Clam Pasta

1 tablespoon of olive oil
2 tablespoons of water
2 large white onions, sliced thin
8 to 10 cloves of garlic, minced
6 ounces of fresh mushrooms, quartered
4 cans (6½ to 7 ounces each) of clams, with their juice
2 tablespoons of butter
2 tablespoons of whole-wheat flour
⅛ cup of evaporated skim milk
⅓ cup of skim milk
2 tablespoons of nonfat dry milk

1 pound of spaghetti
1 pound of bay scallops, drained
¼ cup of grated Parmesan cheese (OR 1 ounce in weight)
¼ teaspoon of cayenne
⅛ teaspoon of cloves
⅛ teaspoon of ginger
⅛ teaspoon of mace
Fresh-ground black pepper to taste

1. Heat the oil and water in a large saucepan. Add the onions, garlic, and mushrooms. Cover and let sauté/steam for a few minutes. Add the clams and their juice and let cook, covered.

2. In another pan, melt the butter. Blend in the whole-wheat flour, stirring constantly, to form a roux. Add the evaporated milk, skim milk, and nonfat dry milk. Pour the resulting sauce into the clam mixture.

3. In a large pot, cook spaghetti in boiling water following package directions.

4. While the spaghetti is cooking, add the scallops to the clam sauce. Stir in the Parmesan cheese. Let simmer on

very low heat for a few minutes, until the scallops are tenderly cooked. Stir in the seasonings and serve. You can add more Parmesan at the table, if desired.

MAKES 10 SERVINGS.

Per serving: 258 calories, 85 mg. cholesterol, 1 g. dietary fiber, **9 g. fat,** 350 mg. sodium

POULTRY

In comparison with red meats, chicken is a low-fat source of protein. A cooked half breast of chicken, about 3 ounces of white meat *without skin*, averages around 140 calories. Only about 20 percent of its nutrient weight, or 27 calories, comes from fat. Compare this to a *small* rib-eye steak of around 3½ ounces cooked, which could contain as much as 440 calories, with 360 of those calories coming from fat. You can see that, as a rule, chicken is the choice to make.

White meat of chicken contains about 25 percent less fat than dark meat. When whole chickens are used, the nutritional analyses assume half white meat, half dark. When a recipe calls for chicken breasts, split breasts are assumed; that is, 4 chicken breasts means 4 half breasts.

Turkey is also a low-fat favorite. Ground turkey is an excellent "extender" for ground beef, or it can be used in place of ground beef in most recipes.

◆

*Baked Chicken with Tarragon and Fennel

4 chicken breasts, skinned
1 teaspoon of tarragon
¼ teaspoon of fennel seeds, crushed

⅛ teaspoon of cardamom
Salt and fresh-ground black pepper to taste

1. Place chicken breasts on foil-lined baking pan. Sprinkle with seasonings. Cover loosely with foil to help retain moisture.
2. Bake at 350 degrees for 45 to 50 minutes, until cooked through.

MAKES 4 SERVINGS.
Per serving: 165 calories, 84 mg. cholesterol, 0 dietary fiber, 3.5 g. fat, 207 mg. sodium

*Baked Turkey Loaf

1½ pounds of ground turkey
½ medium onion, finely chopped
1 stalk of celery, finely chopped
¼ cup of fresh parsley, minced
1 tablespoon of bell pepper, finely chopped
½ cup of whole-wheat bread crumbs, toasted
¼ cup of skim milk or chicken stock
1 egg white, slightly beaten
¼ teaspoon of fresh-ground black pepper
¼ teaspoon of dried oregano, crushed
1 clove of garlic, crushed

1. Mix all ingredients until just blended. Do not overmix.
2. Press the mixture into a 4 × 9-inch nonstick loaf pan.
3. Bake at 325 degrees for 45 minutes to 1 hour. Serve hot with Mushroom Glaze (page 128) or serve cold.

MAKES 6 SERVINGS.
Per serving: 237 calories, 72 mg. cholesterol, 1 g. dietary fiber, 11.5 g. fat, 179 mg. sodium

*Barbecued Chicken

You can use this recipe with our Barbecue Sauce (page 127), or your own variation. Or substitute store-bought sauce if you wish. Look for the one lowest in sugar and salt.

3½ pounds of chicken pieces   1 cup of barbecue sauce

1. Skin the chicken pieces. Place the pieces "skin" side down in a large, shallow baking pan. (You may wish to line the pan with foil for easy cleaning.)

2. Baste the chicken pieces liberally with barbecue sauce, and place in the oven.
3. Bake at 350 degrees for 20 minutes, basting halfway through. Then turn the chicken pieces over and bake another 25 to 30 minutes, or until chicken is tender, basting occasionally.

MAKES 6 SERVINGS.

Per serving: 174 calories, 78 mg. cholesterol, 1 g. dietary fiber, **5 g. fat,** 86 mg. sodium (analyses include Barbecue Sauce recipe)

Five-Pepper Fajitas

You can buy prepared salsa for these fajitas in the Mexican section of your supermarket, or you can make your own (see Mexican-Style Hot Sauce, page 124). Fajitas ("little bundles" of various ingredients) can be messy if you eat them with your hands, so you may want to use a knife and fork.

4 chicken breasts, skinned, boned	8 whole-wheat tortillas
Juice of 1 lime	1 tablespoon of vegetable oil
2 cloves of garlic, crushed	1 tablespoon of water
3 scallions, chopped	2 to 3 teaspoons of jalapeño peppers, chopped fine (use gloves!)
Fresh-ground black pepper to taste	Salt to taste
½ teaspoon of cumin	Fresh cilantro, chopped, to taste
1 medium red bell pepper	1 medium tomato, diced
1 medium yellow bell pepper	Salsa to taste
1 medium green bell pepper	

1. Slice the chicken into chunks about ½-inch square. Place them in a large bowl. Squeeze the lime juice over chicken. Add the garlic, scallions, black pepper, and cumin, and toss to mix.
2. Slice the bell peppers into strips and set aside.
3. Wrap the tortillas in a thin, clean dishcloth, place them on an ovenproof plate, and put the plate in the oven.

Warm the tortillas at the lowest setting on your oven while preparing the fajita mixture.

4. Heat the oil and water in a large saucepan over medium heat and add the chicken, bell peppers, and jalapeño peppers. Add the greater amount of jalapeño if you like your food very spicy. Sauté, stirring frequently, until the chicken and vegetables are cooked through, about 25 minutes. Add salt to taste.
5. Spread a spoonful of the fajita mixture in a thick line in the middle of each tortilla. Top with cilantro, tomato, and salsa to taste. Roll up the tortillas and serve.

MAKES 4 SERVINGS OF 2 FAJITAS EACH.

Per serving (2 fajitas): 421 calories, 84 mg. cholesterol, 3 g. dietary fiber, **13 g. fat,** 508 mg. sodium

*Light and Easy Lemon Chicken

4 chicken breasts, skinned
2 lemons
1 teaspoon of dried tarragon

Fresh-ground black pepper to taste

1. Remove all visible fat from chicken. Place each breast in the center of a 12-inch-square piece of aluminum foil. Fold the sides of the foil up so the lemon juice won't run out.
2. Halve the lemons and squeeze the juice of ½ lemon over each chicken breast. Sprinkle each breast with ¼ teaspoon of tarragon and the black pepper.
3. Fold the foil together and seal well to secure the chicken inside.
4. Place the wrapped chicken in a shallow baking dish and bake at 350 degrees for about 45 minutes.

MAKES 4 SERVINGS.

Per serving: 166 calories, 84 mg. cholesterol, 0 dietary fiber, **3.5 g. fat,** 74 mg. sodium

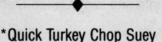

Marinade for Chicken Breasts

½ cup of wine (red or white)
1 teaspoon of soy sauce
1 teaspoon of ground ginger

1 tablespoon of lemon juice
2 scallions, chopped

1. Combine ingredients. Remove the skin from chicken breasts and marinate for several hours, turning occasionally.
2. As you broil the chicken, baste it occasionally with the marinade to prevent dryness.

MAKES ABOUT ½ CUP.
Total per recipe: 90 calories, 0 cholesterol, 0 dietary fiber, **0 fat,** 349 mg. sodium

*Quick Turkey Chop Suey

1 pound of ground turkey
1 can (16 ounces) of bean sprouts, drained
1 cup of chopped celery
½ cup of chopped onion
1 can (8 ounces) of water chestnuts, drained and sliced
1 can (5 ounces) of slices mushrooms, drained

¼ teaspoon of ground ginger
1 can (10½ ounces) of condensed beef or chicken broth
2 tablespoons of soy sauce
2 tablespoons of cornstarch (or ¼ cup of flour)
3 cups of cooked brown rice

1. In a large skillet, brown the ground turkey. Drain off any fat.
2. Add the vegetables, ginger, and all but ¼ cup of the broth. Bring to a boil over medium-high heat. Reduce heat, cover, and simmer 20 minutes.
3. Combine the ¼ cup of reserved broth with the soy sauce and cornstarch. Add to the meat and vegetable mixture, stirring until thickened and bubbly. Serve over the rice.

MAKES 6 SERVINGS.
Per serving: 294 calories, 48 mg. cholesterol, 4 g. dietary fiber, 8 g. fat, 679 mg. sodium

FISH

The many different varieties of fish are usually quick and easy to prepare in a number of delicious, low-fat ways: poaching, broiling, steaming, baking, and grilling. Watch cooking times carefully to avoid overcooking.

As an added bonus, fish also contains "Omega III" fatty acids that can reduce the risk of heart disease. One of these, eicosapentanoic acid (EPA), has been shown to lower serum cholesterol and triglycerides, and to increase high-density lipoproteins (HDL). Lower total cholesterol and higher HDL levels are both associated with a reduced risk of cardiovascular disease. EPA also lessens the risk of blood clots and stroke by causing some changes in the red blood cells and platelets in the bloodstream that are responsible for clotting.

The best sources of Omega III fatty acids are cold-water fish: salmon, mackerel, pollack (bluefish), albacore tuna, and herring. Moderate amounts can be found in halibut, red snapper, swordfish, and shellfish, while cod, monkfish, and orange roughy have a little less. Although the fish richest in Omega III fatty acids contain more fat than other varieties, they are still generally lower in fat than red meat. Flounder and sole, for example, may be very low in fat, but the health benefits and reasonable fat contents of the fattier fish listed above recommend their use on a regular basis.

◆

*Grilled Tuna Mediterranean

You can substitute yellowtail for the tuna with delicious results.

MARINADE:

1 tablespoon of capers
1 tablespoon of olive oil
3 tablespoons of white wine
2 tablespoons of lemon juice
1 clove of garlic, crushed
1 teaspoon of olive oil
½ teaspoon of dried rosemary, crushed
¼ teaspoon of salt
Fresh-ground black pepper to taste

1 pound of fresh tuna steaks, about ½ to ¾ inch thick
Lemon wedges
Fresh cilantro or parsley sprigs

1. Place capers in a strainer and rinse under cold running water. Drain well.
2. Combine all marinade ingredients in a shallow glass or ceramic dish. Arrange the tuna steaks in the dish and marinate for 20 minutes, turning once after 10 minutes.
3. Brush a foil-lined baking sheet with oil and arrange the marinated tuna steaks on the sheet. Pour half the marinade over the steaks.
4. Broil the fish for about 4 minutes, until the tops are slightly seared. Turn the steaks over with a spatula and pour the remaining marinade over them. Broil another 4 minutes, or until fish flakes easily with a fork.
5. Garnish each serving with lemon wedges and fresh cilantro or parsley.

MAKES 4 SERVINGS.

Per serving: 173 calories, 53 mg. cholesterol, 0 dietary fiber, **9 g. fat,** 134 mg. sodium

Lime-Steamed Fish Fillets

These basic directions can be used anytime you want to steam fish.

1½ pounds of fish fillets (try flounder or sole)
Juice of 1 lime

¼ cup of shallots, minced
Fresh-ground black pepper to taste

1. Arrange fillets on a steamer rack over boiling water.
2. Squeeze the lime juice over them, and top with shallots and black pepper.
3. Cover and steam for about 5 minutes, until fish flakes easily with a fork.

MAKES 4 SERVINGS.
Per serving: 124 calories, 66 mg. cholesterol, 0.5 g. dietary fiber, **2 g. fat,** 155 mg. sodium

*Royal Indian Salmon

This recipe is one of our all-time favorites, delicately flavored, and very easy to prepare.

4 salmon steaks, 1 inch thick (about 6 ounces each)
¼ cup of low-sodium chicken or vegetable bouillon
2 tablespoons of lemon juice
½ teaspoon of fennel seeds, crushed

¼ teaspoon of cumin
¼ teaspoon of ground coriander
Dash of salt and fresh-ground black pepper

1. Place the steaks in a shallow pan. Pour the bouillon and the lemon juice over the steaks. Add the seasonings. Marinate, covered, in the refrigerator for at least 2 hours, turning the steaks occasionally.
2. To cook, place the steaks on a foil-covered broiling pan.

Spoon 2 teaspoons of the marinade on top of each steak.
Place under the broiler on low broil for 8 to 10 minutes,
or until slightly brown on the edges. Turn steaks over,
spoon on the remaining marinade, and broil for an additional 8 to 10 minutes.

MAKES 4 SERVINGS, ABOUT 4.5 OUNCES EACH, COOKED
WEIGHT.
Per serving: 285 calories, 120 mg. cholesterol, 0 dietary fiber, 8 g. fat,
225 mg. sodium

Salmon Croquettes Béarnaise

A traditional favorite! Serve with Light Béarnaise (page
128).

1 can (15 ounces) of salmon	¼ teaspoon of fresh-ground
¼ cup of finely chopped onion	black pepper
¾ cup of bread crumbs	¼ teaspoon of nutmeg
1 egg, slightly beaten	Nonstick vegetable cooking spray
1 tablespoon of lemon juice	

1. Combine all ingredients in a bowl and mix well.
2. Cover and refrigerate the salmon mixture for an hour or
   more.
3. After chilling, shape into 4 patties approximately ¾
   inch thick.
4. Spray a nonstick skillet with cooking spray and fry the
   patties over moderate heat, turning once, until browned
   on each side.

MAKES 4 SERVINGS.
Per serving: 173 calories, 90 mg. cholesterol, 1 g. dietary fiber, 5.5 g.
fat, 433 mg. sodium

♦

Saucy Seafood Kebabs

This recipe is delicious with halibut, which holds together well during cooking, but other fish steaks or fillets can be used.

1 pound of fish, cut into 1-inch cubes
16 cherry tomatoes
2 bell peppers, cut into 1-inch cubes
16 mushrooms
16 boiled white pearl onions
Nonstick vegetable cooking spray

1 cup of tomato juice
4 teaspoons of cider vinegar
¾ teaspoon of dry mustard
⅜ teaspoon of garlic powder
⅛ teaspoon of fresh-ground black pepper
1/16 teaspoon of cayenne pepper

1. Thread the raw fish alternately with the vegetables on four skewers. Place the kebabs on a broiler pan sprayed with nonstick cooking spray.
2. Place the remaining ingredients in a saucepan and heat through.
3. Brush the heated sauce on the kebabs. Broil the kebabs about 3 inches away from the heat for about 12 to 15 minutes, turning once halfway through the cooking time. Baste the kebabs with the remaining sauce occasionally while cooking.

MAKES 4 SERVINGS.
Per serving (using flounder): 160 calories, 68 mg. cholesterol, 5 g. dietary fiber, 2 g. fat, 322 mg. sodium

◆

*Sea Bass with Red Bell Peppers

This is also good with regular bass, haddock, or other thick fillets of fish.

1 pound of sea bass fillets
1 tablespoon of fresh parsley, minced
¼ teaspoon of chives
¼ teaspoon of marjoram
¼ teaspoon of tarragon
⅛ teaspoon of rosemary

Juice of ¼ lemon
½ cup of white wine
4 large mushrooms, sliced thin
1 small red bell pepper, diced
3 tablespoons of dry bread crumbs
½ tablespoon of butter

1. Place fish fillets in a shallow baking dish. Sprinkle with the seasonings and lemon juice. Pour the wine around the fish. Arrange the vegetables in the liquid around the fish.
2. Bake at 400 degrees for 15 minutes.
3. Stir the vegetables. Sprinkle the bread crumbs on the fish and dot with the butter. Cook 15 minutes more.

MAKES 4 SERVINGS.
Per serving: 148 calories, 83 mg. cholesterol, 1 g. dietary fiber, 2.5 g. fat, 160 mg. sodium

*Shrimp Florentine

1 onion, chopped
1 tablespoon of butter
2 tablespoons of water
2 large cloves of garlic, minced
1 bell pepper, chopped
2 cups of stock (chicken or fish)
1 cup of uncooked brown rice
Fresh-ground black pepper to taste

1 package (10 ounces) of frozen chopped spinach
1 teaspoon of lemon juice
1 teaspoon of soy sauce
1 pound of shrimp, cooked and peeled
Salt to taste

1. Cook onion in butter and water in a saucepan over low heat until onion is translucent. Add the garlic and cook until lightly browned. Add the bell pepper, cover, and gently steam until somewhat tender. Remove from heat.
2. Meanwhile, bring the stock to a boil in another saucepan. Rinse the rice and add it to the boiling water. Cover, reduce heat to simmer, and let cook about 40 minutes or until rice is tender. Sprinkle with black pepper.
3. In another pan, cook the spinach in water, as directed on the package. Add the lemon juice and soy sauce.
4. Add the shrimp to the onion and bell pepper mixture and toss. Heat gently until heated through.
5. To serve, spoon rice onto a plate, top with spinach and then the shrimp mixture. Season with extra soy sauce or salt as desired.

MAKES 4 SERVINGS.
Per serving: 368 calories, 175 mg. cholesterol, 4.5 g. dietary fiber, 6.5 g. fat, 768 mg. sodium

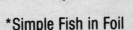

*Simple Fish in Foil

A delicious and simple solution for those fish fillets (flounder, sole, haddock, grouper, orange roughy) in the freezer!

1 pound of frozen fish fillets	¼-inch strips
¼ teaspoon of dried dill weed	2 medium carrots, cut into
2 tablespoons of lemon juice	⅛-inch slices
4 slices of onion	1 cup of frozen Italian green
2 medium potatoes, cut into	beans

1. Place each frozen fish fillet in the center of an individual piece of foil, 12 × 18 inches.
2. Combine dill and lemon juice. Drizzle over fillets.
3. Top with onion slices. Arrange potatoes and carrots on sides of fillets. Top with green beans.

4. Seal foil tightly and place on ungreased baking sheet.
5. Bake at 425 degrees till fork tender, about 30 minutes.

MAKES 4 SERVINGS.

Per serving: 189 calories, 59 mg. cholesterol, 3 g. dietary fiber, 1.5 g. fat, 157 mg. sodium

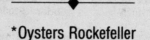

*Oysters Rockefeller

3 tablespoons of dry bread
  crumbs
2 teaspoons of olive oil
1 tablespoon of grated onion
Tarragon, pepper, and/or
Tabasco sauce to taste
1 package (10 ounces) of
  chopped frozen spinach,

thawed and drained
6 ounces of raw or canned
  oysters (not smoked)
2 tablespoons of grated part-
  skim mozzarella cheese
1 tablespoon of Parmesan

1. Combine the bread crumbs, oil, onion, and seasonings. Toss together with the spinach.
2. Broil the oysters, if using raw, for 5 to 7 minutes. Drain liquid if using canned.
3. Top oysters with spinach mixture and broil 3 to 4 minutes. Sprinkle with the cheeses and broil just until melted.

MAKES 4 SERVINGS.

Per serving: 103 calories, 24 mg. cholesterol, 2.5 g. dietary fiber, 4.5 g. fat, 169 mg. sodium

◆

Swordfish with Tarragon

4 swordfish steaks, 6 to 8
   ounces each
1 tablespoon of olive oil
1 tablespoon of lemon juice

2 teaspoons of tarragon
2 tablespoons of grated
   Parmesan cheese
1½ teaspoons of paprika

1. In a foil-covered baking pan, swish the fish in the olive oil and lemon juice to coat both sides. Broil 4 to 5 minutes on each side.
2. Meanwhile, combine the remaining ingredients in a small bowl. Sprinkle the fish with the seasoning mixture in the last minute of cooking time.

MAKES 4 SERVINGS.
Per serving: 228 calories, 68 mg. cholesterol, 0 dietary fiber, 8.5 g. fat, 158 mg. sodium

MEAT

Beef

Although beef is high in saturated fat as compared to poultry and seafood, I eat low-fat cuts in moderation (once or twice a week). I don't feel there is strong evidence against eating it even three to four times a week, provided your cholesterol level is normal and there is no history of heart disease in your family.

The low-fat cuts of beef are top and bottom round, eye of round, sirloin tip, flank steak, London broil, tenderloin (including filet mignon, chateaubriand, fillet steak, and tournedos), and, of course, extra-lean hamburger. However, there is no national standard for fat content in so-called "lean" or "extra-lean" hamburger. "Extra-lean" can contain anywhere from 5 to 15 percent total fat. Sometimes you will find the percentage marked on the package.

Trim all visible fat from other cuts of beef before cooking, and try using beef as a condiment combined with lots of vegetables, as in Oriental cooking.

◆

*Baked Flank Steak

1½ pounds of flank steak	4 tablespoons of minced celery
1 tablespoon of vegetable oil	⅛ teaspoon of fresh-ground
1 cup of hot water	black pepper
1 bay leaf	2 teaspoons of lemon juice
1 large clove of garlic, crushed	1 medium carrot, diced
1 teaspoon of salt	¼ medium bell pepper, diced

1. Trim away any visible fat from the steak. Sear the steak in the oil over medium to medium-high heat. Place the steak in a casserole dish.
2. For extra flavoring, pour the water into the skillet you seared the meat in, and stir. Pour this over the meat, then add all the other ingredients.
3. Cook uncovered at 350 degrees for 30 minutes, or longer if you prefer your meat well done.

Light Gravy (Optional): Heat 1 tablespoon of vegetable oil, and stir in 2 tablespoons of whole-wheat flour. Take a cup of liquid from the meat and stir into the roux. Stir until thickened, and serve over the meat.

MAKES 4 SERVINGS, 4.5 OUNCES EACH, PLUS SAUCE, BUT WITHOUT OPTIONAL GRAVY.
Per serving: 273 calories, 88 mg. cholesterol, 1 g. dietary fiber, **12 g. fat,** 630 mg. sodium (gravy adds 30 calories and 3 grams of fat; nutrient values of the meat liquid and other ingredients are included in the original analysis)

◆

Chili-Bean Meat Loaf

2 cans (15½ ounces each) of
  red kidney beans
1 pound of lean ground beef
¾ cup of dry bread crumbs
2 tablespoons of soy sauce

½ teaspoon of dried oregano
1 tablespoon of dried basil
1 can (15 ounces) of tomato
  puree
Dash cayenne pepper

1. Drain the liquid from the cans of kidney beans.
2. Mix the contents of one can of beans with the meat,
   bread crumbs, soy sauce, oregano, and basil.
3. Press mixture into a 9 × 5 × 3-inch loaf pan, and cover
   with the other can of beans and the tomato puree.
   Sprinkle with cayenne pepper.
4. Bake uncovered at 350 degrees for 1 hour.

MAKES 8 SERVINGS.
Per serving: 252 calories, 38 mg. cholesterol, 8 g. dietary fiber, **9 g. fat,** 761 mg. sodium

◆

Chinese Beef with Vegetables

1 teaspoon of peanut oil
2 teaspoons of water
12 ounces of round steak,
  trimmed of fat, cut diagonally
  into thin strips
1 medium onion, chopped
¼ teaspoon of ground ginger
2 cups of broccoli, chopped

2 carrots, sliced
1 cup of beef stock
1 cup of snow peas
½ cup of water chestnuts,
  drained and sliced
½ cup of bean sprouts
1 tablespoon of soy sauce
1 tablespoon of cornstarch

1. Place oil and water in large skillet or wok and heat over
   medium-high heat. Add meat and onion and brown
   lightly. Add remaining ingredients except soy sauce and
   cornstarch. Cover and cook until vegetables are just
   tender.
2. Mix the soy sauce and cornstarch together to make a

paste. Stir into the other ingredients and cook, stirring occasionally, until thickened. Serve with brown rice.

MAKES 4 SERVINGS.

Per serving: 201 calories, 61 mg. cholesterol, 4.5 g. dietary fiber, 8 g. **fat,** 160 mg. sodium (analyses do not include the rice, which is generally 1 gram of fat per ½ cup)

Japanese Beef Stir-Fry

Here is an example of Oriental-style cooking in which meat is only part of the "main course." Serve this dish as soon as it's ready, or, if you are making enough for leftovers, use regular or Chinese cabbage instead of red, as the red cabbage tends to turn other ingredients purple when cooked and stored.

4 beef tenderloin steaks (about 4 ounces each)
1 tablespoon of peanut oil
2 packages (6 ounces each) of frozen pea pods, thawed
¼ head of red cabbage, sliced thin

¼ inch of fresh ginger root, minced, or ground ginger to taste
1 tablespoon of sake (Japanese rice wine, optional)
Dash of Tamari or soy sauce

1. Heat a wok or heavy skillet over medium-high heat for several minutes. Meanwhile, trim the beef of all visible fat and slice it into thin slices.
2. Add the oil to the pan, then the beef. Cook, stirring constantly, until browned.
3. Turn the heat down to medium, remove the meat from the pan, and set aside.
4. Add the pea pods, cabbage, and ginger root to the wok, and cook for 5 minutes, stirring constantly.
5. Return the meat to the wok, and stir in the sake and the soy sauce. Cover, and let simmer for a few more minutes, until the vegetables are just tender and the meat is cooked the way you like it.

MAKES 4 SERVINGS.
Per serving: 281 calories, 82 mg. cholesterol, 8 g. dietary fiber, **13 g. fat**, 81 mg. sodium

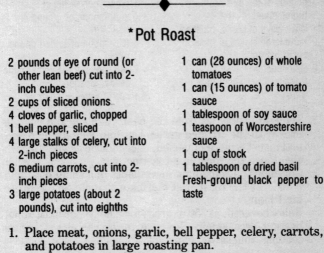

*Pot Roast

2 pounds of eye of round (or other lean beef) cut into 2-inch cubes
2 cups of sliced onions
4 cloves of garlic, chopped
1 bell pepper, sliced
4 large stalks of celery, cut into 2-inch pieces
6 medium carrots, cut into 2-inch pieces
3 large potatoes (about 2 pounds), cut into eighths

1 can (28 ounces) of whole tomatoes
1 can (15 ounces) of tomato sauce
1 tablespoon of soy sauce
1 teaspoon of Worcestershire sauce
1 cup of stock
1 tablespoon of dried basil
Fresh-ground black pepper to taste

1. Place meat, onions, garlic, bell pepper, celery, carrots, and potatoes in large roasting pan.
2. Cover with canned tomatoes, tomato sauce, soy sauce, Worcestershire, and stock. Sprinkle with basil and ground black pepper.
3. Bake covered at 350 degrees for 45 minutes. Reduce heat to 250 degrees and bake for 3 hours or until meat is very tender to the fork. Baste occasionally.

MAKES 6 SERVINGS OF 4 OUNCES OF BEEF (COOKED WEIGHT) EACH WITH ASSORTED VEGETABLES.
Per serving: 473 calories, 78 mg. cholesterol, 8 g. dietary fiber, **8 g. fat**, 667 mg. sodium

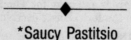

*Round-Roast Oriental

3 pounds of top or bottom round roast
1 large clove of garlic, crushed
2 more large cloves of garlic, cut in halves
2 tablespoons of sake (Japanese rice wine) or sherry

1 tablespoon of honey
1½ tablespoons of ground dry mustard
1 tablespoon of Tamari or soy sauce
2 teaspoons of toasted sesame seeds, crushed
1 cup of water or stock

1. Trim all visible fat from the beef, then rub the beef all over with the crushed garlic. Cut four slits in the roast, and insert a piece of peeled, sliced garlic clove into each slit. Place the roast in a roasting pan.
2. Combine the remaining ingredients in a small bowl and pour over the roast. Let marinate at room temperature for 1 hour.
3. Bake, covered, at 350 degrees for 2 hours, or until done, basting occasionally. Remove the garlic cloves before serving, unless you like a lot of garlic!

MAKES 12 SERVINGS, 3 OUNCES EACH.
Per serving: 207 calories, 82 mg. cholesterol, 0 dietary fiber, **9 g. fat,** 136 mg. sodium

*Saucy Pastitsio

Nonstick vegetable cooking spray
½ pound of very lean ground beef (10 percent fat)
½ cup of chopped onion
1 can (8 ounces) of low-sodium or regular tomato sauce
¼ teaspoon of salt
¼ teaspoon of fresh-ground black pepper

⅛ teaspoon of nutmeg
8 ounces of elbow macaroni, cooked according to package directions
2 tablespoons of grated Parmesan cheese
1¼ cups of 1% or 2% milk
2 tablespoons of all-purpose flour

⅛ teaspoon of cinnamon
⅛ teaspoon of allspice

3 drops of liquid red pepper
  seasoning

1. Spray an $8 \times 8 \times 1\frac{1}{2}$-inch square baking pan with cooking spray.
2. Spray a medium nonstick skillet with cooking spray. Brown meat and onion in hot skillet for 3 minutes or until meat is no longer pink. Pour off and discard any excess fat. Stir tomato sauce, ⅛ teaspoon of the salt, ⅛ teaspoon of the pepper, the cinnamon, allspice, and nutmeg into meat mixture. Stir in hot cooked elbow macaroni and Parmesan cheese. Spoon into prepared baking pan.
3. Stir together milk and flour in a medium saucepan until very smooth. Bring to a boil. Lower heat and cook 1 minute or until mixture thickens slightly. Stir in liquid red pepper seasoning and the remaining salt and pepper. Pour white sauce over meat mixture in baking pan.
4. Bake at 375 degrees for 25 minutes or until center is hot. Serve with a crisp mixed green salad, if you wish.

MAKES 4 SERVINGS.
Per serving: 395 calories, 39 mg. cholesterol, 3 g. dietary fiber, **10 g. fat,** 259 mg. sodium

◆

Steak Marinade

Here are two marinades for flank steak, London broil, or any other lean cut of beef that you might want to use for oven or pan broiling, or outdoor grilling. The wine and soy sauce have a tenderizing effect, so marinate overnight in the refrigerator, in a large covered bowl or plastic bag. Turn the meat once or twice while it is marinating, to be sure all of it has been well covered.

These amounts will do nicely for 2 pounds of meat.

BASIC MARINADE:
1 tablespoon of olive oil
½ cup of dry red wine (you can use white wine for light-colored meats)
¼ teaspoon of Herb Salt (pages 125–126)
1 bay leaf
1 teaspoon of chives
1 small onion, minced

ORIENTAL MARINADE:
1 tablespoon of olive oil
¼ cup of Tamari (or soy sauce)
¼ cup of dry red wine
4 cloves of garlic, minced
4 scallions, minced
6 whole peppercorns
⅛ teaspoon of ground coriander
1-inch cube of fresh ginger, peeled and grated or minced

Olive oil contains approximately 120 calories and 12 grams of fat per tablespoon. The other ingredients provide negligible calories, including the wine, since the alcohol will evaporate and the sugar content is very low. Soy sauce is quite high in sodium, but it is difficult to predict how much will penetrate or adhere to the meat. My guess is that the sodium content per serving, for example, 4.5 ounces of flank steak, would be moderate, perhaps 500 milligrams.

◆

*Swedish Meatballs

Here is an example of how you can adapt your favorite recipes that call for ground beef by combining the beef with other meats. You get the flavor of beef yet reduced fat and cholesterol. Add a pound of drained, crumbled tofu to this recipe to extend it even further if you like, and adjust seasonings accordingly. These are delicious served over saffron or yellow rice, which you can find in your super- market.

2 cups of whole-wheat bread crumbs	½ teaspoon of pepper
1 cup of skim milk	2 teaspoons of sugar
1½ pounds of ground turkey	½ teaspoon of ginger
½ pound of extra-lean ground beef	½ teaspoon of nutmeg
2 whole eggs	½ teaspoon of allspice
2 egg whites	½ teaspoon of dry mustard
1 large onion, finely chopped	3 cups of beef stock
1 teaspoon of salt	4 tablespoons of flour
	2 teaspoons of instant coffee

1. Soak the bread crumbs in the milk for several minutes.
2. Meanwhile, combine the ground turkey and ground beef.
3. Beat the whole eggs and egg whites together and add to the meat mixture. Add the moistened bread crumbs, onion, and seasonings to the meat mixture and mix well.
4. Form into 1½-inch balls (makes 40–50) and refrigerate overnight.
5. Line up the meatballs on a large pan-like cookie sheet (with edges) and bake at 350 degrees for 25–30 min- utes, turning halfway through cooking time.
6. While meatballs are cooking, heat stock in a large pot. Gradually add the flour, stirring constantly. Cook and stir until slightly thickened. Stir in the instant coffee.
7. Remove the meatballs from the oven and transfer them to the beef stock using a slotted spoon to allow grease to drain away. Simmer for 45 minutes and serve.

MAKES 10 SERVINGS OF 4 MEATBALLS EACH.
Per serving: 313 calories, 122 mg. cholesterol, 1 g. dietary fiber, **14 g. fat,** 712 mg. sodium

Pork

Although pork in any form is not a mainstay of my diet, some cuts can be lean. The butt, blade, or sirloin runs about 30 to 35 percent fat per ounce. Combined with vegetable side dishes, fresh salad, and whole-grain bread, or in an Oriental-style main dish, the percentage of fat for the whole meal can be reduced considerably. Be sure to trim away all visible fat, however.

Bacon, on the other hand, is much higher in fat (65 percent), calories, and sodium. If you just can't bear to live completely without it, try substituting lean ham (about 33 percent fat per ounce) or Canadian bacon (about 40 percent fat per ounce) in recipes that call for bacon. (We have just heard of a "turkey bacon" that our informant said was very good, but we have not tried it. It is only 5 percent fat per ounce.)

*Pork Chops Parmesan

3 tablespoons of cornmeal, whole-wheat flour, or bread crumbs
1 tablespoon of grated Parmesan cheese
½ teaspoon of fresh-ground black pepper
½ teaspoon of salt
½ teaspoon of basil
4 pork loin rib chops, about ½ inch thick
1 tablespoon of vegetable oil
3 green onions, chopped
1 clove of garlic, minced
¼ teaspoon of fennel seeds, crushed

1. Combine the cornmeal, Parmesan cheese, black pepper, salt, and basil.
2. Trim the pork chops of all visible fat, pat them dry, and dredge in the cornmeal mixture.
3. Heat a skillet over medium heat, and add the oil. When

the oil is hot, place the chops in the skillet, and reduce the heat to low.

4. Fry the chops for 10 minutes on each side. Then add the onions, garlic, and fennel, and continue frying for another 10 minutes, turning as necessary to keep from sticking.

MAKES 4 SERVINGS.

Per serving: 198 calories, 56 mg. cholesterol, 1 g. dietary fiber, 12 g. fat, 340 mg. sodium

◆

*Pork Tenderloin with Orange Marmalade

1 pork tenderloin (1 pound)
1½ tablespoons of grainy, coarse, prepared mustard
1 clove of garlic, minced
¼ teaspoon of fresh rosemary, finely chopped

Pinch of fresh-ground black pepper
¼ cup of low-sugar orange marmalade
½ cup of water
¼ cup of chicken stock

1. Make a cut lengthwise down the center about halfway through the pork tenderloin.
2. In a small bowl mix together mustard, garlic, rosemary, and black pepper. Spread mixture along the cut surface of the tenderloin. Reshape and tie in several places. Place on rack above roasting pan. Brush with 2 tablespoons marmalade. Add water to pan.
3. Bake in a 400-degree oven for about 40 to 45 minutes or until internal temperature of meat reaches 160 degrees.
4. Mix together remaining orange marmalade and chicken stock in a small saucepan. Simmer 2 to 3 minutes until thickened. Spoon sauce over sliced tenderloin and serve immediately.

MAKES 4 SERVINGS.

Per serving: 160 calories, 74 mg. cholesterol, 0 dietary fiber, 3 g. fat, 175 mg. sodium

◆

Stir-Fry Pork with Pea Pods

4 pork chops
1 tablespoon of peanut or
   vegetable oil
¼ teaspoon of fresh-ground
   black pepper
1 tablespoon of soy sauce
1 clove of garlic, crushed
1 slice of fresh ginger, about ½-

thick, minced
2 teaspoons of sesame seeds
⅓ cup of water
¼ cup of green onions or leeks,
   diced
1 package (6 ounces) of frozen
   pea pods

1. Trim all visible fat from the chops, and slice the meat
   into thin strips, about ¼-inch thick, and ½- to 1-inch
   wide.
2. Heat the oil in a wok or large skillet over medium heat,
   then add the pork and brown, stirring often.
3. Mix together the black pepper, soy sauce, garlic, ginger, sesame seeds, and water, and add to the browned
   meat. Add the onions.
4. Cover, reduce heat, and let simmer for about 30 minutes, until the pork is cooked through, stirring occasionally. Add more water if necessary to prevent
   sticking.
5. Meanwhile, cook the pea pods according to package
   directions, without added salt. Add the cooked pea pods
   to the pork, stir, and serve.

MAKES 4 SERVINGS.
Per serving: 237 calories, 55 mg. cholesterol, 2 g. dietary fiber, **14 g.
fat,** 316 mg. sodium

Lamb

Lamb, like pork, is a fatty meat that requires careful
trimming to meet T-Factor guidelines. As with the other
meat recipes in this book, this recipe illustrates how to
serve lamb in combination with high-fiber, low-fat foods so
that you end up with a meal that's relatively low in fat.

◆

Curried Lamb with Vegetables

4 lamb loin or shoulder chops, about ¾-inch thick
2 cloves of garlic, minced
1 tablespoon of vegetable oil
1 cup of water or low-salt stock
1 teaspoon of cumin
½ teaspoon of ground ginger
¼ teaspoon of ground coriander
¼ teaspoon of cayenne

½ teaspoon of turmeric
1 medium zucchini, cut in chunks
2 medium carrots, sliced
1 medium onion, cut in chunks
Fresh-ground black pepper to taste
1 package (10 ounces) of frozen green peas

1. Trim any visible fat from chops, and brown with the garlic in the vegetable oil in a large skillet.
2. Remove the lamb, and add the remaining ingredients except for the peas. Cover and bring to a boil. Reduce heat to simmer, and put the lamb back in the pan. Cover, and simmer for 30 minutes.
3. Add the peas, and simmer another 10 minutes, until vegetables are tender and lamb is cooked.

MAKES 4 SERVINGS.
Per serving: 223 calories, 60 mg. cholesterol, 10 g. dietary fiber, **10 g. fat,** 120 mg. sodium

VEGETABLE AND GRAIN SIDE DISHES

Fresh raw or steamed vegetables are a low-fat complement to any meal. Cooked in a microwave, vegetables retain their nutrients perhaps better than through any other way of cooking. Check your microwave manual for the simple instructions for cooking vegetables.

Leave edible skins on most vegetables and fruits, such as apples, carrots, and potatoes. The skins contain healthful nutrients and fiber.

Frozen vegetables are good to have on hand in a pinch, but canned are usually overcooked, over-salted, or preserved with ingredients you may prefer to avoid, so read labels carefully.

Nutritionists now believe that we should eat a leafy green vegetable every day not only for the vitamin A content, but also for the calcium. Collards, for example, have about the same amount of calcium as milk products, and no fat!

*Apple-Sweet Sweet Potatoes

3 large sweet potatoes
¾ cup of water
3 medium apples, cored, peeled, sliced ½-inch thick
1 cup of unsweetened apple juice
2 tablespoons of cornstarch

3 tablespoons of unsweetened apple juice
1 tablespoon of honey
¼ cup of wheat germ
¼ cup of graham cracker crumbs

1. Cook whole sweet potatoes in water until tender, about 20 minutes. Peel and slice lengthwise about ½-inch thick. Layer slices in a 2-quart casserole dish. Top with apple slices.
2. In a saucepan, bring the 1 cup of apple juice to a boil.
3. Dissolve the cornstarch in the 3 tablespoons of apple juice and add to the hot apple juice. Stir until thickened. Stir in honey. Pour the sauce over the apples and sweet potatoes.
4. Combine the wheat germ and graham cracker crumbs. Sprinkle on top of casserole.
5. Bake at 350 degrees for 45 minutes or until apples are fork tender.

MAKES 8 SERVINGS.

Per serving: 168 calories, 0 cholesterol, 4 g. dietary fiber, **1 g. fat,** 34 mg. sodium

Baby Carrots

1 pound of whole baby carrots
½ cup of water
½ teaspoon of dry chicken
  bouillon

½ teaspoon of Mrs. Dash
Fresh-ground black pepper to
taste

1. Trim stems from carrots.
2. Combine all ingredients in a casserole dish and bake at
   350 degrees for about 45 minutes until carrots are
   tender.

MAKES 4 SERVINGS.
Per serving: 52 calories, 0 cholesterol, 4 g. dietary fiber, 0 fat, 646 mg.
sodium

*Beets a l'Orange

3 tablespoons of grated orange
  rind
1 cup of orange juice
½ teaspoon of salt

1 tablespoon of cornstarch
4 cups of beets, cooked and
  sliced
Fresh-ground black pepper

1. Combine the orange rind, juice, salt, and cornstarch in
   the top of a double boiler. Cook and stir until thickened.
2. Add the beets and heat through. Sprinkle with black
   pepper.

MAKES 6 SERVINGS.
Per serving: 61 calories, 0 cholesterol, 3 g. dietary fiber, 0 fat, 234 mg.
sodium

Broccoli with Almonds

2 teaspoons of butter
2 tablespoons of almonds,
  chopped or slivered
2 stalks of fresh broccoli,
  chopped in flowerettes, stems

diced (about 2 cups)
About 4 teaspoons of water

1. Melt the butter in a frying pan over medium heat. Add the almonds and toast, stirring frequently, until browned, about 2 to 3 minutes.
2. Add the broccoli and stir to coat with the almonds.
3. Add the water, cover, and reduce heat to low. Sauté/steam for 10 to 15 minutes, until tender, stirring frequently and adding more water if necessary.

MAKES 4 SERVINGS.
Per serving: 54 calories, 5 mg. cholesterol, 2 g. dietary fiber, 4 g. fat, 27 mg. sodium

*Brussels Sprouts with Caraway Seeds

1 pound of brussels sprouts
  (about 2½ cups)
½ cup of water or chicken stock
1 teaspoon of caraway seeds

¼ teaspoon of salt
¼ teaspoon of fresh-ground
  black pepper

1. Wash brussels sprouts and trim wilted leaves. Make a gash in the bottom of each to speed cooking.
2. Place in ½ cup of boiling water or stock. Reduce heat, cover, and cook until fork tender. Do not overcook.
3. Pour off liquid. Add seeds and seasonings.

MAKES 4 SERVINGS.
Per serving: 45 calories, 0 cholesterol, 3.5 g. dietary fiber, 1 g. fat, 233 mg. sodium

Creamed Spinach and Turnip Greens

1 package (10 ounces) of
  chopped frozen spinach
1 package (10 ounces) of
  chopped frozen turnip greens
1 tablespoon of butter
2 tablespoons of whole-wheat
  flour

1 cup of skim milk
2 teaspoons of Mrs. Dash
Garlic powder to taste
Salt to taste
1 tablespoon of bread crumbs

1. Defrost and combine greens (with their liquid) in a casserole dish.
2. Melt butter in a saucepan and add flour gradually, stirring well. Add milk slowly, mixing constantly. Add seasonings (not crumbs) and heat until thickened. Pour over greens.
3. Top with crumbs and bake at 325 degrees until bubbly, about 30 minutes.

MAKES 8 SERVINGS.
Per serving: 53 calories, 4 mg. cholesterol, 2.5 g. dietary fiber, **2 g. fat,** 109 mg. sodium

Green Beans Creole

1 pound of fresh green beans,
  trimmed, or 2 packages (9
  ounces each) of frozen green
  beans
Water
1 can (16 ounces) of tomatoes
1 stalk of celery, finely chopped

¼ cup of chopped bell pepper
½ teaspoon of onion powder
Dash salt
Dash crushed red pepper (optional)

1. Steam green beans over water for 5 minutes, until just tender, or cook frozen beans as package directs.
2. Combine the cooked beans with the remaining ingre-

dients in a large saucepan. Heat over medium heat for
about 15 minutes or until all vegetables are tender.

MAKES 8 SERVINGS.

Per serving: 30 calories, 0 cholesterol, 3 g. dietary fiber, **0 fat,** 140 mg.
sodium

*Scalloped Potatoes

1 large onion, sliced thin	Nonstick vegetable cooking
1 tablespoon of butter	spray
2 large potatoes, sliced thin	1 tablespoon of whole-wheat
2 tablespoons of lemon juice	flour
1 teaspoon of thyme	1 cup of skim milk
½ teaspoon of salt	2 tablespoons of bread crumbs

1. Sauté the onions in the butter until translucent. Add
   the potatoes and combine. Add the lemon juice, thyme,
   and salt, and mix.
2. Spray a casserole dish with vegetable spray. Put half
   the potato mixture in the casserole and sprinkle with
   the flour. Add the rest of the potatoes. Pour in the skim
   milk, and sprinkle with the bread crumbs.
3. Bake at 325 degrees for 1 hour or until potatoes are
   tender and slightly browned on top.

MAKES 4 SERVINGS.

Per serving: 187 calories, 9 mg. cholesterol, 3 g. dietary fiber, **3.5 g.
fat,** 354 mg. sodium

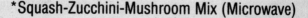

*Scandinavian-Style Potato Casserole

2½ tablespoons of butter
1 can (2 ounces) of anchovy fillets
2 cups of onions (about 2 large), sliced as thin as possible
1 tablespoon of caraway seeds
2 pounds of baking potatoes
(about 3 large), skins on, sliced as thin as possible
¼ teaspoon of salt
Fresh-ground black pepper to taste
1 cup of skim milk
1 cup of part-skim ricotta cheese

1. Melt 2 tablespoons of the butter in a large skillet over medium heat. Drain the anchovies, rinse them in a strainer, and chop them. Add the anchovies, onions, and caraway seeds to the butter and cook just until the onions are soft, about 10 minutes.
2. Combine the potatoes and the onion mixture, tossing to mix. Pour the mixture into a large shallow baking dish. Sprinkle salt and pepper over the top.
3. In a bowl, blend together the milk and ricotta cheese with a wire whisk. Pour this mixture over the potatoes; it will still be a little lumpy, but that's okay. Dot with the remaining ½ tablespoon of butter.
4. Bake at 400 degrees for 1 hour, or until top is nicely browned.

MAKES 12 SERVINGS.
Per serving: 157 calories, 16 mg. cholesterol, 2 g. dietary fiber, **4.5 g. fat,** 107 mg. sodium

*Squash-Zucchini-Mushroom Mix (Microwave)

2 onions, chopped
1 tablespoon of oil
2 tablespoons of water
1 pound each of zucchini and yellow squash, cut in ½-inch chunks
⅛ teaspoon of thyme
Fresh-ground black pepper to taste
8 ounces of fresh mushrooms, sliced thick

1. Sauté onions in oil and water for about 7 minutes on high in the microwave, until the onions are translucent.
2. Add the squashes, thyme, and black pepper and microwave on high for about 12 minutes, until vegetables are just tender, stirring halfway through the cooking time.
3. Add the mushrooms and cook 2 to 3 minutes more on high until the mushrooms are tender. Add more water in small amounts if necessary during cooking.

MAKES 10 SERVINGS.
Per serving: 37 calories, 0 cholesterol, 2 g. dietary fiber, **1.5 g. fat,** 3 mg. sodium

DESSERTS

Yes, you can have your cake and eat it too! If as a rule you will follow the guidelines of the T-Factor Diet, there is room for an occasional dessert, especially a comparatively low-fat dessert such as the ones contained in this section.

You can adapt many of your own favorite recipes as well to lower fat, "higher health" versions. Substitute whole-wheat flour at least in part for refined white flour, for higher fiber and higher nutrient content. Use fresh and dried fruits for sweetness and reduce refined sugar. Instead of making fatty pastry crusts with lard, butter, or vegetable shortening, learn to make crumb crusts with very little fat and honey, as in the scrumptious Pumpkin Cheesecake (page 201) and Chocolate Meringue Pie (see next page). The use of low-fat dairy products instead of their high-fat counterparts (skim milk instead of whole milk or cream, ricotta instead of cream cheese, for example) can reduce fat content considerably.

Of course, "moderation" is a key concept when it comes to sweets that also contain fat. With this in mind, you can enjoy a treat now and then without destroying your waistline or your arteries.

◆

*Chocolate Meringue Pie

1½ cups of graham cracker crumbs	¼ teaspoon of salt
2 tablespoons of honey	2 cups of skim milk
1 tablespoon of oil	1 egg, beaten
¾ cup of sugar	2 teaspoons of vanilla
6 tablespoons of cocoa powder	3 egg whites
⅓ cup of flour or 3 tablespoons of cornstarch	¼ teaspoon of cream of tartar
	½ teaspoon of vanilla
	6 tablespoons of sugar

1. Combine the graham cracker crumbs, honey, and oil. Mix well and press into a 9-inch pie pan. Bake for 10 minutes at 350 degrees.
2. Meanwhile, in a medium saucepan, combine the ¾ cup of sugar, cocoa powder, flour, and salt. Place over moderate heat and gradually stir in milk. Cook and stir until thickened and bubbly. Continue to cook 1 to 2 more minutes.
3. Remove from heat. Stir a small amount of the hot mixture into the beaten egg. Add egg to saucepan, return to heat, and cook 2 more minutes.
4. Stir in the 2 teaspoons of vanilla. Pour the mixture into the prepared crust.
5. To make topping, beat egg whites with cream of tartar and the ½ teaspoon of vanilla until the mixture forms soft peaks. Gradually add the 6 tablespoons of sugar, beating until glossy and the mixture forms stiff peaks.
6. Spread the topping over the filling. Bake at 350 degrees until golden brown, about 12 minutes.

MAKES 8 SERVINGS (⅛ OF 9-INCH PIE).
Per serving: 295 calories, 35 mg. cholesterol, 2.5 g. dietary fiber, **5.5 g. fat**, 265 mg. sodium

*Cocoa Pudding Cake

1 cup of all-purpose flour	2 tablespoons of oil
¾ cup of sugar	1 teaspoon of vanilla
2 tablespoons of cocoa powder	Nonstick vegetable cooking spray
2 teaspoons of baking powder	¾ cup of brown sugar
½ teaspoon of salt	¼ cup of cocoa powder
½ cup of skim milk	1¾ cups of hot water

1. Sift together the flour, sugar, 2 tablespoons of cocoa powder, baking powder, and salt.
2. Add the milk, oil, and vanilla, mixing by hand until smooth.
3. Pour into an 8×8×2-inch baking pan that has been sprayed with nonstick spray.
4. Combine the brown sugar, ¼ cup of cocoa powder, and water and pour over batter.
5. Bake at 350 degrees for 45 minutes.

MAKES 8 SERVINGS.
Per serving: 253 calories, 0 cholesterol, 1 g. dietary fiber, **4 g. fat**, 234 mg. sodium

*Elegant Pears

This is especially good with coffee liqueur. Experiment with your favorite liqueurs.

2 large pears	1 ounce of liqueur of choice
3 cups of water	1 cup of vanilla ice milk
½ cup of Hershey's chocolate syrup	

1. Wash pears and cut in half. Bring water to a boil. Add pear halves, reduce heat, and cover. Cook until pears are soft, about 10 to 15 minutes.

2. While pears are cooking, combine chocolate syrup and liqueur and heat in a small saucepan.
3. Drain pears and wipe off excess moisture. While still warm, top each pear half with ¼ cup of ice milk. Pour approximately 2 tablespoons of chocolate syrup mixture over pear and ice milk. Serve immediately.

MAKES 4 SERVINGS.
Per serving: 204 calories, 5 mg. cholesterol, 3.5 g. dietary fiber, 2 g. fat, 58 mg. sodium

*Lemon Meringue Pie

1½ cups of graham cracker crumbs
2 tablespoons of honey
1 tablespoon of oil
1¼ cups plus 3 tablespoons of sugar
3 tablespoons of cornstarch
3 tablespoons of all-purpose flour
Dash of salt

1½ cups of hot water
2 eggs, slightly beaten
½ teaspoon of grated lemon peel
⅓ cup of lemon juice
3 egg whites
¼ teaspoon of cream of tartar
½ teaspoon of vanilla
6 tablespoons of sugar

1. Combine the graham cracker crumbs, honey, and oil. Mix well and press into a 9-inch pan. Bake for 10 minutes at 350 degrees.
2. In a medium saucepan, combine the 1¼ cups plus 3 tablespoons of sugar, the cornstarch, flour, and salt. Turn the heat to medium high and begin gradually adding the hot water, stirring constantly. Cook and stir until thickened and bubbly. Continue to cook 2 minutes longer.
3. Remove from heat. Stir a small amount of the hot mixture into the 2 beaten eggs, then add the mixture to the saucepan, return to heat, and cook 2 minutes more, stirring constantly.
4. Stir in lemon peel. Gradually add lemon juice, mixing well. Pour into prepared crust.

5. To make topping, beat egg whites with cream of tartar and vanilla until soft peaks form. Gradually add the 6 tablespoons of sugar, beating until glossy and mixture forms stiff peaks.
6. Spread on top of pie. Bake at 350 degrees for about 12 minutes or until golden brown.

MAKES 8 SERVINGS (⅛ OF 9-INCH PIE).
Per serving: 334 calories, 69 mg. cholesterol, 2 g. dietary fiber, 5.5 g. fat, 176 mg. sodium

*Poppy-Seed Cake

⅓ cup of vegetable oil	½ teaspoon of baking soda
¾ cup of sugar	⅔ cup of plain, nonfat yogurt
2 eggs, separated	⅓ cup of poppy seeds
1 teaspoon of vanilla	Nonstick vegetable cooking spray
1 cup of whole-wheat flour	
½ teaspoon of salt	

1. Blend the oil and sugar in a large bowl. Add the egg yolks one at a time, beating well. Add the vanilla.
2. In another bowl, sift together the flour, salt, and baking soda. Alternately fold the flour mixture and the yogurt into the oil and sugar mixture. Set aside.
3. Beat the egg whites until stiff. Fold into the batter. Fold in the poppy seeds.
4. Spray an 8-inch tube pan with nonstick cooking spray, and dust lightly with whole-wheat flour. Pour the batter into the pan.
5. Bake at 350 degrees for about 45 minutes, until top is nicely browned, and a toothpick inserted in the center comes out clean.

MAKES 20 SERVINGS.
Per serving: 131 calories, 34 mg. cholesterol, 1 g. dietary fiber, 7 g. fat, 109 mg. sodium

◆

Pumpkin Cheesecake

1½ cups of graham cracker
   crumbs
2 tablespoons of honey
1 tablespoon of oil
2 whole eggs
3 egg whites
8 ounces of softened
   Neufchâtel cheese

12 ounces of part-skim or "lite"
   ricotta cheese
½ cup of plain, nonfat yogurt
1 can (15 ounces) of pumpkin
¾ cup of sugar
1 teaspoon of vanilla
¼ teaspoon of nutmeg
¼ teaspoon of cinnamon

1. Combine the graham cracker crumbs, honey, and oil. Mix well and press into a 9-inch pie pan.
2. In a mixing bowl, beat together the eggs and egg whites until foamy. Add all other ingredients. Beat until smooth and creamy.
3. Pour into the crust and bake at 350 degrees until slightly browned and firm in the center, about 45 minutes.

Variations: Omit pumpkin, nutmeg, and cinnamon. After baking, top with cherries, blueberries, or other fruit.

MAKES 10 SERVINGS.
Per serving: 294 calories, 102 mg. cholesterol, 2.5 g. dietary fiber, **12 g. fat,** 336 mg. sodium

BEVERAGES

Research has shown that diet drinks are often the bane of overweight people. Though low in calories and fat, drinking them tends to keep alive a person's taste for sweets, which can in turn lead to binging on fat-filled desserts. Studies have shown that people who drink diet drinks do *not* lose weight and keep it off as well as those who don't drink them!

My first recommendation for no-cal beverages is WATER. Water is actually our most essential nutrient. We cannot live without it.

If, like many people, you can't stand the taste of tap water, it may be that the chemicals added in processing it in your town have ruined the taste. Try either bottled spring water or install an activated-charcoal, bacteriostatic filter for your kitchen faucet to remove chlorine and other objectionable organic matter from your water. You can also try sodium-free seltzer water, either plain or with added lemon, lime, or other flavors, but with no sugar added. Check labels carefully.

I don't recommend drinking distilled water, as essential minerals have been removed.

Fruit and vegetable juices, herb teas, and punches made from combinations of these are also good substitutes for soft drinks.

Coffee and black tea, of course, are standard no-cal beverages. Add a little half-and-half or milk if desired, and count up the fat grams accordingly. As long as you limit yourself to no more than two or three cups a day, you will probably suffer no ill effects from the caffeine. Because of increasing demand, many different coffees are now being decaffeinated, but if you use them, use water processed rather than those that are decaffeinated with methylene chloride. The package will carry the words "water processed" if this process has been used. Methylene chloride is carcinogenic.

Iced Fruited Herb Tea

We like a combination of raspberry, apple, orange or lemon, and mint teas in this drink.

16 herb tea bags—your choice	1 quart of unsweetened orange juice
1 quart of boiling water	2 quarts of cold water

1. Soak the tea bags in the boiling water for 20 to 30 minutes.
2. In a gallon jug, combine the orange juice and cold water. Remove the teabags and add the hot tea to the juice mixture. Stir. Chill for at least 1 hour.

MAKES 16 SERVINGS.
Per serving: 56 calories, 0 cholesterol, 0.5 g. dietary fiber, **0 fat,** 1 mg. sodium

Spiced Tea

Pre-mixed instant teas and lemonades are usually high in sugar as well as other additives. Here is a tangy alternative that lets you control the amount of sugar. Serve hot or cold.

4 cups of brewed black tea (4 tea bags)	1 to 2 teaspoons of sugar
	1 teaspoon of ground cloves
2 cinnamon sticks	1 to 2 teaspoons of lemon juice, or 4 slices of fresh lemon
1 cup of unsweetened orange juice	

1. When brewing the tea, place the cinnamon sticks in the same pan or teapot. When the tea is ready, discard the cinnamon sticks
2. Add the remaining ingredients to the pot and serve, or

chill first in a pitcher and serve over ice cubes if you want iced tea.

MAKES 4 SERVINGS.

Per serving: 38 calories, 0 cholesterol, 0 dietary fiber, **0 fat**, 9 mg. sodium

7

The T-Factor Activity Program

I've heard it both ways. Successful people who have lost weight and are keeping it off say, "It's the physical activity that's doing it. I'm not really dieting anymore. My weight stays off as long as I'm active." Unsuccessful people often say just the opposite: "I started an activity program. Three to five times a week, in fact. I didn't lose a pound. I even gained!"

Both are right. Exercise can be the key that makes weight management a snap. However, under certain conditions, exercise can keep you fat. Exercise may even help you gain weight—fat weight. I've talked with many persons who have lost weight only to regain it in spite of religious attendance at their fitness and aerobic dancing classes.[1]

Before I explain how this can occur, I want to say, without qualification, that daily physical activity combined with the T-Factor Diet provides *an absolute guarantee that you will burn body fat and lose weight. In addition, continuing to apply T-Factor principles to your diet and activity program is an absolute guarantee that you will not regain any weight.*

[1] We have had many people enter the Vanderbilt Weight Management Program who have regained weight after previous diets in spite of participation in fitness, calisthenics, and aerobic dance classes. However, no formal research of which I am aware clearly demonstrates how certain forms of exercise, in combination with a high-fat diet, promote weight gain. My discussion and the examples using myself in this chapter are based on other facts pertaining to exercise physiology and theory.

So, what are the conditions under which physical activity can impede weight loss? How can I provide you with such a contrasting guarantee that you will lose weight and keep it off with the T-Factor Activity Program?

Remember that the key to losing fat weight is to burn more fat in your fuel mixture each day than you take in through your diet. Under these conditions, the fat must be withdrawn from your fat cells. Obviously the converse is true: You will gain fat weight easily if you take in more fat than you are burning in your fuel mixture. The surplus fat in your diet ends up in your fat cells. The key is *fat in* vs. *fat out*. The carbohydrate in your diet will play little role in gaining fat weight since so little of it, under normal circumstances, is turned to fat.

Can you see how someone who eats a high-fat diet—in fact, no higher than the typical American diet—*may be replacing all the fat burned through physical activity because of that high-fat diet and never end up losing an ounce of fat weight?*

But the plot thickens. There is a rather complex relationship between diet and activity when it comes to reducing body fat.

Some physical activities do not use body fat as the major component of the fuel mixture that powers them. Other physical activities do. Unfortunately, many of the activity programs that overweight people turn to in an effort to control their weight do not burn body fat as the major component of the fuel mixture.

PUT THE WRONG ACTIVITY PROGRAM TOGETHER WITH THE TYPICAL AMERICAN DIET AND YOU CAN PREVENT WEIGHT LOSS. INDEED, YOU MAY POSSIBLY GAIN WEIGHT!

FACTS ABOUT PHYSICAL ACTIVITY

Some activities burn fat as the major component in the fuel mixture. These activities are most helpful in controlling your weight. Some activities burn carbohydrate (glucose) as the major component in the fuel mixture. THESE ACTIVITIES CAN ALSO BE HELPFUL IN CONTROLLING BODY WEIGHT *PROVIDED* YOU ARE EATING

ACCORDING TO T-FACTOR PRINCIPLES. However, if, after losing weight, you combine carbohydrate-burning exercise with a return to your previous high-fat eating habits, you can regain fat weight quite easily.

Here is how this works.

Start-stop activities at a moderate to vigorous intensity, sometimes referred to as anaerobic activities,[2] will burn in the vicinity of 60 to 70 percent carbohydrate (in the form of glucose) in the fuel mixture, and 30 to 40 percent fat. The more vigorous and taxing each spurt of activity, the more carbohydrate it requires. In fact, among top athletes, a 100-yard dash or a session of high-intensity interval training (alternating laps at top speed and recovery speed) can use 90 percent or more of carbohydrate in the fuel mixture.

But most of us will never exercise at the very highest anaerobic intensity, so I will use the more conservative 60 to 70 percent estimate for carbohydrate burned during our quick start-and-stop activities. Thus, for most of us working about as hard as we care to, sprinting in soccer, football, tennis, racquetball, and working out in most aerobic dance and calisthenic classes, we will force our bodies to burn about 70 percent carbohydrate during any given exercise period, and only 30 percent fat.

I'll show you how this kind of activity combined with improper diet could lead to weight gain in a moment, but first let's contrast this with gentle jogging and brisk walking.

Steady-state activities which move your whole body through space or which require continuous movement of the largest muscles in your thighs and buttocks, some-

---

[2] Anaerobic activities happen so quickly that the energy which drives them is burned without the presence of oxygen. This is possible because your muscles store some fuel in a form that can be used even when the heart and circulating blood cannot supply enough fuel and oxygen to keep up with the demand. Start-stop activities of this kind, including calisthenics, aerobic dance, racket sports, power lifting, and other sports that require sprinting, are characterized by wide swings in your breathing and heart rates. Because these activities have burned fuel without the presence of oxygen, they put you into what is called an "oxygen deficit." That is, in order to catch up and restore energy to the emptied muscles, your heart must continue to beat rapidly and you must breath more heavily for some time after you finish each burst of activity.

times called "aerobic activities," *burn between 50 and 60 percent fat in the fuel mixture and only about 40 to 50 percent carbohydrate.* In steady-state aerobic activities that burn fat at this level, such as jogging and walking, your heart and breathing rates go up, level out, and stay there throughout the activity period. The activities are called aerobic because you burn fuel only as fast as you can supply oxygen for its combustion. The activity feels "moderate" to you—you breathe harder, but you don't get "out of breath." You can do it for forty-five minutes to an hour and while you may get tired in that period of time, you do not become exhausted.

To summarize:

START-STOP ACTIVITIES ARE CARBOHY-DRATE-BURNING ACTIVITIES. IN GENERAL, THEY WILL BURN BETWEEN 60 AND 70 PERCENT CARBOHYDRATE AND 30 TO 40 PERCENT FAT IN THE FUEL MIXTURE.

CONTINUOUS WHOLE-BODY MOVEMENTS ARE FAT-BURNING ACTIVITIES. THEY WILL BURN BETWEEN 50 AND 60 PERCENT FAT IN THE FUEL MIXTURE AND 40 TO 50 PERCENT CAR-BOHYDRATE.

For reference purposes I call the carbohydrate-fueled activities "carb burners" for short, and fat-fueled activities are simply "fat burners."

To demonstrate how diet and activity interact and can either facilitate or interfere with fat loss, let's use tennis and brisk walking, with myself as an example.

In an hour of singles tennis I burn about 500 calories. That will be typical of a man weighing about 153 pounds (my present weight after adopting the T-Factor Diet) who plays at a strong competitive level and who spends his time chasing tennis balls rather than socializing or just picking the balls up after very short rallies. A woman weighing 20 or 30 pounds less than I do may burn only about 400 to 450 calories in the hour since it takes fewer calories to carry the lighter body around. Heavier people will burn more.

Assuming I play quite vigorously, about 70 percent of the calories burned in an hour will come out of my glycogen stores and 30 percent will come out of my fat stores. Thus, about 350 of the calories will be supplied by carbohydrate, and about 150 from fat.

When I walk briskly at 4 miles per hour (or 15 minutes per mile) I burn approximately 400 calories in an hour. This figure will be typical of a man weighing 153 pounds, and, as before, a woman weighing 20 or 30 pounds less may burn 50 to 100 calories less in this period of time. Heavier people will burn more.

I am in pretty good shape and walking at 4 miles per hour elevates my heart rate only about 12 beats above my resting level. That is, it's a comfortable, steady-state aerobic activity. In an hour of walking, when compared with tennis, there will be a change in the ratio of fat to carbohydrate burned—I will burn up to about 60 percent fat to 40 percent carbohydrate. I will burn about 240 fat calories and 160 carbohydrate calories.

Summarizing again: In an hour of vigorous singles tennis I will burn about 350 calories in carbohydrate and 150 calories in fat; in an hour of walking I will burn 160 calories in carbohydrate and 240 calories in fat.

Now, it is important to remember, first of all, that the depletion of carbohydrate in my muscles and liver stores is a stronger factor in the arousal of appetite than is the loss of fat from my fat cells.[3] I am likely to be somewhat hungrier after tennis than after walking. But, second, and much more important in determining whether I gain or lose fat, is whether I am eating a high-fat diet or following the T-Factor Diet.

If I eat a high-fat diet such as is consumed by a majority of overweight persons in this country, which contains about 40 percent of calories from fat and 45 percent from carbohydrate, by the time I have replaced the 350 carbohydrate calories I will also have eaten ⅘ths as much fat, or roughly about 310 fat calories ($^{40}/_{45} = ^{8}/_{9}$). *That's 160 more fat calories than I burned during the exercise.*

Unless I find a way to burn more fat than carbohydrate during the rest of the day, I am going to gain weight.

If you have been weight stable with an exercise program that emphasizes carbohydrate-burning activity, it

[3] The role of glycogen depletion in the arousal of appetite is discussed in Chapter 10.

means that you do burn more fat than carbohydrate during the rest of the day. This compensation is possible because just sitting still or sleeping, while not burning many calories at all, still burns a bit more fat than carbohydrate. You do tend to sit and sleep for longer than you dance or stretch.

But if you have gained weight after losing it on a calorie-reduced diet, and you expected your calisthenics, dance class, or tennis match to prevent it, now you know why your exercise program didn't work.

Now let's take a look at what happens when brisk walking is combined with the T-Factor Diet. I'll use myself again as an example when I first adopted the T-Factor Diet, when walking was my only exercise activity.

When I limited fat intake to about 60 grams a day, I tended to eat about 65 percent of calories from carbohydrates, 15 percent from protein, and about 20 percent from fat. In other words, I was taking in about 3 calories of carbohydrate for every calorie of fat. By the time I'd replaced the 160 calories of carbohydrate that I used in walking for an hour, I had eaten only 50 to 60 calories in fat. This meant that, in order to satisfy the need to refill my glycogen stores, I ended up eating only about 220 calories in all (160 to replace the carbohydrate plus about 60 in fat), which, theoretically, should have resulted in a loss of about 180 calories from my fat stores in that hour of activity (240 fat calories burned during the hour's walk, with 60 replaced). I am sure this emphasis on fat-burning activity during my injury period played a role in losing those 7 pounds, as I described in Chapter 4.

The T-Factor formula is also protecting me from weight gain now that I have resumed playing tennis: Adhering to the same 3 to 1 ratio of carbohydrate to fat in my diet, by the time I have replaced the 350 carbohydrate calories burned in an hour of tennis, I do not consume more fat than the 150 or so fat calories that I have burned in the fuel mixture during the game. Thus, I do not regain any weight.

Can you also see how fat burners make it so much easier to take off body fat and keep it off when they are combined with the T-Factor Diet? When you focus primarily on maximum fat-burning activities in your exercise program, and combine this with a low-fat, high-carbohydrate diet, you keep your glycogen stores at maximum, your appetite satisfied, and your body fat at its healthiest minimum.

THE IDEAL FAT-BURNING ACTIVITY PROGRAM

The fitter you are, the more fat you burn!

Take any aerobic activity: walking, jogging, bicycling, swimming, rowing, cross-country skiing, or any other continuous whole-body movement. If you are out of shape, brisk movement will require considerable effort. You will burn carbohydrate as the principal component in your fuel mixture when you first begin to engage in any of these activities. However, as you increase in fitness, *all of these activities become fat burners*.

How do you develop the ideal fat-burning activity program and increase fitness?

From a physiological standpoint, the ideal program consists in part of a combination of exercises that vary in intensity. This is necessary because, in order to build endurance so that higher levels of exertion begin to feel more and more moderate, you have to exert yourself occasionally.

Here is an example of how walking was transformed from a carb to fat burner, and how it was done by a group of overweight women in the Vanderbilt Weight Management Program. The research subjects were in their thirties and forties and approximately 60 pounds overweight on the average. On the first test walk at 3 miles per hour, their heart rates averaged 138 beats per minute at a 3-mph pace (20 minutes per mile) and most of the women were tired and needed to stop after only 20 minutes. Walking at this level of exertion was, for them, a carbohydrate-burning activity.

Over the next 12 weeks the women walked 6 days a week, with two objectives: Increase time to 45 minutes, then increase speed. In order to increase speed, as their condition improved, they began to intersperse periods of brisk walking, at a 4-mph pace (15 minutes per mile). By the end of the 12 weeks, all of the women were able to walk for 45 minutes at 3 mph without stopping, and many could maintain a 4-mph pace for a good part of the time.

We then did a second test at the 3-mph pace. Their heart rates at this pace had decreased to 112 beats per minute. Walking at 3 mph had become a fat-burning activity, and I estimate that the percentage of fat burned while walking at this pace increased from 30 to at least 50 percent.

THUS, AS PHYSICAL CONDITION IMPROVES, THE FAT-BURNING POTENTIAL OF SIMILAR CONTINUOUS WHOLE-BODY MOVEMENT IMPROVES.

In addition, because the women had been able to increase total walking each day from approximately 1 mile to 3 miles, on the average, the total number of fat calories burned in activity increased significantly: from about 30 (of the total 100 burned in about 20 minutes of walking at the start of the program) to about 150 (of the total 300 burned in the 45 to 60 minutes at the end of 12 weeks).

FAT BURNING WAS THUS ABOUT FIVE TIMES HIGHER THAN AT THE START OF THE WALKING PROGRAM. This is why physical activity of the fat-burning type is so important to weight loss and maintenance. IN ADDITION, BECAUSE TOTAL ACTIVITY WAS GREATER, THEY WERE ABLE TO BURN EVEN MORE CARBOHYDRATE THAN AT THE START OF THE PROGRAM. With daily physical activity you can truly eat more, including more carbohydrate, and still draw more and more body fat from storage and end up weighing less.

Although we know that you will burn more fat calories relative to carbohydrate calories as your condition improves and your heart rate goes down in any physical activity at a given intensity, as it did in the women I've used in my example, it is not possible to give you a precise estimate of the fat-burning to carbohydrate-burning ratio of physical activities by heart rate. It is an entirely individual matter that can be determined only in the laboratory. By that I mean that the same heart rate in two different individuals can have an entirely different implication with respect to both total calories burned in any unit of time and the ratio of fat to glucose burned in the fuel mixture.

But you can be sure of this as you become more active: *In any steady-state activity, as your cardiovascular condition improves, any decrease in heart rate for a given intensity of exercise means more fat burned.*

You can increase your cardiovascular endurance by exercising periodically in what is called the "training range."

THE TRAINING HEART RATE

You can get a rough idea of both your physical condition and your fat-burning ratio from a consideration of what is called the "training heart rate."

Although some kind of moderate to brisk physical activity almost every day for 45 minutes to an hour is extremely helpful if not essential to weight management, if you wish to improve cardiovascular fitness to a greater extent and achieve a high level of fat-burning potential in your more moderate physical activity, you must occasionally exercise at a more intense level.

You can achieve significant cardiovascular benefits by getting your heart rate into the "training range" about four times a week for about 20 to 30 minutes each time. That's all it takes. Any whole-body movement, or use of the major muscles in your buttocks and thighs, that you can perform continuously for that period of time is about as good as any other: walking, bicycling, swimming, rowing (including leg movement), or gentle jogging if you are already at desirable weight. When you exercise in the training range, you bring your heart to a level of exertion that increases its capacity to pump blood with each beat while at the same time increasing the ability of your circulatory system to handle the increased blood flow. In addition, the oxygen-carrying capacity of the blood is increased as well as the ability of your muscles to extract that oxygen and use it to power physical movement. All of this means that physical activity at any given level of intensity begins to feel easier and easier.

For example, at very high levels of fitness, runners

experience little or no elevation in heart rate when going from sitting to walking. In my own case, my heart rate goes from about 54 beats per minute while sitting to 60 when walking at 3 miles per hour and to about 66 at 4 miles per hour. The average sedentary person who embarks on a walking fitness program will notice, at about 12 weeks, about a 20 percent reduction in cardiovascular effort while walking at any given speed (just like the women in my example above). Frequently, but not always, there is a reduction in resting heart rate as well.

There is a simple rule of thumb that you can use to bring your heart into its training range.

Subtract your age from 220.

(On the average, that will be about the fastest your heart can beat during an all-out sprint. Speed decreases with age.)

Multiply that figure by 0.60 (which is 60 percent).

The figure you obtain is the low end of the training range.

Multiply the same figure (220 minus your age) by 0.85 (which is 85 percent).

That is the high end of your training range.

If you exercise within this range for 20 to 30 minutes, four times a week, you will soon begin to experience an improvement in cardiovascular fitness.

To measure your improvement, take your pulse at certain levels of exertion—for example, while walking at 3 and at 4 miles per hour. Over time you will find that your heart rate decreases while performing the same intensity of exercise.

Table 7-1 presents the training levels for age groups by five-year increments in age (p. 215).

Starting Out

When you first begin a training program, stick with the low end of the training range, and do not exceed the upper level of your training range. To achieve very high levels of fitness, however, you do have to exercise at the high end of the training range for 20 to 30 minutes four times a week. Only people in excellent condition should do this, and if you

TABLE 7-1

MAXIMUM HEART RATES AND TRAINING RANGES

Age	Maximum Heart Rate (beats per minute)	60% Level (beats per minute)	85% Level (beats per minute)
20	200	120	170
25	195	117	166
30	190	114	162
35	185	111	157
40	180	108	153
45	175	105	149
50	170	102	145
55	165	99	140
60	160	96	136
65	155	93	132
70	150	90	128

are overweight and out of condition you should definitely check with your physician if you intend to exercise strenuously. It can be dangerous for people with cardiovascular disease and overweight people may be somewhat more likely to have undiagnosed cardiovascular disease than thin people.

REMEMBER THE FIRST RULE OF FITNESS: NEVER HURT YOURSELF!

While world-class athletes must tax themselves to reach maximum levels of skill and fitness, good health does not demand it. In fact, I don't know of any world-class athlete who has not at one time or another had an injury that interfered with training for at least a brief period of time. That's the price they must pay to win championships. Unfortunately, their injuries may haunt them for the rest of their lives and actually be detrimental to their health in the long run. You and I don't need this.

Making Progress

As your condition improves, test yourself at somewhat higher levels of exertion. Listen to your body. Pain is a

TABLE 7-2

APPROXIMATE ENERGY COSTS IN EACH 15 MINUTES OF VARIOUS ACTIVITIES [a]

Activity	Calories per 15 Minutes
Aerobic dancing	105
Badminton	99
*Ballroom dancing, continuous	53
Basketball	141
*Canoeing (recreational)	45
*Cleaning house (steady movement)	63
*Climbing hills (steady pace)	123
*Cooking dinner	47
*Cycling	
5.5 mph, level ground	66
9.4 mph, level ground	102
Football	135
*Gardening (raking)	56
*Golf (walking—no cart)	87
Gymnastics	88
*Horseback riding	
walking	42
trotting (English style)	113
Judo	199
*Piano playing	41
*Rowing (machine, fast pace)	105
*Running	
11 min. 30 sec. per mile	138
10 min. per mile	174
9 min. per mile	197
8 min. per mile	213
7 min. per mile	234
6 min. per mile	260
Skiing	
*cross-country, walking pace	146
downhill	101
Squash	216

Activity	Calories per 15 Minutes
*Swimming	
freestyle, moderate pace	143
sidestroke	125
Table tennis	69
Tennis	111
*Typing (electric typewriter)	27
Volleyball	51
*Walking	
3 mph, level ground	66
4 mph, level ground	99
downstairs, steady pace	50
upstairs, slow steady pace	151

[a]Energy costs are calculated for persons weighing 150 pounds. For each 10 pounds more or less than 150 pounds, add or subtract 7 percent, respectively, from these figures. Activities marked with an asterisk (*) are fat burners—between 50 and 60 percent of the calories listed will be withdrawn from your fat cells. About 30 percent of the calories listed for unmarked items are fueled by fat.

signal to pull back. A feeling of greater effort in and of itself, without pain, is not. However, a bit of *strain*, not pain, is required to reach higher levels of fitness. When you get comfortable exercising at the 60 percent level in the training range, experiment with reaching up to the 70 or 75 percent level. That's plenty high enough. Do not continue in the face of pain. In the end, you can hurt yourself and not be able to exercise at all for a period of time. That can be demoralizing and depressing.

Whatever activity you choose, and I will recommend walking at first, pay special attention to muscular aches and pains. There is far more likelihood of musculoskeletal injury than of any other kind of injury at the start of an exercise program. There is also an increased likelihood of injury any time you make a sudden increase in intensity or duration. Moderation and gradualness should be your guide words.

WHY WALK FOR HEALTH AND SLIMNESS?

Any continuous whole-body movement is about as good as any other for burning body fat and for combining with the T-Factor Diet for permanent weight management.

Walking is easiest and most convenient for most people. Walking burns more calories with less perceived effort than other activities. That's because most of us do at least a little walking every day and that gives us a base to build on. At a 3-mph pace we burn about 100 total calories every 20 minutes. At a 4-mph pace we burn about 100 total calories every 15 minutes.

If walking is impossible for you, then bicycling or rowing, in which you move your legs as well as your arms, is excellent. It requires more perceived effort to burn the same number of calories on a bicycle or on a rowing machine until you become accustomed to those means of exercise. Ski machines can also be good, but don't believe the exaggerated claims for calorie burning that some manufacturers make. No one but highly trained athletes can approach even 1000 calories an hour of energy expenditure, much less 600 calories in 20 minutes!

And, by the way, fitness for exercise is quite specific to each exercise. As a jogger, I hardly notice my heart rate after an hour at a pace of a mile in 10 minutes (6 mph), but at the same level of oxygen consumption on a bicycle I feel considerable strain in my legs after only 20 minutes. That's because I don't use the leg or buttock muscles in the same way for jogging as I do on a bicycle. And, when it comes to swimming freestyle one length of an Olympic-sized pool, I'm out of breath. I occasionally ride a bicycle, but I never swim even though swimming is an excellent exercise. I just don't care for it. However, despite the claims of some experts that swimming won't work for weight loss and might even lead to an increase in body-fat storage, *swimming can be an excellent aid to weight management and overall health and fitness*. I will dispel some myths about swimming below.

If you choose walking as your T-Factor activity, use the principle of gradualness and start out by walking about 15 minutes at a time, at whatever pace feels good to you. *Increase time before you increase your speed.*

Work up to 45 minutes or an hour over a one- or two-month period. For both physiological and psychological reasons (the latter are discussed in Chapter 8), I don't think you can ever fall in love with physical activity of any kind unless you learn to do it well and do it or some other alternating activity for at least 45 minutes to an hour *on an almost daily basis. And the activity or activities have to end up feeling easy to you.*

As you recall, however, for training purposes, you have to occasionally exert yourself. The rules call for you to kick yourself up to a brisk pace for 20 minutes or so, four times a week. As your condition improves, this will result in a feeling of tremendous exhilaration, not exhaustion. For training purposes, check your heart rate occasionally to see that during the periods in which you pick up speed you are actually obtaining training benefits. However, walking is primarily a time to escape the regimentation you may be obligated to apply to the rest of your daily activities. I think you should feel free to bend the rules because, in my experience, people accomplish more by using a whimsical training approach and a "feeling good" principle rather than any mathematical formula or mechanical method. Listen to your body and whenever it says go faster, GO. And when it says slow down, SLOW DOWN.

As I said before, the fitter you get, the more fat you burn in any given aerobic activity. Even without fussing over your heart rate, you can tell that the ratio of fat to carbohydrate that is being burned is increasing when, at any given intensity, the feeling of effort decreases.

And now another important point:

THE LONGER YOU GO THE MORE FAT YOU BURN.

When you first start out in any activity, including walking and other aerobic activities, a major part of the fuel mix is drawn from your glycogen pool. As you continue moving in the steady state, your body switches tanks, as it were, and begins to draw from its fat stores. The fitter you are, the sooner the switch takes place; and the longer you go, the more fat relative to glycogen that you will use. This is one reason why walking for an hour is better than walking for twelve different 5-minute segments during the day. BUT IF BRIEF WALKS ARE ALL YOU CAN MANAGE MOST OF THE TIME, DO THEM. THEN, TRY TO GET A FEW LONGER WALKS IN DURING THE WEEK SO THAT YOUR FITNESS WILL IMPROVE. THIS WILL MAXIMIZE FAT BURNING EVEN IN YOUR SHORTER WALKS.

Once again let me emphasize the importance of the T-Factor Diet in any case where physical activity cannot be pursued for at least 45 minutes at a stretch, or where carb burners form a major part of your exercise program.

I am sure that you are interested in having a list of activities that indicates the ratio of fat to carbohydrate that tends to be burned in the fuel mixture. You will find this in Table 7-2, where I list approximate calories burned per 15 minutes according to standard tables and indicate which activities are fat burners. Outside of the laboratory, however, it is impossible to determine the exact ratio of fat to carbohydrate that is being burned in any given case because there are such large individual differences, some of which, as you now know, are a function of fitness level. The figures given in the footnote to the table assume a level of fitness that you will reach if you customarily perform that particular activity.

AN INCREASE IN EXERCISE TIME OR INTENSITY CAN LEAD TO A BRIEF GAIN OF A FEW POUNDS

If at any time you get turned on and suddenly increase your exercise time or intensity a significant amount, say, by 50 percent, you may gain a couple of pounds overnight. This will be gone in a matter of one to two days. It occurs because a sudden increase in exercise—increasing your walking from 3 to 4½ miles on a weekend hike, for example—will cause your exercised muscles to take in an extra load of glycogen from subsequent meals. Since glycogen is stored with 3 to 4 parts water, it means a considerable weight gain. I gained 2 pounds overnight when I took my first 6-mile run after being accustomed to only 2 or 3 miles per session.

Similarly, if you develop any aches or pains, accompanied by any inflammation of the muscles or joints, it means a gain in water weight since the inflamed area will retain some water.

WHAT ABOUT TIME OF DAY?

Any time that's best for you, in terms of convenience and good feelings, is always the best time to exercise!

But there is evidence that exercise before meals burns the most body fat. That's because the body tends to adjust its fuel mixture to the diet, and, following a typical high-carbohydrate T-Factor meal, it will tend to burn additional carbohydrate. Before meals, your glycogen stores are relatively low, and to conserve glycogen, your body tends to increase its use of fat as fuel.

The combination of walking before meals, which will maximize fat in the fuel mix, and sticking to the T-Factor Diet, which replaces glycogen without replacing the burned fat, will lead to the quickest and greatest permanent fat loss.

Because you are at your lowest ebb in glycogen storage before breakfast, walking before breakfast may lead to the greatest use of fat as fuel. This will be especially true following a cup of coffee or other caffeinated beverage. Caffeine increases the flow of fatty acids from your fat cells. However, if drinking coffee or walking on a completely empty stomach makes you uncomfortable, try eating a slice of toast or a few crackers first. This is what I do before my morning walk or jog. I feel much better with a little something more than coffee inside.

EXERCISE AND APPETITE

Depending on a number of factors, exercise can either decrease or increase appetite.

In sedentary persons who are out-eating their energy needs and gaining weight, exercise may help reduce non–hunger-related overeating. Exercise, by raising body temperature, decreasing the flow of saliva, and diverting blood from the internal organs to the muscles, decreases appetite in the short term. Then, when appetite returns following exercise, it seems to be better attuned to the amount of energy you are expending each day than it is in the sedentary person. In other words, people who exercise tend to eat in a way that does not lead to an increase in weight. It's as though mother nature, in ways that we are unaware of, keeps our bodies adapted to the physical demands we make on them. The active person needs a thinner body in order to be efficient in activity, so appetite becomes regulated to keep you thin. This mysterious adaptive mechanism goes out of whack in the sedentary person.

But certain forms of exercise, under certain conditions, can also increase appetite over its accustomed level. You recall that appetite is, to a large extent, regulated by our glycogen stores. With a steady, ongoing exercise program to which we have become accustomed, glycogen stores fluctuate within the accustomed range together with our appetites, and all is in balance. But we can exceed the usual range and really turn on appetite when we make a drastic change in the nature of our activity.

This was brought home to me the very first time I did a complete strength-training workout under the guidance of an instructor at the YMCA. He was demonstrating the equipment in the weight room, so that I would know what to do on future visits, and I did several sets of exercises covering both the lower and upper body. I did all exercises to virtual exhaustion for all the muscle groups. (Normally you would do upper body on one day, lower body on another.)

I went to my office at the university after the workout, and about an hour or so after arriving, I became ravenous. I have rarely had such an appetite in my life. It was a completely different sensation compared with other times when I have been hungry after going a long time between meals. It reduced me to near criminal activity: I went sneaking around the psychology department, looking for food in my colleagues' offices and in the secretaries' offices. I think the near complete depletion of my muslce glycogen stores was responsible for this. In addition, there may have been an increased need for some protein for muscle repairs, since this was the first time I had ever lifted weights.

Fortunately, one of the secretaries had a package of peanut butter crackers (!), which she gave to me, and my appetite was satisfied until lunch. But once again, as with the sudden increase in running mileage, my glycogen stores were replenished above baseline and I ended up a couple of pounds heavier the next day.

Will strength training interfere with weight loss and fat loss on the T-Factor Diet?

Power lifting—that is, heavy weight lifting with quick explosive movements to exhaustion for each muscle group—burns primarily carbohydrate in the fuel mixture. If you want to lose weight and body fat, and you include power lifting in your regimen, YOU MUST BE SURE THAT YOU FOLLOW THE T-FACTOR DIET in order to replenish carbohydrate without an overconsumption of fat, since power lifting is not a fat-burning activity. I do, however, encourage you to follow my moderate endurance strength-training program (Appendix B) because it will tone you up and you will look and feel better for doing it. Light endurance training, rather than power lifting, will not affect fat loss or weight loss adversely.

Should you walk with weights in your hands, or use some artificial "power" motion? I would approach both of these options cautiously. Carrying light weights (1 pound) can help improve cardiovascular condition more rapidly and build a little more muscular endurance, but I have known persons who sustained joint injuries and lower back pain by adding weights while they walked. Race walking, however, has been a life saver for many joggers who have injured themselves running, so if you learn the motion correctly, you probably won't injure yourself race walking. Simply swinging your arms any old way that feels good to you while walking can significantly increase the intensity of your workout and build endurance. Test out all changes in your natural walking style gingerly, and let your experience be your guide.

THE SWIMMING CONTROVERSY

Noted experts have claimed that you can't lose body fat if you take up swimming as the main component of your exercise program. This is simply not true.

The reason some experts claim that swimming is not a good exercise for weight control is that the temperature of the pool, being perhaps 20 or more degrees cooler than your body, encourages the body to retain the layer of surface fat that lies just under your skin. In thin people who may have little to begin with, swimming may help add a bit of surface fat. This occurs to help prevent heat loss as your body struggles to maintain its internal temperature at around 98.6 degrees Fahrenheit.

However, swimming, when it becomes as easy as walking or jogging for you, is actually a fat-burning exercise, and the struggle to maintain internal temperature is also fueled by fat to a large extent. In combination with the T-Factor Diet, you are assured of burning more fat in your fuel mixture than you are eating if you make swimming your favorite exercise. But you *will* tend to retain a bit more surface body fat than if you walk, jog, or ride a bicycle.

Although I have never learned to be comfortable in the water, I have spoken with persons for whom swimming is as easy and automatic as walking. They can become completely entranced as they glide back and forth in the pool. It's as restful and refreshing as meditation for them. If you have difficulty coordinating your breathing with your strokes and this prevents you from becoming relaxed and enjoying a swim, you may find that learning to use a snorkle will put you completely at ease.

HOW TO DETERMINE THE EQUIVALENCE OF DIFFERENT EXERCISES

I am often asked how a person can determine the equivalence, in terms of calories or fat burned, when they perform different exercises. The best way to do this is to use your pulse rate as your guide. It's done in this way:

Go for a walk at 3 miles per hour (1 mile in 20 minutes) and, after about 5 minutes, measure your pulse rate. Walking at 3 mph burns about three times the calories of sitting still. Assuming a 50/50 ratio of fat to carbohydrate in your fuel mixture, it burns three times the fat as well as three times the carbohydrate as sitting still. Whenever you reach this pulse rate in any other activity in which you are reasonably comfortable, you will be burning about the same number of calories as you do while walking at 3 mph, and half those calories are coming out of your fat cells.

If you are capable of it, walk for 5 minutes at 4 mph (1

mile in 15 minutes) and take your pulse rate. Walking at 4 mph burns almost five times the calories of sitting still, and, assuming that you are in good condition, we can again assume about a 50/50 mixture of fat to carbohydrate in your fuel mixture.[4] Whenever you reach this pulse rate in any other activity in which you are reasonably comfortable, you will be burning about the same number of calories as you do while walking at 4 mph, and about half of these are supplied by fat. Of course the fitter you get, the more fat you burn relative to carbohydrate.

THE COMPLETE FITNESS PROGRAM

I have focused my discussion of physical activity around its role in regulating body fat because that is where our main interest lies. But staying fit and healthy also requires that we maintain our flexibility and muscular strength.

The masters of Yoga say, "You are as old as your spine." That's because, as we age, our spines, as well as other joints, lose flexibility. With loss of flexibility comes an increased likelihood of injury, together with the chronic aches and pains associated with stiffness. To a great extent, however, we can maintain flexibility and agility with appropriate stretching and toning exercises, and in this way we preserve biological if not chronological youth.

While many of us neglect to include a good stretching routine in our fitness programs, even more fail to do anything to maintain muscular strength. The requirements of life today, for most of us, do not include much lifting, pushing, or shoving of heavy objects. In fact, the heaviest things most of us ever carry after our children are grown are the weekly bags of groceries. This means that we do not build and maintain a level of strength that can protect us from injury anytime we find it necessary to exert any

---

[4] A person who is in good condition will be at the low end of, or even below, the training range in heart rate at this speed of walking. If, however, you reach your maximum heart rate, or the top end of your training range, you are burning primarily carbohydrate in your mixture. Many of the participants in aerobic dance classes are actually working out at maximum heart rates and burning as much as 90 percent carbohydrate in their fuel mixtures. Only the instructor in the class is usually in good enough condition to be burning a high-fat fuel mixture.

physical force—even moving a chair, much less a heavier piece of furniture.

You can never experience a fraction of the energy, agility, and vitality you are capable of unless you incorporate a modest level of stretching exercise and strength training into your regimen. In Appendix B, I include a training routine that combines flexibility and modest strength-training exercises.

After you get a sense of what you need to do to maintain flexibility and strength, you can be creative and invent ways to do exercise of this nature and keep it interesting. Here's how I manage it.

A few stretches are essential to keep my back, hips, and leg joints flexible. They must be first in my morning ritual, or I run the danger of becoming too stiff or even injuring myself when I play tennis. Then, two or three times a week, when I am either walking or jogging in the woods near my home, I carry a tree branch that weighs about 6 pounds and invent various exercises to do with it as I move along. At certain points on some trails, I've left large branches weighing 25 pounds or more for more serious weight lifting. At other points I come across picnic tables, which I use to do additional stretches. These exercises have now become part of my routine along these trails and it is hard for me to pass by the appointed spots without doing them.

You now have the facts about exercise that can help you maximize your ability to burn fat, lose weight, and keep it off. I hope these facts, and other hints for incorporating exercise in your life, will motivate you to begin an effective and enjoyable exercise program. *I know that the payoff for a correct program is well worth the investment of time, cost of appropriate clothing and equipment, and physical effort.*

My problem lies in convincing you! I am well aware that facts about its health benefits are often not enough to sustain motivation for exercise. Unfortunately, most people who begin an exercise program in any given year do not continue it the next. If this has been your experience, I think the key to success for you, as for me, may lie in the psychological aspects of exercise. This is the subject of the next chapter.

8

Psychological Aspects of Exercise and Fitness

Have you ever been so fat and so out of shape that you had difficulty getting up out of a chair? It doesn't do much for your self-concept.

Twenty-six years ago I was a fat man. I weighed 230 pounds, which is about 75 pounds more than I weigh today. I was so out of shape that I got out of breath walking one block and up one flight of stairs to the library across from my office at Vanderbilt. I so much hated to get out of my chair that I saved my library work for Friday afternoons in order to make only one trip per week. I was hypertensive and ended up with a minor coronary at the age of thirty-five.

I wish I could take the feeling I have inside me today and put it inside all the fat people in this world who hate exercise. If I could, you would never be fat again!

It's twenty-six years later, and jogs of 5 or 10 miles in the woods are easier today than walking that hated block to the library back in 1963. How did this happen?

There is no question that in many respects I went through a personality transformation. In a matter of two years I went from a person who had never engaged in any physical activity at any period of his life to an amateur tennis player who began to enter and even win tournaments. True enough, I began to exercise for health reasons, but, like the great majority of persons who begin an activity program for health reasons, I would have quit if something much more motivating hadn't occurred as a result of becoming a tennis player and playing every day.

I don't think that any amount of lecturing on the physical benefits of exercise, either for weight control or for cardiovascular health, will ever motivate a majority of sedentary persons to become consistently active individuals. THE KEY IS PSYCHOLOGICAL AND EMOTIONAL.

In spite of all the important information I've given you in the previous chapter on the fat-burning benefits of exercise, I don't think you will succeed in becoming an active person who finds the joy in physical activity that I do unless you find some activity that contributes to your self-concept and builds your self-esteem. There is no question about it: Being a good tennis player and having the strength and endurance to jog easily for miles are, for me, an ego trip. What a contrast with my self-concept as a fat kid, 50 pounds overweight at the age of twelve, so ashamed of my looks that I wouldn't wear short pants. Indeed, so embarrassed with the looks of my legs at the age of thirty-five that it took a whole year on the tennis courts before I discarded long pants and bought my first pair of tennis shorts.

I do not exercise because it keeps me thin. I do not exercise because it may help prevent another heart attack (knock on wood, it must be helping so far). I run and play because running and playing contribute as much to the way I think about myself and describe myself as do being a college professor, health professional, and writer, or for that matter, a husband and father.

Words can't communicate my experience, and the experience I wish you might have. There is an old Oriental proverb which states that there are some things that you can know only by doing. This is one of them.

Here is what you have to do.

1. First you have to believe me! You have to believe it's possible. Somewhere inside you, you must find the fantasy about yourself that can be fulfilled by developing the body and physical skills that you are about to cultivate.

2. You must do something physical every day. Only

DOING can transform your BEING. The key word here is DISCIPLINE. But I don't intend any sense of harsh control or punishment when I use that word. I mean discipline in the sense of your becoming committed to a course of self-directed training that will mold and perfect your mental and physical character. I repeat: Your training sessions must be scheduled daily.

3. You will never experience the "flow," that is, the transformation of your physical state from sluggish to vital, from tense to relaxed, from tired to refreshed, unless just about every day you move about briskly for at least 45 minutes, and preferably for an hour at a time.

4. You must decide on some standard of performance. It has to be one that is yours alone, no one else's. You must choose some standard that you are certain to reach, so that each day your chosen activity takes place as a ritual that can be completed. The standard can involve time, distance, or speed, but it must be reachable and provide a sense of accomplishment.

5. If you choose some activity that is performed alone, it should not require much skill. Fortunately, the fat burners do not require Olympic-level athletic ability.

6. If you choose to engage in competitive activities, you must become as good as time and resources allow. For example, if you ever wanted to be a tennis player, it means lessons and practice. If you engage in the sport in the manner I suggest, you are out to become as good as you can be, which is quite different from going out to win every match. The joy must be found in the game itself, not the outcome.

7. It will take you at least one year, possibly even two years, to experience fully what I'm talking about. You must therefore be prepared to endure a kind of probationary status for this period of time. It will help from a psychological standpoint if you think of yourself as a novitiate. You will need to learn how to get through the change of seasons and the time changes each year. Depending on your choice of activity and the climate where you live, you may need to learn how to deal with the heat and the cold, the rain and the snow, the dogs along your route, and the other vocational and social demands in your life. One day,

you will realize that you are no longer a novitiate, but an "initiate"; you will have become the person you set out to be.

8. If you choose physical activities that are social in nature, you must choose partners who are as sincere as you are. Drop those who disappoint you by not keeping appointments or who try to involve you in supporting their excuses for inactivity. You want partners for whom it is never too hot or too cold to be active!

9. Finally, if you choose some solo activity like walking, jogging, or swimming (and I hope you do, at least as part of your total program), you may have to experiment a bit to find an approach to this activity that leads to the kind of personal growth I'm speaking of. If you normally spend a great deal of time alone, than walking with friends can become an interesting social activity. There are walking groups in many cities, but you can always put notes in your neighbors' mailboxes, informing them that you are looking for walking companions. If you normally work with other people, or are under tension when you work, then walking alone is going to provide you with the greatest benefits. When I have been successful in persuading people to complete their probationary status, and get through a year or two of walking or jogging, they almost always tell me that it has been a period of discovery. While they might have been bored at first, they discovered that walking alone provided them with an opportunity to talk with themselves. They found an opportunity to consider thoughts, emotions, plans, hopes, and dreams that could never have occurred otherwise. They got to know themselves, but best of all, they grew to like themselves a great deal better than before.

That's the final component. Simply put, you will know what I'm talking about when it comes to self-esteem when you can say to yourself, "The real reason I walk [jog, play tennis, dance] is that I feel like a better person for having done it."

9

The T-Factor Program for Children and Adolescents[1]

If you were ever fat as a child, as I was, then you know firsthand the tremendous psychological and social burdens of childhood obesity. As a fat child, you're certain it's your fault you're fat and that it reflects some sort of moral failure. You feel unattractive, of course, and you sense that everyone around you thinks you are, too.[2] Unless you have some special talent, like being the best speller in the class, you expect to be chosen last on just about every team activity during or after school.

Can you remember what it was like to shop for clothes? In my hometown there was only one store back in the 1940s that had "stouts" for fat kids like me, 50 pounds overweight at the age of twelve. I couldn't bear to look in the mirror after the salesperson and my mother had forced me to try something on. I knew I looked fat and ugly no matter what they said. The damn suits were not slimming! My rear end was just as big as it was before I tried the pants on.

Can you remember your first diet? If you were never

---

[1] Much of the material for this chapter, including many of the tips for helping children either lose weight or maintain desirable weight, was furnished by Ms. Jamie Pope-Cordle, M.S., R.D., director of nutrition, Vanderbilt Weight Management Program.

[2] Research shows that children as young as six years of age consider obese children to be less attractive than children with severe physical handicaps.

fat as a child, and are trying to deal with one of your children who has a weight problem, then you have no idea what it feels like to a kid to be "put on a diet" when everyone else is free to eat as they please. You still live in a fat-eating environment. Nothing at school or after changes: Your friends all eat just as they ate before in the school cafeteria and in the fast-food restaurants where the typical meal or snack contains from 40 to 55 percent of its calories in fat! And, most likely, nothing at home changes, either, except for more arguments about food and dieting. You are still surrounded from the moment you wake up in the morning until the moment you go to sleep by all the fatty foods that tempt you. Your mom still cooks exactly as she did before and, suddenly, because you must be "on a diet," you are supposed to have more willpower than a saint—certainly more than anyone else in your family.

Unless you have been there, I don't think you can appreciate that for most overweight children the situation is really quite desperate and quite sad. Perhaps you might have answered as the overweight child of one of the participants in the Vanderbilt Weight Management Program did when his school counselor asked him what he wished for more than anything else in the world. Yes, perhaps you guessed—"To be thin."

Well, he's had his wish granted because his mother took home everything she had learned in the T-Factor program when she lost weight and decided to make it a family affair. In a moment I'll give you the advice that worked for this family because it can work for you, too. First some basics.

WE DO NOT BELIEVE IN PUTTING CHILDREN AND ADOLESCENTS ON DIETS.

A vast number of children, perhaps a majority, come to believe that weight control is a matter of going on and off diets. I see it in many of the young men and women in my classes at Vanderbilt who are not overweight, as well as in the overweight participants in my weight-management groups.

Even when they obviously do not have a weight problem, THE YOUNG ADULTS HAVE EATING PROBLEMS. I don't mean serious binge-and-purge problems, although that does occur occasionally. Frequently these young adults don't know where the fat is coming from in their diets. As I mentioned before, the typical meal in a school or college cafeteria, or in a fast-food restaurant, can contain 40 to 55 percent or even more of its calories in fat. My students eat what they think is quite normal until they gain 5 or 10 pounds. Then they go on a crash diet. Many of them never learn that fat makes you fat, and that there are many things to eat to satisfy your appetite that won't make you fat! Of course, the more they diet the worse it gets, since repeated dieting makes it easier and easier to gain weight, and harder and harder to lose. In the end, many of them do become candidates for weight-control programs!

With children and adolescents, WE DO NOT BELIEVE IN COUNTING ANYTHING, CALORIES OR FAT GRAMS.

We do believe in designing a healthy eating environment, and, at least in the home, you can do that. Of even greater importance, you can use the most powerful tool to encourage appropriate, healthy eating habits: YOUR *SILENT* EXAMPLE. When you adopt the T-Factor Diet, you, as a healthy model, provide the strongest incentive for all your family members to improve their eating habits.

Except for certain nutrients, your children need the same diet you need. Children are growing, of course, and they need more of the nutrients essential for growth. Unfortunately, many children in this country of plenty have diets that are deficient in calcium, iron, vitamins A and C, and the B vitamins.

Your children also need more calories than you do per pound of body weight, because they are growing, *but in a society where food is freely available you can forget about the extra growth calories*. Just provide a healthy eating environment and let your children's appetites determine their food intake.

You can get free pamphlets on the nutrient needs of children and adolescents from any local public health facility as well as from your own pediatrician. These pamphlets will contain rather detailed recommendations for designing diets for children of all ages. I will not burden you with specifics since a complete discussion of childhood nutrition would take at least several hundred pages.[3] But here are some general recommendations[4] that will make sure your children receive adequate nutrition for growth and good health, and will not suffer from the dietary deficiencies (in calcium, iron, vitamins A and C, and the B vitamins) I mentioned above.

Your children should have a wide variety of foods from each of the four food groups each day: (1) low-fat milk products; (2) lean meat, fish, or poultry; (3) vegetables and fruits; and (4) breads and cereals. Recommendations include:

- 4 servings of low-fat milk products
- 2 or more servings of lean meat, fish, or poultry
- 4 or more servings of vegetables and fruits, including one citrus fruit and a green or yellow vegetable
- 4 or more servings of breads and cereals (whole- or mixed-grain preferred).[5]

Notice the "or more" suggestions in these recommendations, especially in vegetables, fruits, and grain products. Children from ages four through ten generally require from 1700 to 2100 calories per day, and adolescents of ages eleven through seventeen generally require from 2100 to 2800 calories per day. The actual amount depends primarily on their increasing age, height, and weight, as well as level of physical activity.

HOWEVER, AS I SAID BEFORE, WE DO NOT BELIEVE IN COUNTING ANYTHING, CALORIES OR FAT GRAMS.

Counting makes me nervous!

---

[3] Parents who are interested should obtain *Parents' Guide to Nutrition*, developed at Boston Children's Hospital, by Susan Baker, M.D., Ph.D., and Roberta Henry, R.D. (Boston: Addison-Wesley, 1986), which offers comprehensive information on nutrition from birth through adolescence.

[4] These suggestions are derived from the Basic Four Food Guide recommended by most experts in childhood nutrition.

[5] Obviously a serving size for a four-year-old is smaller than for a seventeen-year-old, but, in general, when we use the word "serving" we refer to what is considered a standard cafeteria-size portion.

I don't mind counting when I'm in a research project, and Jamie Pope-Cordle and I both counted fat grams when we adopted the T-Factor Diet because we needed to change *faulty* eating patterns and we had no one but ourselves to take charge of our eating environments. Until you learn where the fat in your food is, and in the food you serve your family, you, too, need to count fat grams. But counting encourages obsessional behavior, and we want healthful eating to become second nature, as it did with us, and as it will for you, too, after only a few weeks.

After you learn the fat contents of the various foods you want to include in the diet that you and your family eat we think it best to allow your children to determine what and how much they want to eat of everything you keep in your house. *You, however, have the responsibility to determine what's offered at home, and the manner in which it is served.* Remember: THE T-FACTOR DIET FOR CHILDREN AND ADOLESCENTS IS A FAMILY AFFAIR.

It is simply not fair to ask your children to do anything you aren't willing to do yourself when it comes to healthy eating. With preadolescent children, just do it. It doesn't take any negotiation. Get rid of the junk. Stock up on all the things you feel free to eat, and say, "If you're hungry, just go to the cupboard or refrigerator and have anything you want."

With adolescents, well, we've got a problem. (Who hasn't.)

If you have an overweight adolescent, it takes a kind of mutual non-aggression pact.

Adolescents are trying to establish their own identities and make the long transition to independence. They need to. (Do you really want your kids to hang around all their lives?) If you have an overweight child who has reached the age of twelve or more, seek your opportunity. If, when you see an unhappy expression on your child's face, you ask, in a sympathetic way, "What's wrong, honey," and they say they are tired of being called a fatty, you've got your opening. That's when it's time to tell them the story about dietary fat and how to avoid it, *and to show them all the good things that are left to eat.* Adolescents, just like everyone else, need to be able to eat when they are hungry and they are likely to be hungrier than adults simply because they are growing. Volunteer to set up the kind of home eating environment that will help them fulfill their wish to be thin. Just look back at Tables 3-1 and 3-2 and choose the kinds of foods you want around the house for snacking (we make some specific recommendations for children in Table 9-1 below). Go over the menus in Chapter 3 and the recipes in Chapter 6 and decide which foods will form the foundation for your family meals at home. RE-MEMBER THAT 80 PERCENT OF OBESE CHIL-DREN BECOME OBESE ADULTS! The decisions and choices you make when given this opportunity are likely to affect your children for the rest of their lives.

ADDITIONAL TIPS FOR EVERY DAY AND EVERY PLACE

You cannot control your child's entire eating environment, so don't try. Just controlling the home environment is half the battle and that may be all that is necessary.

Here is what our Vanderbilt Weight Management Program participant did to change her home environment and help her son reduce his pants by two sizes:

She got rid of all the high-fat cookies, snack crackers, chips, and dips, and replaced them with low-fat crackers, pretzels, popcorn, and fresh and dried fruit (see Table 9-1 below for specific suggestions).

She replaced the peanut butter in his afternoon snack of peanut butter, toast, and milk with apple butter.

She began to use only low-fat cuts of meat, prepared as I suggest in Chapter 6 (and her family has not even noticed the change since everything tastes just as good as or better than before).

Instead of candy that contains a major part of its calories from fat, she has substituted plain hard sugar or peppermint candy. In this way no one feels deprived of an occasional sweet. (Obviously we don't want children to overindulge in sugar candy for a variety of health reasons, but we have found that most people, including children, turn off after a maximum of about 100 calories of sugar candy. That's a far cry from the 240 calories in a single 1.65-ounce chocolate bar, of which 50 to 60 percent of the calories come from fat. And when it comes to chocolate, it's not hard to eat 3 or 4 ounces at a time.)

Here are some additional suggestions for dealing with the home environment, school, fast-food establishments, and exercise:

- Find out what is to be offered at school if your child purchases lunches there and obtain advice on the lower-fat food choices.
- Pack a healthful lunch whenever possible (yes, it's extra work, but why wait until your child is even fatter, or becomes a fat adult, and then have even more work to do?).
- If your child eats at any fast-food establishments, check them out, get nutritional information on the foods they serve, and counsel your child on the best choices. If any of your child's friends are also concerned about weight, this is a good time to get some peer cooperation.
- If possible, children should carry appropriate snack foods (such as fruit or low-fat crackers) whenever they have to be away from the house at snack times.
- Offer lots of love and support rather than nagging or criticizing your child about his or her weight.
- Cultivate a positive, healthful attitude toward foods and eating. The enjoyment of good, healthful food is an important part of a satisfying life.
- Set a good example in the foods you choose and the amounts you consume—both at home and away.
- Try new foods, be adventurous, but don't force these new foods on your children. Let them serve themselves a small portion. Young children are especially sensitive to strong tastes or extremes in temperature or texture, but don't forever cast a refused food from the family dinner table, because taste buds change.
- Establish dependable mealtimes. This helps regulate your child's appetite and lends some structure to the day—which facilitates a sense of security.
- Small children have relatively high energy needs, so, since their stomachs cannot hold a lot of food at one time, include at least two snacks a day in addition to meals.
- Do not force children to finish everything on their plates when their appetites are satisfied with less.

- Don't forbid "junk food," but don't keep it around the house all the time. If you feel all your child will eat is junk food, think about who is buying it!
- Don't use food as a reward or as a pacifier.
- Provide a safe environment for your child to run and play.
- Don't carry a child who can walk.
- Make your daily routine and your child's more active by walking more and driving less.
- Ration television time. A child glued to the tube is a child not being active (and there is a direct relationship be-

TABLE 9-1

SMART SNACKING FOR YOUR KIDS

Because 60 to 80 percent of the calories in many snack foods are in the form of fat, it is a good idea to encourage healthful snack foods as early in life as possible. The following chart contains some of our suggestions.

Milk and Dairy Products	Low-fat or nonfat yogurt mixed with fruit, low-fat cottage cheese or part-skim ricotta, other cheeses in moderate amounts, ice milk, low-fat frozen yogurt, hot cocoa made with low-fat milk, sherbert, pudding made with low-fat milk
Vegetables	Fresh, crisp, cut-up raw vegetables with yogurt-based dip; offer a variety of colors, shapes, and sizes; keep in ice water in refrigerator for a quick crunch
Fruit	Fresh or dried fruit, frozen fruit (putting fruit in the freezer, such as bananas and grapes, makes a chilly summertime treat), fruit mixed with no- or low-fat yogurt or milk, fruit mixed with gelatin (Jell-O)
Breads and Cereals	Dry cereals, bagels, pretzels, popcorn, whole-grain pita bread with vegetables or lean meats/cheese, whole-grain breads or rolls spead with low-fat cottage or ricotta cheese and jam, graham crackers, Rice Krispie squares (recipe on back of box), whole-grain crackers, flour tortillas, bread sticks, muffins, raisin bread
Beverages	Water, fruit juices, low-fat or skim milk, seltzer or club soda, hot cocoa made with low-fat milk

tween number of hours spent watching TV as a child and adolescent obesity).

- Encourage your child to play outdoors in all seasons. Appropriate attire will keep them comfortable in cold or hot weather.
- Share enjoyable physical activities with your child. Plan family walks, hikes, bike rides, and other active outings.
- Encourage your child to play with other children.
- Plan active family vacations, reinforcing the idea that exercise is fun and worth pursuing.
- Give an older child responsibility for exercising the family pet.

SOME FINAL ADVICE

Unless your child is severely obese, most experts do not suggest that you make any effort to reduce weight. It is much better to encourage healthy eating habits such as we have designed in the T-Factor Diet, and let the slightly overweight child grow into his or her adult weight.

However, if you feel that your child is seriously overweight, consult your pediatrician or family practitioner for assessment and recommendations or referral. If indicated, check into a local childhood or adolescent obesity treatment program. Often area hospitals will offer programs specializing in pediatric obesity. A team of health professionals, including a registered dietitian, physician, exercise physiologist, and/or psychologist, can work with parents and children on sensible diet and exercise as well as behavior change. You can write the Center for Adolescent Obesity for a list of centers across the country utilizing this team approach (send self-addressed stamped envelope to Center for Adolescent Obesity, University of California, Box 0900 FCM, San Francisco, CA 94143).

10

◆

Myths and Mysteries of Weight Management

◆

IF YOU CRAVE CARBOHYDRATES YOU BETTER SATISFY THAT CRAVING!

A great deal has been written about carbohydrate cravings. If you think you are one of those persons who suffers from some abnormality in this respect because you seem always to crave something sweet, you've probably gotten conflicting and confusing advice. Some experts think of carbohydrate cravings as some sort of malady that requires a cure, while others advise satisfying such cravings with totally inappropriate foods, such as a candy bar.

The truth about carbohydrate cravings is that changes in the body's small store of carbohydrate energy (the glycogen stores) exert a powerful influence on appetite. This influence is much stronger than changes in the much larger fat stores and demands satisfaction.

Since the body only stores about 2000 calories in glycogen and tends generally to burn it over a twenty-four-hour period in equal proportion to fat, it is quite easy for the body to turn over half or more of its glycogen storage every day. In contrast, only about 1 percent or less of the total fat storage may be affected since our bodies may easily store 100,000 calories or more as fat. If the glycogen stores are not replenished in that day's diet as the energy is drained from them to support our activities, the impact is felt immediately.

Experiments with laboratory animals show that a decrease in the intake of carbohydrate on one day results in an immediate increase in food intake on the next day. The reverse is true when more carbohydrate is eaten than is burned in the fuel mixture. That is, when the animals overeat on carbohydrate, they eat less the next day. With fat, on the other hand, there seems to be an unfortunate snowball effect: For some unexplained reason, high fat consumption on a given day seems to lead to continued increased fat consumption on the subsequent day!

Many variables affect appetite. Some we all are acutely conscious of, such as the sight and smell of tasty foods, which do turn on a physiological readiness to eat. However, your body's glycogen stores exert one of the most potent physiological regulators of appetite. The influence is not as direct or as easily recognized as the sight of food or the pangs of an empty stomach, but the impact is almost irresistible. You *will* become ravenous if you do not take in enough carbohydrate to meet the body's daily demand for glucose in its fuel mixture.

For example, if you've been accustomed to skipping breakfast and having a light lunch in an effort to control your food intake, only to find yourself almost out of control from 5 P.M. until you go to bed, it's probably because you have depleted half your glycogen stores and messages are pouring in from every cell in your body, like hundreds of Jewish grandmothers crying "EAT, EAT!"

And eat you should.

In fact, you would have been better off if you had been eating all day long, nibbling on the carbohydrate foods that would have kept your glycogen stores near maximum. Although many nutritionists still recommend eating "three square meals" without snacks, that approach is really not most natural to humankind. It was much more natural to us throughout the long course of our evolutionary history to nibble on whatever was available, usually grains, fruits, or vegetables, whenever we felt the slightest bit hungry. One of the best ways to avoid the development of the "hidden hunger" which suddenly appears to overwhelm you after a period of deprivation and leads to overeating (if not binging) is to eat whenever the urge hits you.

But you must eat the right foods—that is, the kinds of foods that were available to your ancient ancestors.

Unfortunately, the right foods are frequently hard to come by when you need them. I'm talking about fresh fruit and vegetables, and whole-grain breads and cereals, with little or no fat content. These are the foods that can regulate glycogen storage without contributing to fat storage. Processed snack foods have been made more attractive to most people than natural foods; they have been scientifically formulated with added fat combined with sugar and salt to satisfy natural flavor preferences (which I'll discuss later in this chapter) beyond the ability of naturally occurring foods to do so. Thus when you try to satisfy your carbohydrate cravings with anything but naturally occurring foods you end up with fat you really don't need! Let me give you just a few examples: Over 60 percent of the calories in the most popular chips and chocolate candy bars come from fat, while only 30 to 35 percent are carbohydrate; the peanut butter and cheese sandwich crackers that many folks choose as an alternative to candy from the snack machines also generally contain over 60 percent of calories from fat, with only 25 percent of calories from carbohydrate!

Think for a moment about what this can mean if you have a weight problem. Suppose you are down a couple of hundred glycogen calories. The 240-calorie candy bar or package of snack crackers contains only 50 to 75 carbohydrate calories; the rest is fat. The fat will end up in your fat cells and you still won't have satisfied your glycogen needs. You will be hungry again shortly and you will likely overeat at meals because you have not satisfied these glycogen needs. You will get fatter and fatter because you keep on taking in more fat calories than you can burn in your daily fuel mixture, all as a result of an unconscious striving to satisfy your body's natural and healthy drive to replenish glycogen.

I hope you see the point. It bears much repetition and it must sink in! If you choose a food that contains fat in addition to carbohydrate when your appetite has been stimulated by glycogen depletion, you add fat to your fat stores before you get enough carbohydrate to satisfy your legitimate carbohydrate craving. (I discuss the reasons for our fatty food preferences below.)

The T-Factor solution to carbohydrate cravings is to make sure that the majority of calories at all meals comes from carbohydrate, not fat, and to reach for a carbohydrate whenever you are hungry for a snack. You may find that this eliminates cravings completely; it is certainly the only way to satisfy them. Since your body has such a limited ability to convert carbohydrate to fat, there is a built-in protection against putting on weight when you satisfy carbohydrate cravings with real carbohydrate foods rather than fatty foods.[1]

SET POINT: THE POINT THAT ISN'T A POINT

One of the most unfortunate misconceptions to have been foisted on the overweight public is the notion of a set point. It's unfortunate not only because it is a discouraging concept, but because it's simply wrong.

The term "set point" has been used in a descriptive manner to describe the body's apparent preference for a certain weight or amount of body fat. It implies a self-correcting mechanism whereby attempts to change weight or fat storage are met with counterforces that are designed to return you to "THE set point" and defeat any diet or weight-reducing plan.

There are certainly strong genetic influences on body-fat storage. It becomes obvious when anyone compares his or her body build with that of a similarly built ancestor who also deposited fat in identical parts of the body and had a weight problem! In addition, the easy and almost unlimited availability of fatty foods turns on our appetite and constantly tempts us to return to a pattern of high fat

---

[1] Glycogen depletion sets up such a demand for satisfaction that nature seems to have built in a protection against long-term discomfort. People on a fast report how hunger seems to lessen and sometimes almost disappear after twenty-four to forty-eight hours. In part this may be due to the body's ability to switch its fuel requirements to near total fat during a fast, and to produce waste products in the form of ketones, which diminish appetite. Other changes occur with fasting that increase the body's ability to store fat so that once a fasting person starts to eat again, it is easier to gain weight and become fatter than before the fast.

intake. As I've explained before, your excess body fat results from eating more fat in your diet than the amount you burn each day in your fuel mixture. This means that when you combine a given heritage with a given life-style—that is, a certain amount of fat in the diet and a certain amount of exercise—you get a certain body weight.

But there is no such thing as *A* set point! There are, in reality, many set points. Speaking from a biological per-spective, there is *a range of adaptability* within which permanent changes in diet and exercise operate with a certain ease and convenience. The range comprises about 50 to 75 pounds.

If you eat a diet that contains 40 percent or more of its calories in fat and you do no regular fat-burning exercises, you are likely to drift up to the top of your range of adaptability. That is, you may end up weighing perhaps as much as 75 pounds more than necessary.

But you don't have to stay there! If you reduce your fat intake and engage in the kind of exercise that burns a few hundred FAT CALORIES each day, you will drift down to the bottom of your range of adaptability and lose whatever excess weight you have gained—PERMA-NENTLY.

To put it another way, when you follow the T-Factor Diet and Activity Program you adjust your "set point" to its lowest level and it stays there!

Obviously, if you want to weigh even 5 pounds more or less than what you weigh today, forever, you must do something different in the way of your diet or exercise, forever. Both diet and exercise are important, and the T-Factor program makes the necessary changes livable and enjoyable. Exercise, however, may prove to provide the heretofore elusive key. I have already discussed the major role it can play from physiological and psychological stand-points in Chapters 7 and 8, respectively. In addition, a recent research study that compared sedentary and active persons showed that exercise may naturally and automat-ically change your dietary preferences away from fatty foods to carbohydrates. I think you will find that this is likely to occur for you, too, for two reasons. First, car-bohydrate foods tend to contain much more water than fatty foods, and people who exercise find an increased appetite for foods that can replace the water they lose while exercising. Second, even if you concentrate on fat-burning exercise, any exercise at all will deplete glycogen stores beyond the level reached by a sedentary person, and this is likely to increase your appetite for carbohydrate foods.

WHY DO HUMAN BEINGS SEEM TO HAVE A PREFERENCE FOR HIGH-FAT FOODS?

Although glycogen depletion provides a strong internal signal that turns on appetite, human beings seem to turn to *fatty* carbohydrate foods to satisfy that appetite if those foods are present in the environment. The urge to eat fatty carbohydrates, sweetened or salted preferably, has a long evolutionary history. This taste preference was cultivated as a resistance to famine and infectious disease.

Ever since the human race turned from hunting and gathering to agriculture for its food supply, we have faced frequent famines. In fact, two-thirds of the earth's population still faces serious food shortages every two years or so. Only in the Western world, and only for the past few hundred years, has there been anything approaching a stable food supply. Genetic lines that tended to store body fat, and that developed a preference for foods that could put down fat fast (considering that the food supply might be here today and gone tomorrow) were favored under these boom-or-bust conditions.

Infectious disease played a similar selective role. Together with famine, infectious disease often prevented half of newborn infants from reaching their first birthdays. Before antibiotics and immunization, resistance to infectious disease depended in part on the amount of body fat an individual possessed, since the metabolic rate goes up about 7 percent for each degree of fever. With just 4 degrees of fever, energy needs are about 28 percent greater than normal. Thus, individuals with genetic tendencies to obesity, or who liked fatty foods and had laid down a few extra pounds of fat storage, would be favored for survival.

Because in the past individuals who did not possess the capacity to store fat easily or who did not care for fatty foods had less of a chance to reach reproductive age, we tend to be a species with rather strong tendencies to obesity given the availability of high-fat foods. Indeed, just the sight of such foods (not counting the smell and anticipated taste) starts the flow of saliva and gastric juices, and turns on our appetites.

Of course, enterprising food manufacturers capitalize on this natural tendency and design "unnatural" foods that will turn on our appetites even more than anything found in nature. Knowing the preference for fat, salt, and sweetness, scientists can design "super-natural" foods which blend these characteristics and turn on appetite beyond our needs for survival. Just about all human beings have appetites that turn off before they can overeat on apples, or other fruits, vegetables, and grains, but not before they overeat on candy bars, chips, and other confections. Millions of dollars are spent developing such foods, because if we didn't come to prefer them over apples and oranges, these food manufacturers would have a difficult time showing any profits!

Which brings me to a discussion of the role of behavior modification and the reasons for its rather poor showing as a tool in weight management.

LEARNING FROM FAILURE: WHAT CAN BEHAVIOR MODIFICATION DO FOR YOU?

It's been about twenty years since behavior modification techniques were first applied to weight management and the best that can be said is that they help participants in formal weight-management programs lose an average of about 10 to 12 pounds, and that only a small minority is able to keep off that weight for more than one year.

Why?

In theory, the more you apply behavior modification techniques, the more you learn about controlling your eating behavior and the easier it should become. In practice, it doesn't work this way, as I'm sure you know if you have ever been in a behavior modification program for weight control. Behavior modification techniques are a bore and a bother. There is a limit to the extent most people are willing to continue keeping eating records, putting their forks down between bites, eating from tiny dishes, and thinking up artificial, insignificant rewards for controlling their eating behavior. The force of social pressures and emotional pressures to overeat on fatty foods is in the end much greater than any reward or punishment that we can control in a free society!

In my opinion, there is only one behavior modification element that can help you when your normal environment is forever tempting you with super-natural fatty foods that turn on your appetite beyond your needs for energy— AVOIDANCE. I know of no behavior modification strategy that can forever protect you from the innate biological predisposition that turns on appetite when you see, smell, or even imagine the taste of your particular favorite high-fat foods if they are all readily available! You cannot deny mother nature forever; you will succumb.

So the only behavior modification strategy that has a chance of helping you is: CHANGE YOUR ENVIRONMENT.

The highest-ranking response that successful people give when asked what change they have made in their eating behavior is: "I keep junk food out of the house." They do not indicate that they aim for total denial—they occasionally plan a "mini-binge" and enjoy it. *But they customarily AVOID temptation.*

There are a few other ways, however, in which behavior modification techniques may be applied in combination with T-Factor Diet principles to provide you with greater success than ever before.

Normally, behaviorists suggest that you find alternative activities to eating whenever eating urges hit you that appear to be greater than your daily energy needs. That is still a good idea, especially if you turn to physical activity. Remember, however, that eating urges often arise from glycogen depletion after having restrained yourself from eating a nutritious breakfast or lunch. Try my suggestions for breakfast and lunch, and then, AS LONG AS YOU DON'T EAT FATTY FOODS, THERE ARE PLENTY OF GOOD THINGS TO EAT WHENEVER YOU FEEL LIKE MUNCHING.

The most important thing you can learn when it comes to your eating behavior is that, as long as you don't exceed the guidelines for fat consumption, you are likely to be able to eat whenever you wish without harming your weight-control efforts.

Our research also shows that social pressures, especially in situations that make you feel good, such as parties and eating out at restaurants, are frequent reasons for overeating on high-fat foods. One of the best ways to erase the social pressure is to get as many people as you can who interact with you on a daily basis to adopt the T-Factor Diet and start eating in a more nutritious fashion. Once you are all eating in a more nutritious way, it is easier to "save up" for the special occasions, and to return the next day to your basic T-Factor Diet.[2]

Finally, a certain percentage of those who overeat on high-fat foods do so for emotional reasons. After all, when you're feeling down, you don't run to the refrigerator for a carrot. There is something about fatty sweets or fatty salty snacks that is particularly satisfying. The reasons for this are not entirely clear, but some experts feel it has something to do with the impact of fatty foods on the endorphins. In some people, fatty foods may stimulate pleasurable feelings via changes in this or some other hormone secretion.

If you feel that you overeat for emotional reasons, I think you should look for specific help in solving the emotional problems that stimulate your appetite. Learning to deal with that life situation will provide a more satisfactory and more permanent solution than letting the problems continue and trying to find substitute behaviors for eating. But I do have one suggestion: There are plenty of good things to eat on the T-Factor Diet whenever you have an urge to eat for any reason. To be specific, if you haven't learned how to deal with people who aggravate you, you're much better off chewing on a bagel when you feel like biting their heads off than you are downing a bag of potato chips or a box of doughnuts.

---

[2]Other suggestions for choosing nutritious foods when eating out will be found in Chapter 4, where experiences of people on the T-Factor Diet are recounted.

WHY IS IT SO EASY TO GAIN WEIGHT AFTER FASTING OR USING A LOW-CALORIE FORMULA DIET, AND WHAT CAN YOU DO ABOUT IT?

One way to increase your body's ability to gain weight and to encourage higher levels of fat storage is to fast or to use a low-calorie formula diet (600 calories or less per day) for a prolonged period of time. Unfortunately—perhaps out of frustration with the poor results obtained with moderate calorie-reduced diets—many respected health professionals are beginning to encourage the low-calorie formula diets for people 50 pounds or more over desirable weight. While there are certainly some instances where such dieting is called for because of medical reasons to lose weight quickly, there are far too many people for whom such dieting will prove counterproductive.

In my opinion there are many more people who will end up heavier than ever before after using these diets than there are people who will lose weight and keep it off.

There are two important reasons for avoiding low-calorie formula diets unless called for in a medical emergency.

First, there is a severe reduction in metabolic rate. It averages about 25 percent and can reach as high as 40 percent. While the proponents of the formula diets claim that there is "on the average" a return to normal after the diet, there is evidence to show that a certain percentage of users may not return to normal, even after a considerable period of time.

Second, after several weeks on a formula diet, when you start eating again there is a rebound in the activity of the fat-incorporating enzyme, adipose tissue lipoprotein lipase. This enzyme controls the rate at which fat is entered into your fat cells and that rate may be elevated 300 or 400 percent above normal. It's as though the fat is being sucked right out of the bloodstream and soaked up by your fat cells. At least one study has shown that this elevation may last for a year after the diet, and only return to normal or to near-normal levels *once you have regained all your weight*.

Some years ago, following another period of great enthusiasm over these formula diets, I had former users of one popular formula who were having trouble maintaining their weight keep daily eating records for me. Months after losing weight on their formula diet, we found that the women were likely to gain weight whenever they exceeded 1200 calories per day, while the one man in the group gained weight on 1500 calories. This helped explain why people who had lost weight on a formula diet only to regain it were among the hardest to help in any subsequent efforts to lose weight.

There are both principled and unprincipled persons in the business of selling low-calorie formula diets. If you feel you must use such drastic measures to lose weight in spite of my belief that you can deal with the problem in a much simpler, healthier, and less expensive way with the T-Factor Diet, the best programs require your agreement to participate in long-term follow-up and nutritional counseling, with payment in advance to assure commitment. The persons in charge appreciate the tremendous difficulty you will face keeping your weight off after the diet and, rather than just sell their product, where most of the profit lies, they employ a staff of health professionals at a much smaller profit to offer group and personal counseling in order to increase their success rate. *Don't ever consider using a formula diet unless you are willing to make a commitment to the follow-up program.*

If you have ever used a formula diet and now find that it is harder to maintain your weight than ever before, stop thinking calories, start thinking fat grams, and engage in fat-burning physical activity every day! In view of your body's eagerness to refill its fat stores, your best chance of managing your weight lies in controlling your fat intake at the lower levels of the T-Factor Diet. If you are presently using a formula diet, be sure to increase fat intake very slowly when you enter the refeeding phase because there is likely to be a preferential shunting of fat to storage rather than to direct energy use after the diet. That is, you are likely to gain a lot of weight even if you eat very little fat. And remember that if you fail to exercise and you allow total calorie intake to exceed your energy needs every day, you may even force the conversion of carbohydrate to fat.

Epilogue

Compared with the also-rans, champions in all human activities seem to have a cognitive environment that is quite different. They have the highest standards and they have complete confidence that if they follow certain rules, they will reach them. If you could crawl inside their heads, you would hear them say these rules over and over again and you would hear mainly positive conversations with themselves. As a result, when you observe their behavior you see that it is focused and that they work hard to reach their goals.

Here are the kinds of statements that should be flowing around in your head. Let them become rules for you. Practice attaching their meanings to your behavior—that is, SAY these things over and over again as you DO them, and you will never be fat again.

ONLY FAT MAKES ME FAT.

I EAT ANYTHING I WANT EXCEPT FOR FATTY FOODS.

I AM AN ACTIVE PERSON.

DOING IS KNOWING.

I CAN BECOME GOOD AT ANYTHING I WANT IF I PRACTICE EVERY DAY.

EVERY TIME I GO FOR A WALK I LEAVE SOME FAT IN MY FOOTSTEPS.

A LOW-FAT DINNER MAKES ME THINNER.

MY TUMMY STAYS FLAT WHEN I DON'T EAT FAT.

I'M FIT, NOT FAT.

JACK SPRAT COULD EAT NO FAT, WHICH IS
WHY HE WEIGHED 50 POUNDS LESS THAN
MRS. SPRAT.

APPENDIX A

♦

Additional Scientific Background for the T-Factor Diet

♦

Several years ago, certain leading biochemists and physiologists began investigating whether increasing the ratio of carbohydrate to fat in the diet could make a difference in the prevalence of obesity (Danforth, 1985). Based on evidence (already outlined in Chapter 2) that fat is more easily accumulated in the body from dietary fat than from carbohydrate, Danforth concluded that, based on theoretical grounds, an increased ratio of carbohydrate to fat in the diet could make a difference, even if total caloric intake remains the same. The metabolic cost of converting carbohydrate for energy use or storage in the human body is much greater than that of converting fat. Thus, many of the calories contained in carbohydrate foods are simply wasted and given off as heat rather than put to useful work or stored within the body. In addition—and this may be of even greater importance—the body appears to have limited ability to convert carbohydrate to fat even following the consumption of carbohydrate loads far greater than one would spontaneously consume (Flatt, 1987).

In one of the earlier studies on this latter issue, Acheson, Flatt, and Jequier (1982) fed a group of six men a meal containing 500 grams (2000 calories) of carbohydrate. During the next ten hours they found that only 9 grams of fat (81 calories) were produced from the carbohydrate in this meal, and that their subjects went into negative fat balance. That is, the fuel mixture being burned during those ten hours required more fat than could be converted from the carbohydrate in the meal, and this fat had to be withdrawn from tissue storage of fat.

In another study, Acheson et al. (1984) tested the impact of a 2000-calorie carbohydrate load on subjects who had been acclimated to three different diets: a high-fat diet, a standard mixed diet, and a high-carbohydrate diet. On the high-fat diet, glycogen stores were reduced and one would not expect that much of the carbohydrate would be turned to fat since the first priority in the body would be to replenish the depleted glycogen. On the high-carbohydrate diet one might expect considerable conversion of carbohydrate to fat, since the glycogen stores were already quite full. Nevertheless, once again, only about 81 calories of fat were produced from the 2000-calorie carbohydrate load even when the subjects had been eating a high-carbohydrate diet. And again, they went into negative fat balance. In addition, Acheson et al. found that the higher the carbohydrate content of the customary diet, the greater the thermic effect of the single meal, which illustrates the greater thermogenic potential of high-carbohydrate compared with high-fat diets.

In a third study, which I have previously mentioned in Chapter 2, Flatt et al. (1985) varied the fat content of a breakfast containing a set amount of protein and carbohydrate. On each of two days the breakfast contained about 120 calories of protein and about 292 calories of carbohydrate. On one day it contained about 54 calories in fat, and on the other day it contained about 414 calories in fat. On both days, the amount of protein and carbohydrate used in the fuel mixture over the next nine hours very closely approximated the amount contained in the breakfast. That is, all the protein and carbohydrate energy in the breakfast was burned, but on both days, regardless of the fat in the breakfast, the body burned about 360 calories of fat in its fuel mixture. Thus, on the high-fat day there was fat left over for storage, whereas on the low-fat day about 300 calories in fat were withdrawn from fat storage.

It is possible to force the body to convert a portion of dietary carbohydrate to fat following sustained large excesses of carbohydrate in the diet. However, before such conversion takes place it is necessary to maximize the body's ability to store glycogen. In a recent study, Acheson et al. (1988) used a combination of exercise and diet first to deplete glycogen stores and then to saturate them on a high-carbohydrate diet. Each day, in order to saturate glycogen stores, they fed their subjects 1500 more calories than they had burned on the previous day. Before an appreciable conversion of carbohydrate to fat took place, there was a massive increase in glycogen storage until considerably higher than normal levels were reached (an average of 810 grams of glycogen storage versus the more usual average of about 500 grams). In addition, there was a 35 percent increase in the metabolic rate so that by Day 7 of overfeeding in the experiment (the last day of overfeeding) the subjects were consuming over 5000 calories a day, approximately 4000 of which were in the form of carbohydrate. This represented a diet-induced increase in energy requirements (adaptive thermogenesis) of about 1400 calories per day (up from about 3600 on the second day of the overfeeding to 5000 on the seventh) in order to maintain that surplus of 1500 calories above the previous day's energy needs. On the second day of overfeeding by 1500 calories, there was a fat conversion from carbohydrate of about 270 calories and on the fourth day it reached 720 calories. The researchers estimated that thereafter some 70 to 75 percent of the excess intake would be retained in fat storage.

Acheson and his colleagues concluded that while it is possible to force the conversion of carbohydrate to fat, to do so glycogen stores must first increase by about 500 grams over their normal level (about 2000 calories over normal). That is, the body can handle periodic loads of 2000 calories of carbohydrate without contributing to fat synthesis and storage. In order to continue appreciable conversion of carbohydrate to fat, continued massive amounts of carbohydrate over and above daily energy needs, such as they used in their study, would have to be ingested.

When it comes to weight control, the moral of this last study seems to be that while excess dietary fat is easily converted to fat storage, excess carbohydrate is not. Thus, if you want to pig-out occasionally with little danger of gaining fat weight, do it on carbohydrates.

There is one other point worth mentioning with respect to weight control on a high-carbohydrate diet, however, and that is the likelihood of rather large swings in one's daily weight. Since fluctuations in carbohydrate intake within the 2000-calorie (500-gram) range mentioned above have a direct impact on glycogen stores, rather than fat stores, and since glycogen is stored at around 500 calories per pound of body weight due to its solution of 1 part glycogen to 3 to 4 parts water, daily variations in carbohydrate intake can easily cause swings of a pound or two. This is really the weight of the water in solution, and it goes down as easily as it goes up. (Fat variations are not as easily detectable on a daily basis because the body stores fat at around 3500 calories per pound. And, once gained, fat weight, as we all know, does not go down as easily as water weight!)

BODY COMPOSITION IS ADJUSTED TO FAT IN THE DIET

In the steady state, where one is not gaining or losing body fat, the proportion of carbohydrate and fat in the fuel mixture powering the body each day is equal to the proportion of carbohydrate and fat in the diet. If one eats more fat than is being burned each day, it is put into fat storage and the fat reserves increase to the point where energy needs, as a function of increased body weight and increased fat stores, match the intake. At a new higher weight, with greater fat storage, the fat used in the fuel mix reaches the level of the fat in the high-fat diet. As Flatt (1987) pointed out, "On diets with a relatively high fat content (such as the mixed diets consumed in affluent societies), a substantial expansion of the adipose [fat] tissue mass often occurs before the use of fat reaches a rate commensurate with the diet's fat content." And furthermore: "Obesity may be the result of a tendency to achieve the steady state, where the fuel mix oxidized has the same composition as the food consumed only after an undesirably large expansion of the adipose tissue mass has taken place" (p. 305).

The relationship of the body's fat composition to the nature of the diet is being disclosed in a rash of recent studies. The relationship is easiest to illustrate in animals because of our ability to control the diet in laboratory research. In one study, with mice as subjects, as fat intake increased from 1 to 65 percent of calories, obesity increased from 0 to 35 percent. In the range of 20 to 40 percent of daily calories from fat, which pretty much includes the lower and upper ends of the range we are concerned with in humans, body-fat content DOUBLED (Salmon and Flatt, 1985).

Of the human studies, a recent report using data that assessed dietary intake over a one-year period from the Nurses Health Study showed that there was no relationship between total energy intake and obesity in a group of 141 women aged thirty-four to fifty-nine years (Romieu et al., 1988). There was, however, a significant relationship between fat intake (specifically saturated-fat intake) and obesity. These authors also noted a strong relationship between lack of physical activity (such as blocks walked and stairs climbed each day) and obesity.

IMPACT OF A LOW-FAT DIET ON BODY WEIGHT IN HUMANS

There have been several studies in which a low-fat diet was recommended in connection with certain medical problems. Although weight loss was *not* a specific objective, it seemed to occur naturally.

In one study (Asp et al., 1987), as part of their treatment for breast cancer, a group of seventeen women reduced their total daily fat intake from 39 percent of total calories to 22 percent. Over a three-month period they lost approximately 6.5 pounds. While weight loss was not an objective, the increase in bulk of the diet was associated with a lowering of total calories, from approximately 1840 at the start of the change in diet to approximately 1375 at the conclusion. Total daily fat intake went down from about 80 grams, which is quite typical of the American diet, to about 35 grams, which is within the range I recommend on the T-Factor Diet.

A team of investigators at the Division of Nutritional Sciences at Cornell University (Lissner et al., 1987) examined weight changes in twenty-four women who rotated for two-week periods on diets containing 15–20, 30–35, or 45–50 percent of the energy derived from fat. The diets were designed to be equally palatable (although the subjects tended to prefer the low-fat diet) and the women could eat as much of anything as they desired. On the low-fat diet they consumed approximately 2087 calories per day and lost almost a pound each week.[1] On the high-fat diet they consumed about 2714 calories and gained about two-thirds of a pound each week. They maintained their weight on the medium-fat diet, consuming about 2352 calories per day. Once again, on the average, the low-fat diet, on which the subjects lost weight on over 2000 calories per day, contained under 40 grams of fat. The women in this study were maintaining weight on about 98 grams of fat per day, while the high-fat diet, on which they gained weight, contained over 140 grams of fat per day. The amount of weight lost or gained each week corresponds almost exactly to the difference in the energy contained in the dietary fat that was subtracted or added to the maintenance diets. *Weight loss was inversely related to the total amount of carbohydrate and protein in the diet:* Total calories from protein and carbohydrate equaled about 1722 on the low-fat diet and about 1425 on the high-fat diet. In addition, the total weight of the food consumed on the low-fat diet was significantly higher than that on the high-fat diet.[2]

Finally, at the University of Alberta in Canada (Brown et al., 1984), a group of fifty average-weight men and women suffering from peripheral vascular disease were asked to follow either an American Heart Association

---

[1] Interestingly, while this study used normal-weight subjects who used each of the diets for only two weeks, the weight loss achieved on the low-fat diet is approximately what overweight women using the T-Factor Diet obtained in the Vanderbilt Weight Management Program over periods as long as twenty weeks, with calorie intakes as high as 2000 calories a day.

[2] On the low-, medium-, and high-fat diets, approximately 13, 12, and 10 percent of calories was derived from protein, and approximately 70, 55, and 42 percent of calories was derived from carbohydrate, respectively. Because of low energy density (in fruits, vegetables, and grains) the weight and bulk of a high-carbohydrate diet are greater than those of a low-carbohydrate diet.

(AHA) lipid-reducing diet or a higher-fiber, lower-fat version of the Pritikin maintenance diet (HFD). Subjects assigned to either diet benefited greatly, but those in the AHA group ended up twelve months later consuming about 34 percent of their days' total average of 1687 calories in fat, while the HFD group ended up consuming about 16 percent of their days' total average of 1608 calories in fat. In grams, this amounts to about 63 grams of fat per day in the AHA group, and about 28 grams of fat per day in the HFD group. Although the participants in this study were not overweight, the American Heart Association group lost an average of 9 pounds (from 113 percent of average weight to 105 percent), while the group asked to follow a higher-fiber, lower-fat diet lost over 13 pounds (from 109 percent of average weight to 99 percent). Once again, weight loss was inversely related to total carbohydrate and protein consumption (average of 1120 calories, carbohydrate and protein combined, in the AHA group, and 1344 calories, combined, in the HFD group).

You might ask why the participants in these groups did not continue to lose weight indefinitely on a low-fat diet. In other words, how and when does stabilization occur? It works something like this:

When you switch from a high- to low-fat diet, your body pulls fat from your fat cells in order to maintain the present high proportion of fat to carbohydrate in its fuel mix. At the same time as you lose body fat and move toward some new, and lower, body-fat content, you begin to make gradual adjustments in your fuel mixture, moving toward matching the change in diet. When you reach stabilization at some new and lower weight, your fuel mix will now approximate the new dietary ratio of carbohydrate to fat.

Of course, no one can tell what the new weight and body-fat content will be in any individual case when you change the fat content of the diet. You have to find out by experience.

You might also ask, on the basis of the results of the Canadian study, why I am not simply recommending a Pritikin maintenance diet, and the reason is quite easy to understand. Although the Pritikin program is based on what is essentially a good idea, it is carried beyond the tolerance and endurance of very many people! If you have ever tried the Pritikin program, you know that it is a terribly restricted diet and very hard to stick with. Indeed, the subjects in the study I've just discussed were not able to stick with it. But, fortunately, with the modifications they spontaneously added to it, they ended up close enough to the total fat-gram target that I recommend in the T-Factor Diet to be illustrative of what you can expect when you cut total daily fat grams down to 20–40 for women and 30–60 for men.[3]

CONCLUSION

I have referred to a selection of the most pertinent studies illustrating the importance of the composition of the diet to energy balance and fat storage. For a more exhaustive review of the many factors involved in energy balance in human beings, see Sims (1986) as well as Danforth (1985) and Flatt (1987). The unique merits of a low-fat diet for weight control are fully discussed by McCarty (1986) in an article bearing that title. This article closes with an observation that makes the point quite nicely:

> "Calorie counting" is one of the more grotesque manifestations of the modern American scene. While it may be useful for a small percentage of

---

[3] As the type for this book was being set, a study appeared in the *American Journal of Clinical Nutrition* (1989, 49, 77–85) by R. L. Hammer, C. A. Barrier, E. S. Roundy, J. M. Bradford, and A. G. Fisher, titled "Calorie-Restricted Low-Fat Diet and Exercise in Obese Women."

In one experimental condition, subjects ate a low-fat, unrestricted carbohydrate diet, with no attempt to cut calories, and slowly increased their physical activity until they were able to walk or jog about three miles four or five days a week. The calorie and fat intake ended up matching almost exactly what we have been obtaining in clinical practice when we prescribe the T-Factor Diet in the Vanderbilt Program. The weight loss over sixteen weeks was also almost identical, that is, almost a pound a week (14.75 pounds in sixteen weeks). The authors reported that this approach to losing weight was well received by the participants, and the authors concluded, "A low-fat, high-carbohydrate diet combined with daily exercise is effective in causing weight and fat loss in obese women without altering RMR [resting metabolic rate] and results in improved cardiovascular fitness," and "A program similar to the ALX [their ad libitum–carbohydrate diet with exercise] treatment is an effective prescription for weight and health management of obese persons" (p. 84).

the stoic, highly motivated individuals, few fallible humans will submit to this rigorous discipline for a lifetime. The dismal long-term success rates of most weight-control programs bear witness to the futility of calorie counting as a weight-loss strategy. Calorie counters are usually doomed to failure because they continue to eat the fatty Western foods which made them fat in the first place—albeit in restricted quantities. Sooner or later their discipline fails, and their weight goes back up.

Contrast that with the experience of many primitive groups whose traditional diets are low in fat. They have never heard of a "calorie," they eat as much as they want, they get some exercise—and they remain slender throughout life. Here's a weight-control program with a *proven* track record! [page 192]

REFERENCES

Acheson, K. J., Flatt, J. P., and Jequier, E. (1982). Glycogen synthesis versus lipogenesis after a 500 gram carbohydrate meal in man. *Metabolism*, 31, 1234–1240.

Acheson, K. J., Schutz, Y., Bessard, T., Anantharaman, K., Flatt, J. P., and Jequier, E. (1988). Glycogen storage capacity and de novo lipogenesis during massive carbohydrate overfeeding in man. *American Journal of Clinical Nutrition*, 48, 240–247.

Acheson, K. J., Schutz, Y., Bessard, T., Ravussin, E., and Jequier, E. (1984). Nutritional influences on lipogenesis and thermogenesis after a carbohydrate meal. *American Journal of Physiology*, 246, E62–70.

Asp, E. H., Buzzard, I. M., Chlebowski, R. T., Nixon, D., Blackburn, D., Jochimsen, P., Scanlon, E., Insull, W., Elashoff, R., Butrum, R., and Wynder, E. (1987). Reducing total fat intake: Effect on body weights. *International Journal of Obesity*, 4, 397a–397b.

Brown, G. D., Whyte, L., Gee, M. I., Crockford, P. M., Grace, M., Oberle, K., Williams, H. T. G., and Hutchison, K. J. (1984). Effects of two "lipid lowering" diets on plasma lipid levels of patients with peripheral vascular disease. *Journal of the American Dietetic Association*, 84, 546–550.

Danforth, E. (1985). Diet and obesity. *American Journal of Clinical Nutrition*, 41, 1132–1145.

Flatt, J. P. (1987). Dietary fat, carbohydrate balance, and weight maintenance: Effects of exercise. *American Journal of Clinical Nutrition*, 45, 296–306.

Flatt, J. P., Ravussin, E., Acheson, K. J., and Jequier, E. (1985). Effects of dietary fat on post-prandial substrate oxidation and on carbohydrate and fat balances. *Journal of Clinical Investigation*, 76, 1019–1024.

Lissner, L., Levitsky, D. A., Strupp, B. J., Kalwarf, H. J., and Roe, D. A. (1987). Dietary fat intake and the regulation of energy intake in human subjects. *American Journal of Clinical Nutrition*, 46, 886–892.

McCarty, Mark F. (1986). The unique merits of a low-fat diet for weight control. *Medical Hypotheses*, 20, 183–197.

Romieu, I., Willett, W. C., Stampfer, M. J., Colditz, G. A., Sampson, L., Rosner, B., Hennekens, C. H., and Speizer, F. E. (1988). Energy intake and other determinants of relative weight. *American Journal of Clinical Nutrition*, 47, 406–412.

Salmon, D. M. W., and Flatt, J. P. (1985). Effect of dietary fat content on the incidence of obesity among ad libitum fed mice. *International Journal of Obesity*, 9, 443–449.

Sims, E. A. H. (1986). Energy balance in human beings: The problem of plentitude. In *Vitamins and Hormones*, Vol. 43. San Diego/Orlando/New York: Academic Press.

APPENDIX B

◆

Rounding Out Your T-Factor Fitness Program

◆

Cardiovascular fitness is only part of the fitness picture. A total physical activity program also includes flexibility, and muscular strength and endurance.

First, let's talk about flexibility.

Stretching loosens you up before a walk or jog, and cools you down after vigorous exercise. A good stretching routine works the most important areas of the body for active people: calves, hamstrings (the muscles at the rear of your legs), stomach, and lower back. The T-Flex Routine will also address the areas where most of us hold a lot of our tension: the upper shoulders and neck, and again, the lower back.

Remember to stretch comfortably; don't push yourself to the point of pain. In time, with practice, your flexibility will increase naturally.

T-FLEX ROUTINE

This entire series of stretches takes only minutes to perform. Add to it some hatha-yoga postures if you wish for even greater flexibility, health, and relaxation.

T-Flex for the Neck and Shoulders

These first four movements are best performed while standing in the shower with hot water pouring down on your neck.

1. *Shoulder lift*. With head straight and neck relaxed, slowly lift your shoulders toward your ears. When shoulders are as high as they can comfortably go, roll them back, pushing your shoulder blades gently together. Hold for about 10 seconds, then reverse your movements, rolling your shoulders forward to the starting position, then lowering them. Repeat.

2. *Neck roll*. From the same starting position as above, slowly let your neck roll forward and your head drop down, trying to touch your chin to your chest without straining. Hold for several seconds, then roll your head up until you're looking at the ceiling. Hold for several seconds, then return to starting position. Repeat.

3. *Head roll*. From starting position, facing forward, let your head slowly drop sideways to the left. Try to touch your left ear to your left shoulder; you can lift your left shoulder slightly to give yourself an added stretch. Don't strain. Return to starting position and repeat on the other side.

4. *Neck twist*. Facing forward, turn your head slowly to the left as if to look over your shoulder. Hold for several seconds. Return to starting position, then look to your right. Repeat.

T-Flex Floor Routine

1. *Sitting stretch*. Sit on the floor with your legs crossed. Bend forward from the hips, keeping your back relaxed but straight. Reach forward as far as you can to touch the floor with your hands. Stretch your shoulder joints as well as your hips. Hold for 10 to 20 seconds, then relax.

2. *Sitting toe-touch*. This one is good for the hip joints, calves, and hamstrings. While still sitting, straighten your legs out in front of you. Bend forward from the hips, aim your toes back toward your head, and reach for your toes. Many people can only reach to their ankles

or calves when they first do this exercise. If this is true for you, don't force yourself to go beyond the point of comfort. Hold the stretch for 10 to 20 seconds.

3. *Resting twist*. This will increase your lower back flexibility and relieve stiffness. Lie flat on the floor, arms straight out to the sides, legs together. Bend your right knee and place your right foot under your left knee. Keep your shoulders flat to the floor and rotate your lower body to the left, from the hips. Try to touch the inside of your right knee to the floor on your left side. Turn your head to the right and look out over your extended right arm. You

can gently push your right knee toward the floor with your left hand, but don't force the stretch. Hold about 10 seconds. Do the other side (left foot under right knee, etc.).

4. *Back stretch.* This also helps relieve tension in the lower back. Lie flat on the floor, legs together. Bend your right leg and bring your right knee to your chest. Hold the knee with both hands and press it gently toward your chest. Hold for 10 seconds, then reverse legs. Your head and shoulders can come up off the floor if you like, or you can use a pillow under your head for this and the next three exercises.

5. *Back curl*. Another excellent lower back exercise. Still lying on the floor, bring both knees to your chest, gently pressing them closer with your hands. Hold for about 10 to 20 seconds. Then go right on to the next exercise.

6. *Ceiling stretch*. From the position you are already in for the back curl, continue holding your right knee while grasping the big toe of your left foot with your left hand. Straighten the left leg up toward the ceiling as far as you can, continuing to hold the big toe. Hold for at least 10 seconds, then do the other leg. This works the calves, hamstrings, and lower back as a unit. Return to the back curl position.

7. *Bicycle and flutter kicks.* From the back curl position, place your hands palms-down under your buttocks. With your knees about halfway to your chest, do a bicycling motion for 10 seconds (or 10 repetitions). Then lower your legs straight out in front of you to within 6 inches of the floor and do flutter kicks for 10 seconds (or 10 repetitions). Repeat the bicycle motion, alternating with the flutter kicks, until you feel some strain in your stomach area. This exercise can take the place of sit-ups and is an excellent tummy toner and back exercise. *However, if you already suffer from chronic lower back pain, do not do this exercise without getting your therapist's advice. Your problem may require a different stomach muscle strengthener.*

8. *Pelvic curl.* Still lying down, rest your arms flat on the floor with elbows bent and hands near your head, palms up. Bend your knees so that your feet are flat on the

floor about 12 inches from your buttocks. Curl your pelvis so your lower back presses against the floor and your buttocks lift slightly. Hold for about 10 seconds, release, and repeat. This will relieve tension in the lower back.

9. *T-Factor "shoulder stand."* Simply place your legs up on a chair and relax for 30 seconds. This is good for your circulation, helps reduce swelling around the ankles, and will relieve "drawing pains" in the legs. If you experience pain in your extremities during the night, do the T-Factor "shoulder stand" before you go to bed. If you are already fairly flexible and don't have much weight to lose, you can do the more rigorous shoulder stand: Lie flat on the floor

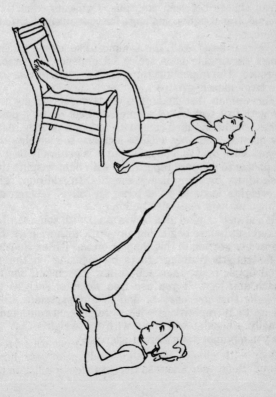

with your arms resting along your sides. Curl your legs up as if for the back curl, but keep rolling your torso up, placing your hands on your back to help keep your balance. Straighten your legs up toward the celing and hold for 30 seconds. *However, if you suffer from hypertension, do not do any exercise that requires you to lift your legs up over your head, as in a shoulder stand, without consulting your physician.*

T-STRENGTH ROUTINE

In recent years, strength-training centers have been popping up everywhere: in spas, YMCAs, and private clubs. You can choose between Nautilus, Dynacam, Cam Two, Universal, free weights, and more for your strength-training equipment.

Which is best? Well, this is almost like asking which is the best car or television set. A lot depends on personal preference. The important thing is that you exercise each of the large muscle groups.

For women just beginning a strength-training program with free weights, it's generally best to use 3-pound weights. Beginning men can go up to 5 or 6 pounds. After a few months, you may wish to increase the weights that you work with by 3 to 6 pounds, but it is generally best for most people to do more repetitions with light weights than to risk injury by using heavy weights. In addition, using light weights leads to good tone, an "alive" feeling, and nice lines without excessive bulking.

It's always a good idea to warm up with some stretching exercises before beginning any work with weights. See the previous section in this chapter on the T-Flex Routine.

T-Strength training starts by focusing on the neglected upper body, then adds a few movements for the stomach and legs. If you use free weights, such as the dumbbells that are easy to find in a department store, work up to 10 repetitions with a weight you can handle. Normally a booklet will come with the weights that will show you a number of different exercises.

Upper Body Series

1. *Two for the shoulders.* Hold arms at your sides with palms facing the rear. Keeping arms straight, raise weights forward to shoulder height and return to down position, slowly and with control. Breathe normally at all times. Work up to 10 repetitions, then rest for at least one deep breath. Then, turn the weights so that your palms face your body, and raise your arms outward to the sides, up to shoulder level. Work up to 10 repetitions.

2. *Biceps curl.* Stand straight with arms at sides, palms facing forward. Curl forearms up to shoulder 10 times at a moderate pace.

3. *Triceps.* Keep elbows next to your body, bend forward at about a 60-degree angle from the hips, and curl forearms, bringing weights up to your shoulders. Then, keeping elbows next to your body, straighten your arms out in back behind you. Repeat until you feel some strain and stop. This will build the muscle on the back of your arms, and help reduce the likelihood of loose skin on your upper arms if you have been losing weight.

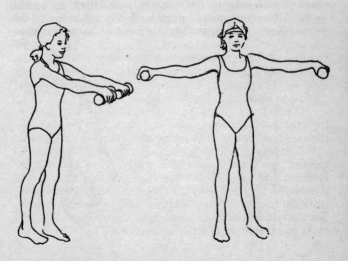

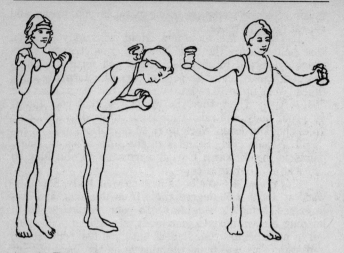

4. *Forward, up, and out.* Standing upright, start with arms at your sides, palms facing body. Curling at the elbows, bring weights forward and up almost to the shoulders. Continuing in one uninterrupted motion, spread arms out to your sides, shoulder level, palms facing forward. Keep your arms slightly bent to avoid excessive

strain. Return along the same path as you began and repeat up to 10 times.

Leg Series

5. *Heel lifts*. With weights at your side, go up and down slowly on your toes several times, resting about a second at the top each time.

6. *Half squats*. (If you are more than a few pounds overweight, don't use any extra weight for this exercise.) With arms at sides, feet at shoulder width, toes facing slightly out, squat down ⅓ to ½ of the way to the floor. Do not go beyond the point where your thighs are parallel to the floor, and keep your knees over your feet when squatting.

Stomach Series

7. *Bent-knee sit-up*. Lie on your back with knees bent and feet close to your buttocks. Curl your head and shoulders about halfway up to your knees to begin with. (As you get stronger, try to get closer to your knees.) Roll back down. Arms can be held out in front of you to start, and then, as you get stronger, they can be folded across your chest. Ultimately, hands are held behind your head.

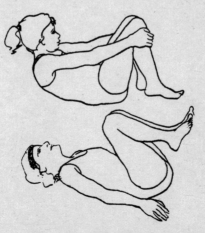

8. *Reverse sit-up.* Lying flat on the floor with arms at your sides, bring your heels back to your buttocks, and then lift knees to your chest, raising hips off the floor. Return to starting position and repeat several times. Breathe normally.

Finally, one of the very best strengthening exercises of all is the push-up, but it should not be undertaken until your stomach muscles are reasonably strong and until you can do a push-up resting on your knees rather than your toes. You can practice some easier versions of the push-up by pushing off against a wall until you get stronger.

Be sure to check with your physician before beginning any new fitness program. Then, get start-up instruction from a qualified teacher at your local YMCA, club, or spa.

APPENDIX C[1]

◆

INSTRUCTIONS FOR KEEPING A DAILY FAT-GRAM RECORD

It's a good idea to keep a pocket notebook and record your fat-gram intake until you are familiar with the fat contents of the foods you normally eat. After a few weeks you will have made the required changes in your diet, committed the new knowledge to memory, and recording will become unnecessary.

Simply write down the food item on the left-hand side of the page and the fat content in grams on the right. Total after each meal and stick within your fat-gram allowance:

20 to 40 grams per day for women
30 to 60 grams per day for men

You may also choose to photocopy this counter, or cut it out of the book, if necessary, so that you can carry it in your pocket or purse.

Since the energy in fat is so concentrated (there is a gram or more of fat in each ¼ teaspoon of fat or oil, which equals 9 calories), accurate measurements of all items that contain fat are important.

For your additional information, this counter also lists the fiber content of various foods. However, unless you are curious, you do not need to keep a record of fiber intake. The suggested range of 20 to 40 grams of fiber per day for women and up to 50 grams for men is easily reached on the T-Factor Diet (our Quick Melt menus average about 30 grams of fiber per day). Many authorities suggest that you slowly increase fiber until you are consuming quantities that are at the high end of the suggested range.

---

[1] Nutrient values in this appendix were obtained from materials provided by the U.S. Department of Agriculture, as well as the food industry, journal articles, and computer data banks in which information is assumed to be public domain.

HOW TO INTERPRET THE LISTINGS IN THE DIFFERENT CATEGORIES OF FOODS IN THIS COUNTER

The category "combination foods" includes examples of a variety, but not all, of the thousands of processed and packaged foods with different brand names. We have chosen representative items from different food manufacturers, or taken an average from several, without naming them. You should be aware that the same dish may vary greatly from one manufacturer to another. The only way to be certain of the fat content of packaged foods under different brand names is to read the nutrient labels. If an item does not say either "homemade" or "frzn." (frozen) in our list, the values tend to be similar and you can use the figures in the table for either.

Values for salads, soups, sandwiches, and other dishes that are in reality combinations of ingredients are for typical recipes. If the values are for low-calorie recipes, the food item will be labeled "low cal." or "reduced cal."

In the meat, fish, and poultry categories, values are for cooked portions, without added fat, unless otherwise specified. In some cases, where values vary according to cooking methods, the cooking method is specified.

Compared with many items with similar labels listed in this counter, T-Factor recipes contain far less fat and more fiber. Be sure to check the nutrient values given with T-Factor recipes in recording your fat intake when you use these recipes.

If an item is not listed in this counter, use the values of a similar food as an approximation.

ORGANIZATION OF THIS COUNTER

The food items in the Fat and Fiber Counter are listed in alphabetical order within a number of different food categories. The categories of foods are organized as follows, with the page numbers on which you will find them:

Fat and Fiber Counter

ITEM	SERVING	FAT GRAMS	FIBER GRAMS
Beverages			
apple juice	6 fl. oz.	0.0	0.0
beer, all varieties	12 fl. oz.	0.0	0.0
carbonated			
diet	12 fl. oz.	0.0	0.0
w/sugar	12 fl. oz.	0.0	0.0
club soda/seltzer	12 fl. oz.	0.0	0.0
coffee, brewed or instant	6 fl. oz.	0.0	0.0
cordials & liqueurs, 54 proof	1 fl. oz.	0.0	0.0
eggnog			
alcoholic, homemade	4 fl. oz.	15.8	0.0
nonalcoholic, store bought	8 fl. oz.	19.0	0.0
fruit juices	6 fl. oz.	0.0	0.0
Gatorade	8 fl. oz.	0.0	0.0
gin	1 fl. oz.	0.0	0.0
Hawaiian Punch	8 fl. oz.	0.0	0.0
Kool-Aid, from mix, all flavors	8 fl. oz.	0.0	0.0
lemonade, frzn. conc. or mix	8 fl. oz.	0.0	0.0
orange juice, frzn. conc.	6 fl. oz.	0.3	0.1
rum	1 fl. oz.	0.0	0.0
Tang			
grape	in water	0.0	0.0
orange	in water	0.0	0.0
tea, brewed or instant	8 fl. oz.	0.0	0.0
vodka	1 fl. oz.	0.0	0.0
whiskey	1 fl. oz.	0.0	0.0
wine	3½ fl. oz.	0.0	0.0

ITEM	SERVING	FAT GRAMS	FIBER GRAMS
Breads and Flours			
bagel, medium	1 bagel	1.0	2.0
biscuit			
from mix	1 medium	3.3	0.8
homemade	1 medium	4.8	0.8
Bisquick mix	½ cup	8.0	0.0
bread			
Boston brown, canned	1 slice	1.2	4.0
cracked wheat	1 slice	0.9	1.5
fruit (e.g., banana), w/o nuts	1 slice	3.4	1.4
fruit w/nuts	1 slice	7.0	0.8
fruit/nut quick, from mix	1 slice, ¹⁄₁₆ loaf	5.4	0.8
honey wheatberry	1 slice	1.1	1.5
Italian	1 slice	0.3	0.5
mixed grain	1 slice	0.9	1.4
raisin	1 slice	0.7	0.9
rye	1 slice	0.9	1.5
rye/pumpernickel	1 slice	0.8	1.3
sourdough	1 slice	0.5	0.8
wheat	1 slice	1.0	0.7
wheatberry	1 slice	1.1	1.4
white	1 slice	0.8	0.4
white, buttermilk	1 slice	0.8	0.4
white, homemade	1 slice	1.2	0.4
whole wheat	1 slice	0.8	1.4
whole wheat, homemade	1 slice	1.0	1.8
bread sticks			
all flavors	1 piece	0.2	0.2
sesame	1 piece	3.7	0.2
breadcrumbs	1 cup	4.0	2.3
coffee cake	1 piece	7.0	0.6
cornbread			
from mix	⅛ prep. mix	4.0	0.8
whole ground	1 piece, 2½" square	6.9	1.3
corn flake crumbs	2 T	0.0	0.0
corn meal	½ cup	0.9	4.9
cornstarch	1 T	0.0	0.0
crackers			
cheese	5 pieces	4.9	0.3
cheese w/peanut butter	2-oz. pkg.	13.5	0.1
goldfish, all flavors	12 crackers	2.0	0.2

ITEM	SERVING	FAT GRAMS	FIBER GRAMS
graham	2 squares	1.3	0.2
graham, crumbs	½ cup	4.5	1.5
Hi Ho	4 crackers	4.4	0.4
melba toast	1 piece	0.2	0.1
oyster	33 crackers	3.3	0.1
rice wafer	3 wafers	0.0	0.3
Ritz.	3 crackers	2.9	0.3
Ritz, cheese	3 crackers	2.9	0.3
rye w/cheese	1.5-oz. pkg.	9.5	0.2
Rye krisp, plain	2 triple crackers	0.2	0.2
Rye krisp, seasoned	2 triple crackers	0.9	0.2
Rye krisp, sesame	2 triple crackers	1.5	0.1
saltines	2 crackers	0.6	0.1
soda	10 crackers	3.2	0.1
Triscuit	2 crackers	1.5	0.1
Uneeda	2 crackers	1.0	0.1
Waverly Wafers	2 crackers	1.6	0.1
Wheat Thins	4 crackers	1.4	0.1
wheat w/cheese	1.5- oz. pkg.	10.9	0.3
croissant	1 medium	12.0	0.4
croutons, herb seasoned	½ cup	2.0	0.2
danish pastry	1 medium	18.0	0.7
doughnut			
cake	1	8.0	0.7
yeast	1	14.0	1.0
English muffin			
regular	1	2.0	0.9
whole wheat	1	2.5	2.0
flour			
white, all purpose	1 cup	1.1	3.0
whole wheat	1 cup	1.6	7.1
French toast			
frzn.	1 slice	5.0	0.3
homemade	1 slice	6.7	0.3
hush puppy	1 medium	11.0	0.8
muffin			
all types, commercial	1 large	10.3	0.8
blueberry from mix	1 medium	4.3	0.2
bran, homemade	1 medium	5.1	1.0
corn	1 medium	4.2	0.6
soy	1 medium	4.4	0.6
white	1 medium	4.0	0.1
whole wheat	1 medium	1.1	0.8

ITEM	SERVING	FAT GRAMS	FIBER GRAMS
pancakes			
buttermilk from mix	3 medium	10.0	0.2
homemade	1 medium	3.2	0.1
pita	1 6" pocket	1.0	1.5
popover	1	5.0	0.1
rice cakes	2	0.6	0.2
rolls			
brown & serve	1	2.2	0.4
butterflake	1	3.0	0.4
buttermilk	1	4.9	0.4
cloverleaf	1	3.2	0.2
crescent	1	5.0	0.5
French	1	0.4	0.5
hamburger	1	2.1	0.8
hot dog	1	2.1	0.7
kaiser/hoagie	1 large	8.4	0.5
Parkerhouse	1	2.1	0.4
raisin	1 large	1.7	0.5
rye	1	1.6	2.2
sandwich	1	3.1	0.7
sesame seed	1	2.1	0.8
sourdough	1	0.4	0.8
sweet roll	1 medium	8.0	1.0
wheat	1	1.7	0.9
Stuffing			
bread, from mix	½ cup	12.2	0.2
cornbread, from mix	½ cup	1.8	0.3
Stove Top	½ cup	8.9	0.4
taco/tostada shells	1	2.2	0.2
toaster pastry, all varieties	1	6.0	0.1
tortilla			
corn	1 medium	1.1	0.6
flour	1 large	3.8	1.3
waffle			
frzn.	1	3.2	0.5
frzn., Eggo	1	5.0	0.5
homemade	1 large	12.6	0.7
Candy			
Almond Joy	1 oz.	7.8	0.0
Bit-o-Honey	1 oz.	21.2	0.0
butterscotch	6 pieces	2.5	0.0
butterscotch chips	1 oz.	7.0	0.0

ITEM	SERVING	FAT GRAMS	FIBER GRAMS
caramels			
plain or choc. w/nuts	2 pieces	4.6	0.1
plain or choc. w/o nuts	3 pieces	2.9	0.1
chocolate			
chips	¼ cup	12.2	1.2
kisses	6 pieces	9.0	0.3
special dark, Hershey	1.02 oz.	8.6	0.3
stars	7 pieces	8.1	0.1
Chunky			
milk choc.	1 oz.	4.4	0.0
original	1 oz.	7.1	0.0
fudge			
choc.	1 oz.	3.4	0.1
choc. w/nuts	1 oz.	4.9	0.1
Good & Plenty	1.5-oz. pkg.	0.0	0.0
gum drops	28 pieces	0.2	0.0
hard candy	6 pieces	0.3	0.0
jelly beans	10 pieces	0.0	0.0
Kit Kat	1.13 oz.	8.5	0.1
Krackle	1.2 oz.	9.7	0.2
Life Savers	5 pieces	0.1	0.0
M&M's			
peanut	1.67-oz. pkg.	12.0	0.0
regular	1.59-oz. pkg.	10.0	0.0
malted milk balls	14 pieces	7.0	0.1
Mars	1.7-oz. bar	10.0	0.0
marshmallow	1 large	0.0	0.0
milk choc.			
plain	1 oz.	9.0	0.3
w/almonds, Hershey	1 oz.	9.0	0.3
Milky Way	2.1 oz.	9.0	0.0
mints	14 pieces	0.6	0.0
Mounds	1 oz.	6.9	0.0
Mr. Goodbar	1.27 oz.	11.9	0.4
Nestle's Crunch	1.06 oz.	8.0	0.0
peanut brittle	1 oz.	4.4	0.0
peanut butter cups, Reese's	2 pieces	10.7	0.3
Peppermint Pattie	1 oz.	2.3	0.0
Reese's Pieces	1.7-oz. pkg.	10.0	0.3
Snickers	2 oz.	13.0	0.0
Three Musketeers	2.28 oz.	8.0	0.0
Twix	1.73 oz.	6.0	0.0

ITEM	SERVING	FAT GRAMS	FIBER GRAMS
Cereals			
All Bran	¾ cup (1 oz.)	0.5	16.0
Alpha-Bits	1 cup	0.6	0.6
Apple Jacks	1 cup	0.1	0.6
Bran Buds	⅓ cup	0.7	3.0
Bran Chex	⅔ cup	0.8	5.5
Bran Flakes, 40%	¾ cup	0.5	4.5
bran, 100%	½ cup	1.4	12.1
Cap'n Crunch	¾ oz.	2.6	0.6
Cheerios	1¼ cups	1.8	2.5
Corn Chex	1 cup	0.1	0.1
corn flakes	1 cup	0.1	0.4
corn grits, w/o added fat	1 cup	0.5	0.2
Cracklin' Bran	⅓ cup	4.1	1.0
Cream of Wheat, w/o added fat	¾ cup	0.4	0.5
Froot Loops	1 cup	0.5	0.6
Frosted Mini-Wheats	4 biscuits	0.3	0.7
Fruit & Fibre			
w/apples & cinn.	½ cup	0.3	3.1
w/dates, raisin, walnut	½ cup	0.7	3.0
Golden Grahams	¾ cup	1.1	0.6
granola, Nature Valley	⅓ cup	6.5	1.8
Life, plain or cinn.	⅔ cup	0.5	1.6
Most	⅔ cup	0.3	2.0
Nutri-Grain			
barley	¾ cup	0.2	1.4
corn	⅔ cup	0.7	1.5
wheat	¾ cup	0.3	2.5
oats, w/o added fat			
instant	1 packet	1.7	1.2
regular	¾ cup	1.8	1.2
Product-19	¾ cup	0.2	0.4
Puffed Rice	1 cup	0.1	0.1
Raisin Bran	¾ cup	0.7	6.5
Rice Chex	1⅛ cups	0.1	0.6
Rice Krispies	1 cup	0.2	0.4
Shredded Wheat	1 cup	0.6	2.4
Special K	1⅓ cups	0.1	0.2
Sugar Frosted Flakes	¾ cup	0.2	0.6
Sugar Smacks	¾ cup	0.5	0.6
Team	1 cup	0.5	0.8
Total	1 cup	0.6	2.9

ITEM	SERVING	FAT GRAMS	FIBER GRAMS
Wheat Chex	⅔ cup	0.7	2.6
wheat germ, toasted	¼ cup	3.0	4.0
Wheaties	1 cup	0.5	2.5
whole-wheat hot natural cereal	¾ cup	0.7	0.7
Cheeses			
American			
reduced cal.	1 oz.	2.2	0.0
regular	1 oz.	8.9	0.0
blue	1 oz.	8.2	0.0
brick	1 oz.	8.4	0.0
Brie	1 oz.	7.9	0.0
cheddar	1 oz.	9.4	0.0
Colby	1 oz.	9.1	0.0
cottage cheese			
1% fat	½ cup	1.0	0.0
2% fat	½ cup	3.0	0.0
creamed	½ cup	5.0	0.0
cream cheese			
"lite"	1 oz. (2 T)	7.0	0.0
regular	1 oz. (2 T)	9.9	0.0
feta	1 oz.	6.0	0.0
Gouda	1 oz.	7.8	0.0
Monterey Jack	1 oz.	6.1	0.0
mozzarella			
part skim	1 oz.	4.5	0.0
whole milk	1 oz.	7.0	0.0
Muenster	1 oz.	8.5	0.0
Parmesan, grated	1 T	1.5	0.0
pimiento cheese spread	1 oz.	8.8	0.0
provolone	1 oz.	7.6	0.0
ricotta			
part skim	½ cup	9.8	0.0
whole milk	½ cup	16.1	0.0
Roquefort	1 oz.	8.7	0.0
Swiss	1 oz.	7.8	0.0
Combination Foods			
beans & franks, canned	7¾ oz.	14.5	1.5
beans			
refried, canned, w/o added fat	½ cup	2.0	10.5

ITEM	SERVING	FAT GRAMS	FIBER GRAMS
refried, w/added fat	½ cup	13.0	10.0
refried w/sausage, canned	½ cup	13.0	10.0
Beef Oriental, Stouffer's Lean Cuisine	9⅛ oz.	9.0	0.0
beef pie			
frzn. variety	8 oz.	23.0	0.0
homemade	8 oz.	32.9	0.9
beef stew	1 cup	13.0	0.0
beef stroganoff	1 cup	44.4	0.8
beef teriyaki, frzn. variety	10 oz.	11.0	0.0
beef veg. stew, homemade	1 cup	10.5	1.0
burrito, beef	1 large	24.8	2.2
Caesar salad w/o anchovies	1 cup	7.2	0.6
cannelloni, meat & cheese	1 piece	29.3	0.6
carrot-raisin salad	½ cup	5.8	1.7
casserole: meat, veg., rice, sauce	1 cup	11.1	3.1
chef salad w/o dressing	1 cup	4.3	0.7
chicken & noodles, homemade	1 cup	18.5	NA
chicken & rice, homemade	1 cup	14.6	0.0
chicken a la king, homemade	1 cup	14.3	NA
chicken & dumplings	1 cup	10.5	0.8
chicken & veg. stir-fry	1 cup	6.9	3.2
chicken cacciatore, frzn. variety	11¼ oz.	11.0	0.0
chicken divan, frzn. variety	8½ oz.	22.0	0.0
chicken parmigiana, homemade	7 oz.	14.8	0.0
chicken pie			
frzn. variety	8 oz.	25.0	0.0
homemade	8 oz.	31.4	1.0
chicken salad	½ cup	21.0	0.3
chili			
w/beans, homemade	1 cup	13.7	7.8
w/o beans, homemade	1 cup	24.8	0.2
chow mein			
chicken	1 cup	4.0	0.0
homemade	1 cup	4.0	0.7
chop suey,			
beef, homemade	1 cup	17.0	1.3
coleslaw	½ cup	16.2	0.9
corned beef hash	1 cup	29.3	2.0
creamed chipped beef	1 cup	22.0	0.3
curry w/o meat	1 cup	6.6	1.7
eggplant Parmesan, fried version	1 cup	24.0	3.0

ITEM	SERVING	FAT GRAMS	FIBER GRAMS
eggroll	1 (3½ oz.)	10.5	1.0
enchilada			
cheese, frzn.	4	21.0	0.0
chicken, frzn.	7½ oz.	11.0	0.0
homemade	1 piece	14.0	3.3
green pepper, stuffed	1 average	10.2	0.0
ham salad	½ cup	24.3	0.0
Hamburger Helper, all varieties	1 serving	16.0	0.0
lasagna with meat	1 piece	19.3	1.5
macaroni & cheese			
from package	1 cup	8.7	0.2
frzn.	6 oz.	12.0	0.0
macaroni salad w/mayo	½ cup	9.5	1.2
manicotti, cheese & tomato	1 piece	11.8	1.7
meatloaf	1 slice, 2½ oz.	16.3	0.3
moo goo gai pan	1 cup	16.9	0.5
pizza			
cheese	1 slice	10.0	0.9
cheese, French bread, frzn.	5⅛ oz.	13.0	0.0
deep dish, cheese	1 slice	13.3	3.9
pork, sweet & sour	1½ cups	21.7	0.5
potato salad			
German	½ cup	3.5	1.4
w/mayo dressing	½ cup	11.5	1.0
ratatouille	½ cup	7.4	1.5
ravioli, canned	1 cup	7.3	2.7
Salisbury steak, w/gravy	8 oz.	27.3	0.0
sandwich			
BLT	1	15.6	0.6
chicken & mayo on white	1	14.4	0.3
club	1	20.8	1.2
corned beef on rye	1	10.8	0.2
cream cheese & jelly on white	1	16.0	0.1
egg salad on white	1	12.5	0.3
ham & mayo on white	1	15.4	0.1
ham salad on white	1	16.9	0.4
peanut butter & jelly on white	1	15.1	0.6
roast beef & gravy on white	1	24.5	0.1
roast beef & mayo on white	1	22.6	0.8
reuben	1	38.0	5.9
tuna salad on white	1	14.2	0.1
turkey & mayo on white	1	18.4	0.1

ITEM	SERVING	FAT GRAMS	FIBER GRAMS
spaghetti w/meat sauce	1 cup	16.7	0.7
sweet & sour pork	1 cup	21.7	0.5
tabouleh salad	½ cup	9.5	2.2
taco, beef	1 medium	17.8	1.3
taco salad w/o dressing	1 cup	14.0	1.7
tamale	1 piece	6.0	1.3
three-bean salad	½ cup	11.2	3.4
tortellini, meat or cheese	1 cup	14.4	1.4
tuna noodle casserole	1 cup	11.8	0.0
tuna salad w/mayo	½ cup	16.3	0.4
veal parmigiana	1 piece	25.0	1.7
Desserts			
apple brown betty	½ cup	4.9	0.7
brownie			
choc., plain	1 small	5.0	0.0
choc. w/nuts & icing	1 small	8.5	0.1
choc., Little Debbie	2 small	7.3	0.0
Hostess	1 small	6.0	0.0
cake, w/o icing			
angel food	¹⁄₁₂ cake	0.2	0.1
banana	¹⁄₁₂ cake	11.0	0.0
carrot, w/o nuts	¹⁄₁₂ cake	11.0	0.0
choc.	¹⁄₁₂ cake	11.0	0.6
lemon	¹⁄₁₂ cake	11.0	0.0
pineapple upside down	2½" square	9.2	0.2
pound	¹⁄₁₂ cake	9.0	0.0
spice	¹⁄₁₂ cake	5.9	0.0
sponge	¹⁄₁₂ cake	3.1	0.0
white	¹⁄₁₂ cake	10.0	0.1
cheesecake	⅛ cake	22.0	0.2
cookies			
animal	15	2.9	0.1
choc., plain	1	3.3	0.1
choc. chip	1	2.7	0.0
choc. sandwich (Oreo type)	1	2.1	0.0
fig bars	1	1.0	0.2
gingersnaps	3 small	1.1	0.0
graham crackers			
choc. covered	1	3.1	0.1
regular	2 squares	1.3	0.2
macaroons	1	3.2	0.3
Milano, Pepperidge Farm	1	3.6	0.0

ITEM	SERVING	FAT GRAMS	FIBER GRAMS
molasses	1	2.9	0.0
oatmeal	1	3.0	0.0
oatmeal raisin	1	2.6	0.1
Orleans, Pepperidge Farm	1	1.8	0.0
peanut butter	1	2.6	0.1
shortbread	1	2.3	0.0
sugar	1	3.4	0.0
sugar wafers	2	2.1	0.0
van. creme sandwich	1	3.1	0.0
cream puff	1	16.6	0.0
Creamsicle	1 bar	3.1	0.0
cupcake			
choc. w/icing	1 small	4.5	0.1
yellow w/icing	1 small	6.0	0.1
custard	½ cup	5.0	0.0
danish			
cheese	1 medium	7.2	0.3
fruit	1 medium	5.5	0.4
plain	1 medium	8.8	0.2
Devil Twin, Little Debbie	1 square	3.4	0.0
Ding Dong, Hostess	1 cake	10.2	0.0
dumpling, apple	1	17.0	0.0
eclair			
w/choc. icing & custard	1	15.4	0.0
w/choc. icing & whipped cream	1	20.7	0.0
fruitcake	2″ square	6.2	0.2
Fudgesicle	1	0.2	0.0
gelatin, regular or low cal.	½ cup	0.0	0.0
gingerbread	2½″ square	12.9	0.1
granola bar	1 bar	5.0	0.2
Ho Ho's, Hostess	1 cake	5.4	0.0
ice cream			
choc. reg. (10% fat)	1 cup	16.0	0.0
choc. rich (16% fat)	1 cup	26.5	0.0
drumstick	1	9.9	0.0
sandwich	1	6.2	0.0
strawberry	1 cup	12.0	0.0
van. reg (10% fat)	1 cup	14.3	0.0
van. rich (16% fat)	1 cup	23.7	0.0
van. soft serve	1 cup	22.5	0.0
ice cream cone (cone only)	1	0.3	0.0

ITEM	SERVING	FAT GRAMS	FIBER GRAMS
ice milk			
choc.	1 cup	6.1	0.0
strawberry	1 cup	4.1	0.0
vanilla	1 cup	5.6	0.0
ices	1 cup	0.0	0.0
icing			
choc.	3 T	5.3	0.0
cream cheese	3 T	7.6	0.0
lemon or van.	3 T	4.0	0.0
lady finger	1	16.6	0.0
peach cobbler	⅓ cup	6.4	0.2
pie			
apple	⅛ pie	11.9	0.5
banana cream	⅛ pie	14.0	0.0
blueberry	⅛ pie	17.3	1.1
Boston cream	⅛ pie	12.5	0.0
cherry	⅛ pie	18.0	0.2
choc. cream	⅛ pie	17.0	0.2
coconut cream	⅛ pie	14.0	0.0
lemon chiffon	⅛ pie	13.0	0.0
lemon meringue	⅛ pie	13.1	0.1
mincemeat	⅛ pie	18.4	0.6
peach	⅛ pie	17.7	0.7
pecan	⅛ pie	18.3	0.4
pumpkin	⅛ pie	16.8	0.8
rhubarb	⅛ pie	17.1	1.0
strawberry	⅛ pie	9.1	0.9
sweet potato	⅛ pie	18.2	0.3
Popsicle	1 bar	0.0	0.0
pudding pops, all flavors	1	2.6	0.0
pudding			
all flavors except choc., w/whole milk	½ cup	5.5	0.1
choc., w/whole milk	½ cup	8.5	0.6
sherbet	1 cup	0.0	0.0
snack pie, fruit, Hostess	1	20.2	0.0
Snoballs, Hostess	1 cake	4.8	0.0
turnover	1	20.0	0.0
Twinkies, Hostess	1 cake	4.2	0.0
yogurt, frzn.			
low fat	1 cup	8.0	0.0
nonfat	1 cup	1.0	0.0

ITEM	SERVING	FAT GRAMS	FIBER GRAMS
Eggs			
boiled/poached	1	5.6	0.0
Egg Beaters, Fleishmann's	¼ cup	0.0	0.0
fried	1 large	6.4	0.0
omelet			
plain, 3 eggs	1 large	21.3	0.0
cheese (2 oz.), 3 eggs	1 large	40.0	N/A
scrambled w/milk & fat	1 large	7.1	0.0
soufflé			
cheese	4 oz.	18.8	0.0
cheese, Stouffer's	6 oz.	26.0	0.0
veg., Stouffer's	4 oz.	7.0	0.0
white	white of 1 large	0.0	0.0
yolk	yolk of 1 large	5.6	0.0
Fast Food			
Arby's			
club sandwich	1	30.0	NA
ham & cheese sand.	1	17.0	NA
junior roast beef sand.	1	9.0	NA
roast beef sand.	1	15.0	NA
turkey sand.	1	24.0	NA
Arthur Treacher			
chicken fillet, fried	1	21.6	NA
chicken sand.	1	19.2	NA
chips (fried potatoes)	1	13.1	NA
coleslaw	1	8.0	NA
fish chowder	1	5.4	NA
fish sand.	1	19.2	NA
fish, fried	2 pieces	19.7	NA
Krunch Pup (hot dog)	1	14.9	NA
Burger King			
apple pie	1	12.0	NA
cheeseburger	1	17.0	NA
cheeseburger, double	1	32.0	NA
french fries, reg.	1 order	11.0	NA
hamburger	1	13.0	NA
onion rings, reg.	1 order	16.0	NA
shake			
choc.	1	10.0	NA
van.	1	11.0	NA
Whopper	1	36.0	NA

ITEM	SERVING	FAT GRAMS	FIBER GRAMS
Whopper w/cheese	1	45.0	NA
Whopper, double beef	1	52.0	NA
Whopper, double beef w/cheese	1	60.0	NA
Whopper Junior	1	20.0	NA
Whopper Junior w/cheese	1	25.0	NA
Church's Fried Chicken			
dark meat, fried	3½ oz.	21.0	0.2
white meat, fried	3½ oz.	23.0	0.1
Dairy Queen			
banana split	1	15.0	0.1
Buster bar	1	22.0	NA
cheeseburger	1	14.0	NA
chili dog	1	20.0	NA
choc. sundae med.	1	7.0	NA
Dilly bar	1	15.0	NA
fish sand.	1	17.0	NA
float	1	8.0	NA
freeze	1	13.0	NA
french fries, reg.	1 order	10.0	NA
frozen dessert	1	6.0	NA
hamburger	1	9.0	NA
hamburger, super	1	48.0	NA
hot dog	1	15.0	NA
hot fudge brownie	1	22.0	NA
ice cream in cone			
small	1	3.0	NA
medium	1	7.0	NA
large	1	10.0	NA
ice cream dipped in choc.			
small	1	7.0	NA
medium	1	13.0	NA
large	1	20.0	NA
ice cream sandwich	1	4.0	NA
onion rings	1 order	17.0	NA
shake			
small	1	11.0	NA
medium	1	20.0	NA
large	1	28.0	NA
Jack in the Box			
apple turnover	1	24.0	0.2
Breakfast Jack sand.	1	13.0	0.1
cheeseburger	1	15.0	0.2

ITEM	SERVING	FAT GRAMS	FIBER GRAMS
french fries	1 order	15.0	0.6
french toast	1	29.0	0.9
hamburger			
Jumbo Jack	1	29.0	0.7
regular	1	11.0	0.2
Moby Jack sand.	1	26.0	0.1
omelette, ham & cheese	1	23.0	0.2
onion rings	1 order	23.0	0.3
pancakes	1 order	27.0	0.7
scrambled eggs	1 order	44.0	1.3
shake, choc.	1	10.0	0.3
taco	1	11.0	0.6
Kentucky Fried Chicken			
breast	1	11.7	0.1
breast, ex. crispy	1	17.8	0.2
breast fillet sand.	1	22.5	0.5
coleslaw	1	7.5	0.5
french fries	1 order	6.7	0.8
gravy	1	1.8	0.0
leg & thigh dinner	1 order	35.2	0.8
leg & thigh dinner, ex. crispy	1 order	44.0	1.0
thigh	1	17.5	0.1
wing	1	9.0	0.2
wing & thigh dinner	1 order	37.8	1.0
wing & thigh dinner, ex. crispy	1 order	48.2	1.0
Long John Silver's			
Chicken Planks	4 pieces	23.0	NA
clam chowder	1	3.0	NA
clams, breaded	1 order	34.0	NA
coleslaw	1	8.0	NA
fish sand.	1	31.0	NA
fish w/batter	2 pieces	22.0	NA
french fries	1 order	16.0	NA
hush puppies	3 pieces	7.0	NA
ocean scallops	6 pieces	13.0	NA
Peg Leg w/batter	5 pieces	28.0	NA
shrimp w/batter	6 pieces	13.0	NA
McDonald's			
Big Mac	1	33.0	0.6
cheeseburger	1	14.1	0.2
Chicken McNuggets	6 pieces	19.0	0.0
cookies			
choc. chip	1	16.3	0.0

ITEM	SERVING	FAT GRAMS	FIBER GRAMS
McDonaldland	1	10.8	0.1
Egg McMuffin	1	14.8	0.1
English muffin w/butter	1	5.3	0.1
Filet-o-Fish	1	25.0	0.1
french fries	1 order	11.5	0.5
hamburger	1	9.8	0.3
hash browns	1 order	7.0	0.3
hot cakes w/butter & syrup	1	10.3	0.2
ice cream			
in cake cone	1	5.2	0.1
in sugar cone	1	4.5	0.1
pie	1	14.0	0.2
Quarter Pounder	1	21.7	0.7
Quarter Pounder w/cheese	1	30.7	0.8
sausage, pork	1	18.6	0.1
scrambled eggs	1	13.0	0.0
shake, choc.	1	9.0	0.3
sundae, hot fudge	1	10.8	0.2
Taco Bell			
burrito			
bean	1	10.8	1.1
beef	1	21.0	NA
combination	1	16.0	NA
supreme	1	22.0	NA
enchirito	1	16.9	1.4
frijoles w/cheese	1	6.0	1.9
taco	1	8.6	0.4
tostada	1	6.0	NA
tostada w/beef	1	15.0	NA
Wendy's			
cheeseburger			
single	1	34.0	1.0
double	1	48.0	1.3
triple	1	68.0	1.6
chili con carne	1	8.0	2.3
french fries	1 order	16.0	1.2
hamburger			
single	1	26.0	0.8
double	1	40.0	1.1
triple	1	51.0	1.4
shake. choc. (frzn. dessert)	1	16.0	0.0

ITEM	SERVING	FAT GRAMS	FIBER GRAMS
Fats			
bacon fat	1 T	14.0	0.0
beef, separable fat	1 oz.	23.3	0.0
butter			
regular	1 t	4.1	0.0
whipped	1 t	3.1	0.0
cream			
light	1 T	2.9	0.0
medium (25% fat)	1 T	3.8	0.0
whipping, heavy	1 T	5.6	0.0
cream substitute			
liquid	½ fl. oz.	1.5	0.0
powdered	1 T	0.7	0.0
half-and-half	1 T	1.7	0.0
margarine			
solid or liquid	1 t	4.0	0.0
reduced calorie	1 t	2.0	0.0
mayonnaise			
regular	1 T	11.0	0.0
reduced calorie	1 T	5.0	0.0
Mazola no-stick spray	2-sec. spray	0.8	0.0
oil, all types	1 T	13.6	0.0
pork fat (lard)	1 T	12.8	0.0
salt pork, fried	1 oz.	19.6	0.0
sandwich spread (Miracle Whip type)	1 T	3.4	0.0
shortening, solid veg. (Crisco type)	1 T	12.0	0.0
sour cream			
cultured	1 T	2.5	0.0
reduced fat	1 T	1.3	0.0
whipped topping, pressurized or frozen	1 T	1.0	0.0
Fish (cooked weights unless otherwise noted)			
abalone, canned	3½ oz.	0.3	0.0
anchovy, canned	3 fillets	1.2	0.0
bass			
freshwater	3½ oz.	2.6	0.0
saltwater, striped	3½ oz.	2.7	0.0

ITEM	SERVING	FAT GRAMS	FIBER GRAMS
bluefish, baked or broiled, w/o fat	3½ oz.	6.5	0.0
catfish	3½ oz.	3.1	0.0
caviar, sturgeon, granular	1 round t	1.5	0.0
clams, canned, solids only	½ cup	2.5	0.0
cod	3½ oz.	0.3	0.0
crab			
cake	3½ oz.	10.8	0.4
canned	½ cup	2.1	0.0
salad	½ cup	8.5	0.4
fillets			
batter dipped, frzn.	2 pieces, approx. 8 oz.	31.0	0.0
light & crispy, frzn.	2 pieces, approx. 8 oz.	23.0	0.0
fish cakes	3½ oz.	18.0	0.0
fish sticks, frzn.	4, baked	8.9	0.0
flounder/sole/haddock/grouper	3½ oz.	0.5	0.0
halibut	3½ oz.	1.2	0.0
herring, pickled	1 oz.	6.0	0.0
jack mackerel	3½ oz.	5.6	0.0
lake trout	3½ oz.	11.0	0.0
lobster			
cooked, plain	3½ oz.	1.0	0.0
Newbury	7 oz.	21.2	0.0
salad	3½ oz.	6.4	0.0
ocean perch	3½ oz.	1.2	0.0
oysters			
canned	3½ oz.	2.2	0.1
fried	3½ oz.	13.9	0.0
raw	5–8 medium	1.8	0.0
red snapper	3½ oz.	0.9	0.0
rockfish, oven steamed	3½ oz.	2.5	0.0
salmon			
canned	3½ oz.	12.2	0.0
fresh, broiled/baked	3½ oz.	7.4	0.0
sardines, in oil	8 medium	24.4	0.0
scallops			
frzn., fried	3½ oz.	10.5	0.0
steamed	3½ oz.	1.4	0.0
shrimp			
canned, wet pack	½ cup	0.8	0.0
fried	3½ oz.	10.8	0.0

ITEM	SERVING	FAT GRAMS	FIBER GRAMS
raw	3½ oz.	0.8	0.0
sole, fillet, baked w/o fat	3½ oz.	1.1	0.0
swordfish, broiled w/o fat	3½ oz.	6.0	0.0
trout, rainbow			
baked w/o fat	3½ oz.	3.6	0.0
fried	3½ oz.	13.4	0.0
tuna			
canned in oil	6½ oz.	22.1	0.0
canned in water	6½ oz.	1.7	0.0
salad, w/water-pack tuna	½ cup	10.5	0.0

Fruit

ITEM	SERVING	FAT GRAMS	FIBER GRAMS
apple			
dried	½ cup	0.1	4.5
whole w/peel	2¾" diam.	0.4	3.5
applesauce	1 cup, unsweet.	0.1	2.0
apricots			
dried	5 halves, ½ cup	0.3	6.0
fresh	3 med. (about 12 per lb.)	0.4	1.5
avocado	1 med. (about 8 oz.)	30.0	3.7
banana	1 med. (8¾" long)	0.6	2.0
blackberries, fresh	1 cup	0.5	7.0
blueberries, fresh	1 cup	0.6	5.0
cantaloupe	½ melon, 5" diam.	0.7	3.0
cherries, sweet	10, ½ cup	0.7	1.5
cranberries, fresh	1 cup	0.2	4.0
dates, whole, dried	½ cup	0.4	7.5
figs, dried, uncooked	½ cup	1.0	16.0
fruit cocktail, canned	1 cup	0.3	5.0
grapefruit	½ med., 3¾" diam.	0.1	0.5
grapes, seedless	½ cup	0.3	0.7
honeydew, fresh	¼ small	0.3	1.0
kiwi, fresh	1 medium	0.3	1.5
Mandarin oranges, canned	½ cup	0.1	3.5
mango, fresh	1 medium	0.6	4.0
nectarine, fresh	1 medium	0.6	2.3
orange, fresh	1 medium	0.2	3.8
papaya, fresh	1 medium	0.4	2.4

ITEM	SERVING	FAT GRAMS	FIBER GRAMS
peach			
canned	1 cup	0.2	4.0
fresh	1 medium	0.1	1.3
pear			
canned	1 cup	0.3	5.5
fresh	1 medium	0.7	4.5
pineapple			
canned	1 cup pieces	0.2	2.1
fresh	1 cup pieces	0.7	3.2
plum, fresh	1 medium	0.6	2.5
prunes, dried, uncooked	½ cup	0.4	9.5
raisins, seedless	¼ cup	0.2	3.0
raspberries, fresh	1 cup	0.2	6.0
strawberries, fresh or frzn.	1 cup	0.2	3.0
tangerine, fresh	1 medium	0.2	0.3
watermelon, fresh	1 cup	0.2	0.5
Gravies, Sauces, and Toppings			
au jus	½ cup	0.4	0.0
barbecue sauce	1 T	0.3	0.1
beef gravy, canned	½ can	3.4	0.0
brown gravy			
from mix	½ cup	0.1	0.0
homemade	¼ cup	14.0	0.0
butterscotch, caramel, fruit			
sauces	1 T	0.0	0.0
chicken gravy			
canned	½ can	8.5	0.0
from mix	½ cup	0.9	0.0
giblet, from can	¼ cup	2.0	0.0
chili sauce	1 T	0.0	0.0
chocolate			
fudge topping	1 T	1.9	0.4
syrup, Hershey's	1 T	0.2	0.1
enchilada dip	1 oz.	1.2	0.2
fruit topping	1 T	0.0	0.0
hard sauce	1 T	2.8	0.0
hollandaise	¼ cup	18.5	0.0
home style gravy, from mix	¼ cup	0.5	0.0
horseradish sauce	1 T	0.0	0.2
jalapeño bean dip	1 oz.	1.1	0.3
ketchup, tomato	1 T	0.1	0.0

ITEM	SERVING	FAT GRAMS	FIBER GRAMS
marshmallow creme topping	1 T	0.0	0.0
mushroom gravy			
canned	½ can	4.0	0.0
from mix	½ cup	0.4	0.0
mustard	1 T	0.7	0.1
onion gravy, from mix	½ cup	0.3	0.0
picante sauce	6 T	0.6	0.4
pork gravy, from mix	½ cup	0.9	0.0
sour cream sauce	¼ cup	11.9	0.0
soy sauce	1 T	0.0	0.0
spaghetti sauce, meatless, in jar			
or can	½ cup	3.8	0.0
Steak sauce			
regular	1 T	0.0	0.1
w/mushrooms	1 fl. oz.	0.1	0.2
stroganoff sauce, from mix	¼ packet prep.	2.9	0.2
sweet & sour sauce	¼ cup	0.2	0.0
taco sauce	2 t	0.0	0.0
tartar sauce	1 T	7.9	0.0
teriyaki sauce	1 T	0.0	0.0
tabasco sauce	1 T	0.0	0.0
turkey gravy			
canned	½ can	3.1	0.0
from mix	½ cup	0.9	0.0
white sauce			
thin	2 T	2.6	0.0
medium	2 T	4.1	0.0
thick	2 T	5.2	0.0
Worcestershire sauce	1 T	0.0	0.0
Meats (cooked weights unless otherwise noted)			
beef			
7.5–12.4% fat	3½ oz.	9.4	0.0
12.5–17.4% fat	3½ oz.	15.2	0.0
17.5–22.4% fat	3½ oz.	19.6	0.0
22.5–27.4% fat	3½ oz.	26.5	0.0
27.5–32% fat	3½ oz.	30.0	0.0
brisket, lean & marbled	3½ oz.	30.0	0.0
chipped	2 slices (approx. 2 oz.)	1.8	0.0
chipped, creamed	½ cup	13.1	0.0
chipped, creamed, frzn.	5½ oz.	16.0	0.0

ITEM	SERVING	FAT GRAMS	FIBER GRAMS
chuck, ground	3½ oz.	23.9	0.0
chuck, lean & marbled	3½ oz.	23.9	0.0
chuck, separable lean	3½ oz.	9.5	0.0
corned, med. fat	3½ oz.	30.4	0.0
cubed steak	3½ oz.	15.4	0.0
flank steak, fat trimmed	3½ oz.	9.4	0.0
hamburger, extra lean	3-oz.patty	13.9	0.0
hamburger, lean	3-oz. patty	15.7	0.0
hamburger, regular	3-oz patty	17.6	0.0
jerky	1 oz.	4.0	0.0
meatballs	1 oz.	5.5	0.0
meatloaf	3½ oz.	15.6	0.0
porterhouse steak	3½ oz.	19.6	0.0
porterhouse steak, lean	3½ oz.	9.4	0.0
rib roast	3½ oz.	30.0	0.0
rib roast, lean	3½ oz.	15.2	0.0
ribeye steak	3½ oz.	30.0	0.0
round, broiled	3½ oz.	15.2	0.0
round, lean	3½ oz.	9.4	0.0
round, bottom, broiled	3½ oz.	15.2	0.0
round, bottom, lean, broiled	3½ oz.	9.8	0.0
round stew meat	4 oz.	15.3	0.0
rump, lean, pot-roasted	3½ oz.	15.2	0.0
rump, pot-roasted	3½ oz.	19.6	0.0
short ribs	3½ oz.	31.7	0.0
short ribs, lean only	3½ oz.	18.0	0.0
sirloin, broiled	3½ oz.	19.6	0.0
sirloin, ground	3½ oz.	26.5	0.0
sirloin, lean, broiled	3½ oz.	9.4	0.0
steak, chicken-fried	3½ oz.	30.0	0.0
t-bone, broiled	3½ oz.	24.4	0.0
t-bone, lean, broiled	3½ oz.	10.3	0.0
tenderloin	3½ oz.	15.2	0.0
tenderloin, lean, broiled	3½ oz.	9.4	0.0
bologna, beef or beef & pork	1 oz.	8.0	0.0
bratwurst (pork or beef)	2-oz. link	18.8	0.0
braunschweiger or liverwurst	1 oz.	7.8	0.0
corned beef, jellied	1 oz.	2.9	0.0
frog legs, cooked w/o fat	4 large (4 oz.)	0.3	0.0
hot dog			
beef	1	13.2	0.0
chicken	1	8.8	0.0

ITEM	SERVING	FAT GRAMS	FIBER GRAMS
kielbasa (Polish sausage)	1 oz.	14.2	0.0
knockwurst	2-oz. link	18.9	0.0
lamb			
leg, roasted	3½ oz.	14.5	0.0
loin chop	1 chop, approx. 2 oz.	15.5	0.0
loin chop, lean	1 chop, approx. 2 oz.	5.2	0.0
shoulder chop, lean	1 chop, approx. 2 oz.	8.9	0.0
liver			
beef	3½ oz.	3.8	0.0
beef, fried	3½ oz.	10.6	0.0
calf	3½ oz.	4.7	0.0
calf, fried	3½ oz.	13.2	0.0
pâté (goose)	1 oz.	12.4	0.0
pastrami			
beef	1 oz.	8.3	0.0
turkey	1 oz.	1.8	0.0
pepperoni	1 oz.	13.0	0.0
pork			
bacon, cured, broiled	1 slice (⅓ oz.)	3.1	0.0
bacon, cured, raw	1 slice (⅘ oz.)	16.2	0.0
blade	3½ oz.	28.8	0.0
blade, lean	1 slice (2 oz.)	9.2	0.0
Boston butt	3½ oz.	28.0	0.0
Boston butt, lean	3½ oz.	11.2	0.0
Canadian bacon, broiled	1 slice (2 oz.)	4.2	0.0
ham, chopped, sandwich	1 oz.	4.3	0.0
ham, cured, butt	3½ oz.	28.0	0.0
ham, cured, butt, lean	1 slice (1 oz.)	6.5	0.0
ham, fresh, lean	1 slice (1 oz.)	4.7	0.0
ham, lean, cured	3 oz.	8.5	0.0
ham, turkey	1 oz.	1.5	0.0
loin chop	1 chop, approx. 2 oz.	22.5	0.0
loin chop, lean	1 chop, approx. 2 oz.	7.7	0.0
picnic shoulder	2 slices (2 oz.)	14.3	0.0
picnic shoulder, lean	2 slices (2 oz.)	2.7	0.0
sausage	2 patties	25.9	0.0
sausage, brown & serve	1 oz.	10.6	0.0

ITEM	SERVING	FAT GRAMS	FIBER GRAMS
spareribs, roasted	3½ oz.	30.1	0.0
tenderloin, lean, roast	3½ oz.	12.1	0.0
salami			
cooked	1 oz.	10.0	0.0
dry or hard	1 oz.	10.0	0.0
turkey, cooked	1 oz.	3.7	0.0
sausage			
Italian	2-oz. link	17.2	0.0
smoked	2-oz. link	20.0	0.0
Vienna	1 sausage (½ oz.)	4.0	0.0
Spam	1 oz.	7.4	0.0
tongue, beef, smoked	3½ oz.	28.8	0.0
veal			
blade	3½ oz.	16.8	0.0
blade, lean	3½ oz.	8.4	0.0
chuck, med. fat	3½ oz.	12.8	0.0
cutlet, breaded	3½ oz.	15.0	0.0
cutlet, round	3½ oz.	15.0	0.0
cutlet, round, lean	1	12.8	0.0
loin chop with fat	1	43.8	0.0
loin chop, lean	1, approx. 2 oz.	4.8	0.0
sirloin, lean, roasted	3½ oz.	5.9	0.0
sirloin, roasted	3½ oz.	12.2	0.0
venison, roasted	3½ oz.	2.2	0.0
Milk and Yogurt			
buttermilk			
<1% fat	1 cup	2.2	0.0
dry	1 T	0.4	0.0
choc., hot (cocoa)			
w/skim milk	1 cup	2.0	0.2
w/whole milk	1 cup	9.1	0.2
choc. milk			
1% fat	1 cup	2.5	0.2
2% fat	1 cup	5.0	0.2
whole milk	1 cup	8.5	0.2
cocoa			
from mix w/water	1 cup	3.0	0.1
reduced cal., w/water	1 cup	0.8	0.1
condensed, sweetened	½ cup	14.0	0.0
evaporated milk			
skim	½ cup	0.5	0.0

ITEM	SERVING	FAT GRAMS	FIBER GRAMS
whole	½ cup	10.0	0.0
instant breakfast	1 cup	8.0	0.0
lowfat milk			
1%	1 cup	2.6	0.0
2%	1 cup	4.7	0.0
malted milk	1 cup	9.9	0.1
milkshake			
choc., thick	1 cup	17.0	0.8
soft serve	1 cup	7.0	0.3
van., thick	1 cup	15.0	0.2
Ovaltine	1 cup	8.8	0.0
skim milk			
liquid	1 cup	0.4	0.0
nonfat dry	¼ cup	0.2	0.0
whole milk			
3.5% fat	1 cup	8.0	0.0
dry	¼ cup	8.6	0.0
yogurt			
fruit flav., low fat	1 cup	5.0	0.2
plain, low fat	1 cup	2.5	0.0
plain, skim	1 cup	0.4	0.0
plain, whole milk	1 cup	7.4	0.0

Miscellaneous

ITEM	SERVING	FAT GRAMS	FIBER GRAMS
Bac o Bits, General Mills	1 T	1.3	0.0
baking powder	1 t	0.0	0.0
baking soda	1 t	0.0	0.0
candied fruit	1 oz.	0.1	0.5
chewing gum	1 stick	0.0	0.0
choc., baking	1 oz.	15.0	0.7
cocoa, dry	⅓ cup	3.6	1.5
fruit butter	1 T	0.2	0.2
honey	1 T	0.0	0.0
icing, decorator	1 t	0.0	0.0
jam, all varieties	1 T	0.1	0.1
jelly, all varieties	1 T	0.0	0.0
marmalade, citrus	1 T	0.1	0.1
meat tenderizer	1 t	0.0	0.0
molasses	1 T	0.0	0.0
olives			
black	2 large	4.0	0.3
Greek	3 medium	7.1	0.8

ITEM	SERVING	FAT GRAMS	FIBER GRAMS
green	2 medium	1.6	0.2
pickle relish	1 T	0.1	0.2
pickles			
bread & butter	4 slices	0.1	0.1
dill or kosher	1 large	0.2	0.5
sweet	1 large	0.4	0.5
Shake & Bake, General Foods	¼ packet	2.6	0.2
sugar			
all varieties	1 T	0.0	0.0
substitutes	1 t	0.0	0.0
syrup, all varieties	1 T	0.0	0.0
vinegar	1 T	0.0	0.0
yeast	1 T	0.1	0.0

Pasta and Rice

ITEM	SERVING	FAT GRAMS	FIBER GRAMS
macaroni, cooked	1 cup	0.8	1.1
noodles			
chow mein	½ cup	8.0	NA
egg	1 cup	2.5	1.4
enriched	1 cup	0.9	1.1
ramen, all varieties	1 cup	6.5	1.2
rice			
brown	½ cup	0.6	1.8
fried	½ cup	7.2	1.0
long grain & wild	½ cup	2.1	1.9
pilaf	½ cup	7.0	0.8
Spanish style	½ cup	2.1	1.2
white	½ cup	1.2	0.3
spaghetti			
enriched	1 cup	0.7	0.6
w/tomato sauce	1 cup pasta, ½ cup sauce	2.5	0.7

Poultry

ITEM	SERVING	FAT GRAMS	FIBER GRAMS
chicken			
breast w/skin, roasted	½ breast	7.6	0.0
breast, w/o skin, roasted	½ breast	3.1	0.0
breast, w/skin, fried	½ breast	8.7	0.0
fried, frzn.	8 oz.	38.9	0.0
fryers, w/o skin, fried	3½ oz.	9.1	0.0
fryers, w/o skin, roasted	3½ oz.	7.4	0.0
fryers, w/skin, fried	3½ oz.	17.4	0.0

ITEM	SERVING	FAT GRAMS	FIBER GRAMS
fryers, w/skin, roasted	3½ oz.	13.6	0.0
leg, w/o skin, roasted	1	2.5	0.0
liver, cooked w/o added fat	3½ oz.	5.5	0.0
roll	1 oz.	1.3	0.0
thigh, w/o skin, roasted	1	5.7	0.0
w/skin, roasted	3½ oz.	28.4	0.0
w/o skin, roasted	3½ oz.	11.2	0.0
turkey			
breast, cold cuts	1 oz.	1.3	0.0
breast, smoked	3½ oz.	4.0	0.0
ground	3½ oz.	14.0	0.0
processed	1 oz.	4.5	0.0
w/skin, roasted	3½ oz.	9.7	0.0
w/o skin, roasted	3½ oz.	5.0	0.0
Salad Dressings			
blue cheese			
low cal.	1 T	0.8	0.0
regular	1 T	8.0	0.0
buttermilk, from mix	1 T	5.8	0.0
Caesar	1 T	7.0	0.0
French	1 T	6.4	0.1
garlic, from mix	1 T	9.2	0.0
Green Goddess			
low cal.	1 T	2.0	0.0
regular	1 T	7.0	0.0
herb & spice, low cal.	1 T	0.0	0.0
Italian			
low cal.	1 T	1.5	0.0
regular	1 T	7.1	0.0
zesty, from mix	1 T	9.2	0.0
mayonnaise type			
low cal.	1 T	1.8	0.0
regular	1 T	4.9	0.0
oil & vinegar	1 T	7.5	0.0
ranch style, prep. w/mayo	1 T	5.7	0.0
Russian			
low cal.	1 T	0.7	0.0
regular	1 T	7.8	0.0
sesame seed	1 T	6.9	0.1
Thousand Island			
low cal.	1 T	1.6	0.2

ITEM	SERVING	FAT GRAMS	FIBER GRAMS
regular	1 T	5.6	0.3

Snacks
almonds	12–15 nuts, 2 T	10.0	1.9
Brazil nuts	4 medium	11.5	1.3
Bugles	1 oz.	8.0	0.0
cashews, roasted	6–8 nuts, 2 T	7.8	1.5
cheese puffs, Cheetos	1 oz.	10.0	0.1
chestnuts, fresh	3 small	7.9	1.0
coconut, dried, shredded	⅓ cup	9.2	0.6
corn chips, Fritos	1 oz.	9.7	0.3
Cracker Jack	1 oz.	1.0	0.0
hazelnuts (filberts)	10–12 nuts, 2 T	10.6	1.0
macadamia nuts, roasted	6 medium, 2 T	12.3	0.9
mixed nuts	8–12 nuts, 2 T	10.0	1.6
peanut butter	1 T	7.3	0.7
peanuts, roasted	1 oz., 3 T	15.0	2.7
pecans	12 halves, 2 T	9.1	1.0
pistachios	30 nuts, 2 T	8.0	1.2
popcorn			
air popped	1 cup	0.2	0.3
microwave, unbuttered	1 cup	2.0	0.3
microwave, w/butter	1 cup	3.5	0.3
popped w/oil	1 cup	2.0	0.3
w/sugar coating	1 cup	1.2	0.3
pork rinds, fried, Frito-Lay	1 oz.	9.3	0.2
potato chips	10 chips	8.0	0.3
potato chips	1 oz.	11.2	0.5
pretzels	1 oz.	1.0	0.1
pumpkin seeds	2 T	8.0	1.1
sesame seeds	2 T	8.9	1.3
sunflower seeds, kernel	2 T	8.7	1.1
tortilla chips			
Doritos	1 oz.	6.6	0.3
round, Tostito	1 oz.	7.8	0.4
trail mix	2 T	5.1	1.2
walnuts	8–15 halves, 2 T	8.7	0.8

Soups (canned unless specified dry)
asparagus, cream of			
w/milk	1 cup	8.2	0.7
w/water	1 cup	4.1	0.7

ITEM	SERVING	FAT GRAMS	FIBER GRAMS
bean			
regular	1 cup	3.0	4.5
w/bacon	1 cup	5.9	1.5
w/bacon, dry, w/water	1 cup	3.5	1.5
w/franks	1 cup	7.0	1.5
w/ham	1 cup	8.5	4.0
beef			
barley	1 cup	1.4	0.4
broth	1 cup	0.5	0.5
broth, cube, w/water	1 cube	0.1	0.0
chunky	1 cup	5.1	0.7
noodle	1 cup	3.1	0.4
noodle, dry, w/water	1 cup	0.8	0.1
w/mushrooms	10¾ oz.	7.0	0.4
black bean	1 cup	1.5	2.3
Campbell's chunky w/meat	1 cup	5.0	2.0
Campbell's chunky w/o meat	1 cup	4.0	3.0
cauliflower, cream of,			
w/cream & milk	1 cup	21.4	0.4
cheese	1 cup	21.0	0.5
chicken			
and dumplings	1 cup	5.5	0.5
broth	1 cup	1.4	0.2
broth, cube, w/water	1 cube	0.2	0.0
cream of, w/milk	1 cup	11.5	0.2
cream of, dry, w/water	1 cup	5.3	1.2
cream of, w/water	1 cup	7.4	0.2
gumbo	1 cup	1.4	1.5
mushroom	1 cup	9.2	0.5
noodle, chunky	1 cup	6.0	0.5
noodle, w/water	1 cup	2.5	0.2
noodle, dry, w/water	1 cup	1.2	0.1
rice, chunky	1 cup	3.2	0.5
rice, dry, w/water	1 cup	1.4	0.0
rice, w/water	1 cup	1.9	0.1
veg., w/water	1 cup	2.8	0.1
veg., chunky	1 cup	4.8	0.5
clam chowder			
Manhattan chunky	1 cup	3.4	0.5
Manhattan, dry, w/water	1 cup	1.6	0.6
New England	1 cup	6.6	0.5
New England, dry, w/water	1 cup	3.7	0.2

ITEM	SERVING	FAT GRAMS	FIBER GRAMS
consommé, w/gelatin	1 cup	0.0	0.4
corn chowder	1 cup	12.0	3.0
crab	1 cup	1.5	0.5
minestrone			
chunky	1 cup	2.8	0.6
w/water	1 cup	2.5	0.7
dry, w/water	1 cup	1.7	0.4
mushroom			
barley	1 cup	2.3	0.7
w/beef stock	1 cup	4.0	0.5
cream of, condensed	1 cup	23.1	0.6
cream of, w/milk	1 cup	13.6	0.3
cream of, w/water	1 cup	9.0	0.5
dry, w/water	1 cup	4.9	0.1
noodle or veg.			
w/meat	1 cup	3.0	2.0
w/o meat	1 cup	2.0	2.0
onion			
dry, w/water	1 cup	0.6	0.2
French, w/o cheese	1 cup	5.8	0.2
regular	1 cup	1.7	0.5
oyster stew	1 cup	12.8	0.4
pea			
green	1 cup	2.9	1.7
split	7½ oz.	0.5	1.2
split, w/ham	1 cup	4.4	1.2
potato, cream of, w/milk	1 cup	7.4	2.0
shrimp, cream of, w/milk	1 cup	9.3	0.5
tomato			
beef w/noodle	1 cup	4.3	0.5
dry, w/water	1 cup	2.4	0.4
w/milk	1 cup	6.0	0.5
w/water	1 cup	1.9	0.5
rice	1 cup	2.7	0.6
turkey			
chunky	1 cup	4.4	0.9
noodle	1 cup	2.0	0.2
vegetable			
beef, dry, w/water	1 cup	1.1	0.2
w/beef broth	1 cup	1.9	0.7
beef, chunky	10¾ oz.	4.0	0.8
chunky	1 cup	3.7	1.2
won ton	1 cup	2.0	0.4

ITEM	SERVING	FAT GRAMS	FIBER GRAMS
Vegetables			
alfalfa sprouts	3½ oz.	0.6	3.0
artichoke	1 large, edible parts	0.2	3.4
asparagus, cooked w/o fat	½ cup	0.3	1.5
avocado			
California	1 medium	30.0	3.7
Florida	1 medium	27.0	6.4
bamboo shoots	1 cup	0.4	2.0
beans			
baked, brown sugar or molasses	½ cup	3.0	4.5
refried, canned, w/o added fat	½ cup	2.5	10.5
refried w/added fat	½ cup	13.0	10.5
white, cooked w/o fat	½ cup	0.4	8.7
beets, pickled	1 cup	0.0	4.1
black-eyed peas (cowpeas), cooked w/o fat	½ cup	0.6	2.2
broccoli			
au gratin, frzn.	5 oz.	12.0	2.5
cooked w/o fat	1 cup	0.4	4.0
frzn. in butter sauce	⅔ cup	2.3	1.9
frzn. w/cheese	½ cup	11.6	1.2
brussels sprouts, cooked w/o fat	6–8 medium	0.3	2.8
butter beans, cooked w/o fat	½ cup	0.6	3.8
cabbage	2 cups	0.1	3.6
carrots			
cooked w/o fat	⅔ cup	0.2	3.0
frzn. in butter sauce	½ cup	2.3	1.8
raw	1 large	0.2	1.5
cauliflower			
cooked w/o fat	1 cup	0.2	3.4
raw	1 cup	0.2	3.6
celery, diced, raw	1 cup	0.1	3.3
Chinese style veg., frzn., cooked	½ cup, prep. per pkg.	4.7	2.8
collard greens, cooked w/o fat	½ cup	0.1	1.7
corn			
cream style	½ cup	0.4	3.5
frzn., cooked w/o fat	½ cup	0.2	4.0
frzn. in butter sauce	½ cup	2.6	3.8
on the cob	4-inch ear	0.9	4.3

ITEM	SERVING	FAT GRAMS	FIBER GRAMS
crowder peas, cooked w/o fat	½ cup	0.6	2.2
cucumber, raw	½ medium	0.1	0.8
eggplant, cooked w/o fat	½ cup	0.1	1.8
endive lettuce	1 cup	0.1	1.4
garbanzo beans (chick-peas), cooked w/o fat	½ cup	2.1	5.2
green beans, cooked w/o fat	½ cup	0.1	2.4
hominy (grits), cooked w/o fat	1 cup	1.0	2.8
Italian style veg. frzn., cooked	½ cup, prep. per pkg.	7.0	1.8
kale, cooked w/o fat	½ cup	0.5	1.8
kidney beans, red	½ cup	0.8	7.5
lentils, cooked w/o fat	½ cup	0.1	7.5
lettuce, iceberg	1 cup	0.2	0.8
lima beans, cooked w/o fat	½ cup	0.4	4.8
mushrooms			
fried/sautéed	4 medium	7.4	0.7
raw	10 small	0.1	1.0
mustard greens, cooked w/o fat	½ cup	0.4	1.9
okra, cooked w/o fat	½ cup	0.2	2.8
onions			
french fried	5 pieces	10.0	0.6
raw	¼ cup	0.1	0.7
parsnips, cooked w/o fat	½ cup	0.2	3.0
peas, green, cooked w/o fat	½ cup	0.2	3.5
pepper, bell, raw	1 large	0.2	1.5
pimientos	3 medium	0.5	0.6
potato			
baked	1 medium, w/skin	0.1	3.8
boiled, w/o skin	½ cup	0.1	1.5
french fries	10 pieces	7.6	1.4
hashbrowns	½ cup	11.7	2.0
mashed from flakes	½ cup	2.3	1.5
mashed w/milk & butter	½ cup	4.3	1.4
pancake	1	6.4	0.9
puffs, frzn.	½ cup	11.6	3.0
scalloped	½ cup	4.8	1.4
scalloped w/cheese	½ cup	9.7	1.4
pumpkin, canned	½ cup	0.3	4.0
radish, raw	½ cup	0.3	1.3
sauerkraut	½ cup	0.2	4.0
scallions, raw	5 medium, ½ cup	0.2	3.6

ITEM	SERVING	FAT GRAMS	FIBER GRAMS
soybeans, cooked w/o fat	½ cup	0.4	1.8
spinach			
creamed	½ cup	3.0	0.8
raw	½ cup	0.5	1.1
squash			
summer, cooked w/o fat	½ cup	0.3	1.9
winter, baked w/o fat	½ medium	0.2	3.5
succotash, cooked w/o fat	½ cup	0.8	3.0
sweet potato			
baked	1 medium, or ¾ cup	0.3	7.3
candied	½ cup	4.3	4.5
tofu (soybean curd)	4 oz.	4.8	0.3
tomato			
raw	1 medium, ½ cup	0.2	1.4
stewed	3½ oz.	0.1	1.2
tomato paste	½ cup	1.2	4.0
turnip greens, cooked w/o fat	½ cup	0.2	2.0
turnips, cooked w/o fat	½ cup	0.1	1.7
water chestnuts, canned	16 medium	0.2	1.8
wax beans, cooked w/o fat	½ cup	0.2	2.2
yam, cooked w/o fat	½ cup	0.4	2.9
zucchini, cooked w/o fat	½ cup	0.1	1.9

Index

Boldfaced page numbers refer
to recipes.

313

We Deliver!
And So Do These Bestsellers.